WHEN SHERMAN MARCHED
NORTH FROM THE SEA

CIVIL WAR AMERICA

Gary W. Gallagher, editor

When Sherman Marche

The University of North Carolina Press   Chapel Hill and London

North from the Sea

RESISTANCE ON THE CONFEDERATE HOME FRONT

JACQUELINE GLASS CAMPBELL

© 2003
The University of North Carolina Press
All rights reserved
Set in Quadraat, Rosewood, and Egiziano
by Keystone Typesetting, Inc.
Manufactured in the United States of America

The paper in this book meets the guidelines for
permanence and durability of the Committee on
Production Guidelines for Book Longevity of the
Council on Library Resources.

Library of Congress
Cataloging-in-Publication Data
Campbell, Jacqueline Glass.
When Sherman marched north from the sea : resistance on
the Confederate home front / Jacqueline Glass Campbell.
    p. cm.—(Civil War America)
Includes bibliographical references and index.
ISBN 0-8078-2809-2 (cloth: alk. paper)
1. Sherman's March to the Sea—Social aspects. 2. United
States—History—Civil War, 1861–1865—Social aspects.
3. Passive resistance—Confederate States of America—
History. 4. United States—History—Civil War, 1861–1865—
Women. 5. Women—Confederate States of America—
Social conditions. 6. United States—History—Civil War,
1861–1865—African Americans. 7. African Americans—
Confederate States of America—Social conditions.
8. Slaves—Confederate States of America—Social
conditions. 9. Confederate States of America—Social
conditions. I. Title. II. Series.
E476.69 .C36 2003
973.7'378—dc21   2003004583

07 06 05 04 03   5 4 3 2 1

FRONTISPIECE: Sherman's Seventeenth Corps
crossing the South Edisto River on pontoons at
Bennaker's Bridge, South Carolina, February 9, 1865
(Frank Leslie's Illustrated History of the Civil War).

To my children, Stephanie, Justin, and Daniel

CONTENTS

Acknowledgments, xi

Introduction, 3

Chapter 1
Savannah Has Gone Up the Spout, 8

Chapter 2
Rocking the Cradle of Secession, 31
When the Wind Blows, 33
When the Bough Breaks, 44

Chapter 3
The Most Diabolical Act of All the Barbarous War, 58

Chapter 4
God Save Us from the Retreating Friend and Advancing Foe, 75

Chapter 5
With Grief, but Not with Shame, 93

Epilogue, 105

Notes, 111

Bibliography, 145

Index, 167

A map showing the route of Sherman's March appears on page 2.

ACKNOWLEDGMENTS

On the last occasion that I sat down to write acknowledgments, I had just completed my dissertation at Duke University. I described the process as consisting of hysteria, hair tearing, tears, and frustration. Although revising and editing the manuscript for publication has been equally challenging, the process has been greatly eased by my relationship with the University of North Carolina Press. Stevie Champion's meticulous copyediting both clarified and enriched my prose. The support and encouragement I received from Charles Grench and series editor Gary Gallagher were powerful tools in my survival arsenal. Both of these men offered insightful criticism in a manner that never made me feel insecure or defensive. This book is the result of that collaboration. I trust they are as pleased with the results as I am.

My work environment at the University of Connecticut has also enhanced this period of my life. Altina Waller, Richard Brown, Nina Dayton, and Karen Spalding deserve special mention for their mentorship; I look forward to many years of collegial interaction with them.

Other colleagues and institutions are equally deserving of mention. Three people were extraordinarily important to me during the writing phase. I have never met a better storyteller than Sydney Nathans, whose skills I have tried to emulate. Bill Blair's scholarship was an inspiration, and his frequent reminders to root my story "in my folks" constantly echoed in my mind. Finally, it gives me enormous pleasure to publicly express my gratitude to Nancy Hewitt. My relationship with her goes back many years, during which she has nurtured my intellectual growth and has been a constant source of strength, humor, and compassion. No one could ask for a better mentor or friend. Crucial financial support came from the History Department at Duke University, an Ann Firor Scott Research Award, and an Archie K. Davis Fellowship. The Blue and Gray Education Society provided both financial and professional assistance, sponsoring my attendance at a conference where I was fortunate enough to meet John Marszalek and Mark Grimsley who nourished the seeds of a nascent project. Archivists astounded me with their patience and courtesy in Durham, Chapel Hill, Raleigh, and Columbia.

As far as friends and family are concerned, I consider myself blessed. Ellen Babb and Melissa Seixas are sisters of my heart. We have shared many hours of deep conversation, as well as raucous laughter, both of which I consider necessities of life. I know my dear friend Peter Thompson would agree with this sentiment. I also wish to thank Jane Mangan and Derek Chang who provided intellectual challenge and inspiration, as well as sound shoulders on which to lean. My parents, Sylvia and Gerald Glass, and my siblings, Karen and David, have been great sources of strength from across the Atlantic. Even when they found my decisions difficult to understand, they offered me continuous support and have taught me the true value of family. Bruce Campbell came into my life at the beginning of this project and influenced my work in fundamental ways. I thank him for his love and support. Credit must go also to Michael Bindman, whose willingness to shoulder the responsibilities of single parenthood made my path much easier. This book is dedicated to my children, Stephanie, Justin, and Daniel, who made many involuntary sacrifices while I struggled through graduate school. They are sources of great pride to me, and I trust that they are now equally as proud of their mother.

WHEN SHERMAN MARCHED
NORTH FROM THE SEA

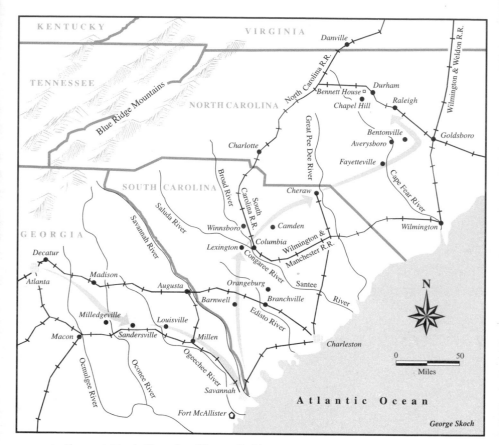

Sherman's March, November 1864–April 1865

INTRODUCTION

In February 1865 a Confederate officer learned that William T. Sherman's soldiers were an imminent threat to his South Carolina family. He warned his mother and sisters that they were likely to lose all their material possessions, yet his words expressed no concern over their physical safety. In fact, he advised his female kin that, "should any scoundrel intrude or go rummaging round the place, don't hesitate to shoot." Ten days later, hearing that his family had survived the ordeal, he thanked God for having provided him with "such a brave mother & Sisters," and he renewed his own commitment to the Confederate cause. "With such a spirit emanating from you," he wrote, "how could we [soldiers] do else but perform our duty noble and manfully." At the same time a Union officer surveyed the charred remains of Columbia, the South Carolina capital, and openly wept at the distress of homeless women and children. An ex-slave who had decided to remain on her South Carolina plantation, rather than flee with the Union army, also remembered that month with bitterness. All she had to thank the Yankees for was "a hungry belly and freedom."[1]

These three commentaries on the nature of Sherman's campaign through the Confederate heartland convey a very different picture from traditional accounts of a military strategy that destroyed both the war resources and the morale of the Southern people. But by integrating evidence from soldiers and civilians, black and white, at a moment when home front and battlefront merged, Sherman's March becomes a far more complex story—one that illuminates the importance of culture for determining the limits of war and how it is fought. If we understand war as culturally sanctioned violence, we can place a military campaign in a much broader social context, one that takes into account a wider array of behavioral patterns. These patterns include racial attitudes, gender ideology, and perceptions of the military as a cultural entity.

Sherman's March was an invasion of both geographic and psychological space. The Union army constructed a vision of the Southern landscape as military terrain. When they brought war into Southern households, however, soldiers were frequently astounded at the fierceness with which many white Southern women defended their homes. Whereas some lauded women's bravery, many others concluded that such inappropriate displays crossed the boundaries of acceptable feminine behavior. But in the rural South, where the household remained the political center, white women could see themselves as both mothers and warriors, giving them material and ideological reasons to resist. African Americans' reactions to Union soldiers were even more complex. Their initial delight at the coming of the "army of emancipation" was often replaced with terror as Yankees plundered black homes and assaulted black women.

This work differs from other studies of Sherman's March in yet another, and extremely important, way. It has its starting point in Savannah, Georgia, the culmination of the general's much-studied March to the Sea. Sherman himself saw the campaign of the Carolinas as crucial and a great deal more difficult than his all-but-unobstructed advance through Georgia; his soldiers frequently referred to this first stage in their journey in festive terms. Nevertheless, both in academic circles and in popular culture, Sherman's entire offensive is often called his "March to the Sea," completely obscuring the importance of his continuing advance.[2]

It was in the wake of a major turning point in the war that Sherman devised his plan to take the conflict to the Southern home front. In September 1864 Ulysses S. Grant and Robert E. Lee were entrenched around Petersburg, Virginia. In Georgia, Sherman's campaign to take Atlanta was being frustrated by a determined Confederate force that, despite having sustained heavy losses, still clung to the city. This apparent stalemate in the field, coupled with increasing casualties, escalated a downward slide of morale in the North that could only be reversed by a major Union victory. Sherman's capture of Atlanta could hardly have come at a more propitious time, and his success had major political and military repercussions. The fall of the city ensured Abraham Lincoln's election to a second term, which, in turn, indicated to the Confederacy that the North would continue the fight. This message was clearly brought home to the South when, on November 16, 1864, Sherman left Atlanta with an army of sixty thousand handpicked men on a path to the Atlantic Ocean.

Conventional wisdom tells us that in wartime men are both the protectors and the threat. The army regulates the exercise of violence against an enemy and exacts kudos and support from the protected. Logically then, if noncombatants find their guarantees of protection gone, they will withdraw their support and help end the war.[3] When Sherman led his army through the Confederate heartland, he recognized this relationship of battlefront and home front. Although fighting had occurred on home ground before, he deliberately targeted the Southern home front. His hardened veterans, who had seen the worst war had to offer, were now engaged in a campaign designed to simultaneously destroy the military resources and the morale of the Southern people. By Christmas 1864 Sherman's troops had swept through Georgia, cutting a path that penetrated the very heart of the Confederacy.

This is the story we have become accustomed to, yet neither the official record nor the private papers of Union soldiers reflect the March to the Sea as either grueling or devastating. It was, in fact, the psychological rather than the physical aspects of the campaign that had the most effect on soldiers and civilians alike. In the wake of Sherman's March to the Sea, Georgians were dazed, confused, and humiliated; Union troops, on the other hand, arrived in Savannah elated and confident. It was the ongoing journey of Sherman's men through the Carolinas that would test the endurance of soldiers and civilians, blacks and whites, and this confrontation forms the heart of our story.

We begin, in Chapter 1, with the occupation of Savannah. The study of this city highlights the nature of the Georgia campaign as Union soldiers perceived it. It also opens up a new story of the city itself, which was surrendered without a struggle and offered as a Christmas present to Abraham Lincoln. But a closer examination of the seemingly orderly interactions between citizens and the army reveals that, while many cold and hungry people welcomed the arrival of Federal troops and the consequent distribution of supplies, others hid burning resentments and sought to survive through enterprise or manipulation. By the time Sherman's men reached Savannah, many had determined that Confederate women were the staunchest supporters of the war, and this perception was confirmed by their month-long hiatus in the city.[4]

Chapter 2 follows Sherman and his army into South Carolina. Armed with weapons, detailed maps, and a spirit of revenge, these veterans overcame harsh weather and hostile terrain in ways that fueled white Southerners' increasing panic. The anticipatory elements among soldiers and civilians add a special dimension to the story and help to explain why confrontations often played out differently from the grand narrative of pillage and destruction. This chapter also focuses on the experiences of African Americans and the difficulties they faced in deciding whether to flee with, or from, Union troops.

In Columbia, the wrath of the army reached its zenith as a large part of the city was consumed by flames. Chapter 3 uses the destruction of this city to explore the concept of female honor and white women's relationship to the Confederate nation. It also examines the dynamic nature of Southern morale, arguing that civilians showed more resiliency than previously noted. Here I test the hypothesis that an initial wave of despondency might, in fact, be only the first step in a longer process of rededication and resistance.[5]

The North Carolina home front has most often been the focus of studies of conflict within the Confederacy, particularly along class lines.[6] In Chapter 4, I argue that, although many North Carolinians protested the burdens of war, this did not necessarily mean that they were disloyal; rather, they sought to negotiate a moral economy of war by which hardships would be more equitably distributed. The arrival of Sherman's forces in the state served as a catalyst to redirect these resentments toward the enemy. Consequently, many citizens proved more loyal than previous studies suggest.[7]

Finally, Chapter 5 examines the peace treaty that Sherman negotiated with Confederate general Joseph Johnston. All but reinstating the status quo in the South, this document was harshly criticized and rejected by the Union government. Although the victorious North forgave Sherman this political error, he became the devil incarnate in the Southern mind. It was this demonization of Sherman and Southerners' quest to win a moral victory that served, in the postwar period, to obscure elite white women's active role in the shaping of Confederate nationalism.

The most daunting challenge of this work, which blends civil war, gender, and military history, was to find a language acceptable to scholars from each of these fields. Equally as important to me, however, was to make this study accessible to the Civil War enthusiast. Historians constantly struggle with balancing narrative and analysis, often choosing a language so heavy with theoretical jargon that it speaks only to other academics. I believe that history can, and should, be both engaging and thought provoking, and that has been my goal. Practitioners of each of the aforementioned subfields strongly disagree on what constitutes accessible language, and I cannot expect to satisfy all of my colleagues. I have, therefore, chosen the path that I believe will come closest to providing my colleagues with a sophisticated analysis, as well as engaging the general reader who desires both historical knowledge and a good read!

Thus, while the body of the text contains sufficient analysis to inform, without disrupting the narrative flow, I have consigned questions of historiography and larger theoretical implications to the endnotes. In the Epilogue I stray most from this path. Although I have endeavored to avoid obscure language, this section is highly speculative and may be of more interest to academicians. Still, I trust that a broader audience will share my fascination with these intriguing ideas.

1 : SAVANNAH HAS GONE UP THE SPOUT

On December 22, 1864, William T. Sherman offered President Abraham Lincoln a special Christmas gift, namely the city of Savannah. When the Yankee press published the news, it made for a particularly joyous holiday in the North and earned Sherman the title of the "Military Santa Claus."[1] The fact that Sherman offered such a gift to the Union president, neatly tied up and conveyable, suggests a tidy transfer of a city from Confederate to Union hands. This picture is underscored by the fact that Confederate troops under General William J. Hardee had evacuated during the night, and Mayor Richard Arnold had surrendered the city. The March to the Sea was over, and the Union soldiers felt a growing confidence in their ability to end the war. An officer from New Hampshire wrote to his sister of the "satisfaction in being with a victorious army." Unlike his experience in the Army of the Potomac, where it was "always defeat, except at Gettysburg," under Sherman's command, victory was the norm.[2]

On the surface, the Georgia campaign had ended in an easy victory, and the orderly interaction between citizens and the Union army in Savannah tends to support this image of a "subjugated" people in Georgia. A closer examination of the month-long hiatus of Sherman's troops between their glorious march through Georgia and their ongoing campaign through the Carolinas reveals other aspects of the invasion—the complacent mood of the soldiers, the difficulties of families living on the outskirts of the city, who were subjected to repeated raids by foraging troops, and the resentments and acts of resistance of civilians who felt both anger and humiliation at the Federal occupation.[3]

For many Union soldiers, the Georgia campaign had seemed "easy, comfortable and jolly." A Captain Divine described it as a "gay old campaign." In fact, his regiment had enjoyed "the best health they have since leaving the States."[4] Little wonder that the troops felt so satisfied, for the countryside had provided them with a rich abundance of food. Sherman was well aware that his men "like[d] pigs, sheep, chickens, calves and Sweet potatoes better than Rations." He had thoroughly studied the Georgia census and correctly predicted that there was little chance his men would starve. An Iowan soldier told his cousin that he "had never lived better." He had fed on everything the general had promised, as well as "Geese, Turkeys, Honey, Molasses, Shugar [sic]." A New York private thought there had never been an army "that lived as well as Gen. Sherman's on his last campaign." Soldiers were quick to lay their hands on all the bounty of the Georgia countryside. They had little need of "Uncle Samuel's rations," which they regarded "with disdain."[5] This greatly eased Chief Commissary Officer George Balloch's job. He had been "worn out" when he left Atlanta but had little to do on the march across Georgia. "The troops gathered from the country what supplies we did not bring with us and the novelties that presented themselves continually gave a healthy excitement to the journey so that the whole thing looked more like an old fashioned muster than the march of an invading army." His health was now excellent, he told his wife, "and I feel quite like a man again." So much food had been available that one soldier found the idea of starving the South utterly ridiculous.[6]

Foraging for food and valuables had, in fact, become so easy that a sense of monotony was setting in. While main columns took everything by the roadside, others were looking for distractions and becoming expert at discovering hidden items. By early December one soldier noted a change in the behavior of Sherman's troops. "It is becoming apparent that unprincipled men are taking advantage of the license given to them to forage, and are pillaging," he wrote in his diary. "Almost an endless variety of articles have been exhumed. Some are bringing away clothing, others blankets, others fine dishes, silver spoons, etc. One man has just passed us dressed as a lady, only his toilet was rather crudely made."[7]

For the white citizens of Georgia, of course, Sherman's March had seemed far from agreeable but was instead a "bitter quaff." Union soldiers who took pride in discovering hidden caches no doubt conveyed a sense that they were able to outsmart as well as overpower Southerners. Furthermore, when they engaged in the not uncommon ritual of parading around in clothes wrested from a Southern lady's wardrobe, they only intensified her humiliation and resentment. "Those of us who have suffered," wrote the editor of the *Georgia Countryman*, "can hardly be expected to love our tormentors, and persecutors, and we can hardly be expected to look with much favor upon anything that has the remotest resemblance to reunion with the Yankees." This resentment masked feelings of dishonor that Georgians had allowed Sherman to pass through "comparatively uninjured. . . . This should mantle with the blush of shame the cheek of every Georgian, and every Confederate. . . . We, for one, feel deeply mortified—humbled, chagrined—even degraded."[8]

Georgia had, in fact, received far more of a psychological blow than material damage at the hands of Sherman.[9] In the capital of Milledgeville, for example, only two plantation residences and two private city homes were destroyed. Soldiers did, however, ridicule Southerners by holding a mock session of the legislature in the abandoned statehouse and destroying books and papers. In the absence of any government officials, who had all fled before Sherman's forces, a young girl of the town felt her "cheeks glow with shame."[10]

Just as Northern soldiers were prone to trivialize their transgressions, Southerners tended to exaggerate them. Recent scholarship suggests that the amount of destruction of private property in Georgia fell far short of what was popularly believed.[11] Furthermore, in the countryside inhabitants also had to contend with Confederate cavalry under the command of Major General Joseph Wheeler. A resident of Griffin complained to Confederate president Jefferson Davis that Wheeler's cavalry were "burning up all the corn and fodder" and carrying off "mules and horses." Unless some speedy action was taken, he warned, citizens who had been loyal to the Confederacy "will not care one cent which army is victorious in Georgia."[12] In a letter to the *Countryman*, a Georgia woman confirmed that the people were suffering from both the "depredations" of Yankees and the "shameful" behavior of Wheeler's men. "While the enemy were burning and destroying property on one side . . . they [Wheeler's men] were stealing horses and mules on the other."[13]

The limits of war depended to a great extent on geography. The apparent order in Savannah was in direct contrast to the confusion in the countryside. A correspondent from the *New York Herald* noted the difference in behavior. "While marching through the country, where military restraint cannot control all, excesses may be committed; but where military influence is concentrated, it is impossible for them to go unpunished."[14] Civilians also understood this distinction. A refugee from the city told her sister that although she had heard property was respected in Savannah, the surrounding countryside was "devastated." A Savannah woman reported that although women in the city were not molested, "in the country of course it was different."[15]

In Liberty County, surrounding the city of Savannah, residents were subjected to repeated raids by soldiers stationed in the town. An Iowan soldier told his cousin that he had "a very pleasant time" on just such a five-day foraging excursion.[16] The experiences of Georgians who lived in an area that one historian has described as "no-man's land" were an exception to the normal rule of foraging on Sherman's campaign. Yet they also represent what was typical in confrontations between Union soldiers and Southern civilians—namely, that Southern women frequently faced the enemy alone.[17]

When white men of the South went off, eager to display their manhood on the battlefield, Confederate women celebrated their bravery, prayed for them, sewed for them, and wept for them. When the home front became a battlefront, however, it was primarily women and children who faced enemy troops. Even the men who remained at home frequently hid, leaving their families without a male protector. When Joseph LeConte, a doctor from Columbia, South Carolina, heard of Sherman's advance across Georgia, he traveled to Liberty County to bring some female members of his family out of harm's way. After a long and arduous journey, the doctor arrived to find his sister's house subjected to recurrent Union raids. Although the house was ransacked, the women suffered no bodily harm. It was, in fact, the doctor whose life was considered to be in jeopardy, and he hid in the surrounding woods for a week. A Union colonel detailed one of the few occasions on which his regiment came across Confederate soldiers who had taken shelter behind a house. After driving the enemy away, Colonel Oscar Jackson found the house filled with women and children. "This was chivalry indeed—to hide behind women and children," was his sarcastic comment.[18] Why would Southern men hide from an approaching enemy, leaving their female kinfolk to face the onslaught alone? The explanation for this behavior rests in the culture of the Old South and its variance from gender ideologies accepted in the North.

One could well make the argument that both Yankees and Confederates shared a belief that privileges of race and class offered certain women a guarantee of protection. Nevertheless, there were also conflicting interpretations of gender ideology. One of the keys to understanding why Confederate men felt that their women were well prepared and equipped to serve as defenders of the home is that they interpreted female strength differently from their Northern counterparts.[19]

The industrializing and urbanizing areas of the North encouraged the development of a separate sphere ideology molded around the model of burgeoning middle-class families. Women assumed the role of moral guardian to provide stability and shelter for men involved in the increasingly hostile world of business and politics. As gender became an especially salient political division in the North, women's economic roles were obscured and they were assigned a superior moral strength, based on the belief that they were inherently less passionate than men. This designation may well have eased the minds of middle-class men as their wives left the confines of the home to pursue acts of benevolence and reform.[20]

Southern ladies did not enjoy the same liberties of movement as their Northern counterparts. Although this was the result of practicalities as much as ideological tenets, such limited mobility has been interpreted as undermining the development of feminist consciousness. This argument, however, is based on a flawed model of Southern society. The enduring significance of the Southern household as the center of both production and reproduction delayed the full flowering of the separate sphere ideology. In the mid-nineteenth century, Northern industrialization and urbanization shifted the political focus from personal influence to public institutions, highlighting the exclusion of women. But in the South, where race was the primary determinant of social and political power, and deference remained central to its exercise, women could function as virtuous and active citizens so long as they supported the existing system.

Both North and South placed great importance on women's outward display of submission to male authority. In the South, however, this was not based on a belief that women were inherently delicate creatures, but that they *chose* to restrain their inner strength for the benefit of social harmony and family honor. Consequently, women were not merely vicarious beneficiaries of male honor but could share in this concept and see their own roles as vital in the shaping of Confederate nationalism. Furthermore, it was permissible for white women to display passion and proficiency provided it was in support of the family.[21]

In the antebellum period it was not unusual for white women of the South to be left alone on plantations or farms.[22] A series of letters from a young New York woman who married a North Carolina planter described to her family the major differences between the lives of Northern and Southern women. She explained that even privileged plantation women worked "harder than any Northern farmer's wife." With a workday that began at dawn, she found herself "tired enough to sleep like a rock" by dusk. During her husband's frequent absences she ran his business and suspected that she could be a farmer herself. Even though she felt lonely when left "quite alone in the midst of the pine woods with the Negroes," she did not feel fear.[23] On the basis of this understanding, Southern women frequently managed farms and plantations alone and saw themselves as responsible for the material and cultural survival of the family. When threatened by an invading army, they were more than able to respond with a passion worthy of both mothers and warriors.[24]

During an invasion, women often recognized the advantage of having no men present. A Jasper County, Georgia, woman who lived with her mother, her niece, and two female refugees from Tennessee expressed relief that there was "no gentleman at our house" when Sherman's men passed. "He would have been no protection," she continued, and may have "been badly treated." A Virginia woman hoped that her father in Georgia would not consider staying at home. "Here, in this raid-visited section, the men are wiser," she wrote. "They all leave home, as a matter of course on the approach of the enemy—for long experience has taught them that women are the best defenders of themselves and their property under such circumstances."[25] Some men actually feared the passion that might be revealed by their female kin's overzealous defense of the hearth. The editor of the *Georgia Countryman* advised his mother, who waited alone for the Yankees, to be "polite." In his own home, even though he was present, he begged his wife to stay in her room "lest she should betray her indignation, and give vent to her feelings, in words which might cause the hyenas to insult her."[26]

Northerners, for their part, used such examples of Confederate women's behavior as propaganda, particularly to encourage women's patriotism on the Union side. In 1863 a New York woman addressed accusations that "women of the North have not equaled those of the South in patriotic interest, labors, and sacrifices." She acknowledged "radical differences between the women of the two sections," claiming that Northern women could never embrace such a "ferocious patriotism." It was obvious to her that Southerners were more "demonstrative," whereas "northern women are rather deep than violent; their sense of duty is a quiet and constant rather than a headlong or impetuous impulse." She accused Southern women of placing passion before principle and encouraged Northern women to express their patriotism "without public demonstration."[27]

Though both North and South embraced gender distinctions, they understood and interpreted them in different ways. Overt manifestations of female power disconcerted Union soldiers, who carried their own set of domestic values into the war based on the image of home as "haven." This image fed into a biologically deterministic view of women as mothers and wives and conflated the moral superiority assigned to women with an innate pacifism. Thus when Northern soldiers encountered defiant and vituperative Southern women, they frequently concluded that such displays crossed the boundaries of acceptable feminine behavior. Branding them "she-devils," some Union men even blamed Southern women for prolonging the war, demonstrating a vindictiveness and zeal for blood that, to the soldiers, seemed unprecedented.[28]

The tenacity and rebellious spirit of many Confederate women struck Union soldiers as remarkable. One officer encapsulated the link between the Confederate army and Southern women. In his opinion most people in Alabama, Georgia, and the Carolinas were ready to submit, "but the real country is the army—it & the vast majority of the women are unconquered & unconquerable."[29] Even those who were weary of the war had not renounced their belief in independence. A Georgia woman admitted to a Yankee chaplain that she thought it foolish to continue the war. Yet she professed that although they were "whipped," they were "not subdued in spirit." "We hate you," she told Reverend Bradley, "but you have the power in your own hands, and sooner or later we must come under." But defiance was a two-edged sword—by the time Bradley reached Savannah, this indomitable spirit of Southern womanhood had influenced his thinking. Acknowledging his wife's concern over the suffering of women and children of the South, he countered, "So far as the women are concerned, we might as well spare our pity, for they are the worst secessionists, and why should they not suffer?"[30]

That fierce spirit was tested to its limits in the case of Mrs. Mary Jones and her daughter of Liberty County. The first Union soldiers arrived at their home on December 15, 1864, and reappeared continuously for eight more days. Thereafter they came sporadically until January 5, 1865. This episode is representative of the experiences of white Southern women of the planter class who, along with their slaves, encountered Sherman's army. Yet their trial was atypical in a geographic sense. Whereas residents in other parts of the Georgia countryside watched the soldiers march past, the Jones family endured three weeks of constant raids by Yankees. During that time these women showed both political savvy and strength, as well as desolation and hope.

On one day fifty soldiers swept through the Jones's house. During a hiatus from stealing food and rifling through the women's personal belongings, one Kentuckian engaged Mrs. Jones in a political debate. She was more than adequately prepared for the exchange. "My countrymen have decided that it was just and right to withdraw from the Union," she said. "We wished to do it peaceably[.] You would not allow it. We have now appealed to arms & I have nothing more to say with you upon the subject." For several days squads of soldiers came until darkness fell. "It is impossible to imagine the horrible uproar &

stamping through the house every room of which was occupied by them, all yelling, cursing, quarreling, & running from one room to another in wild confusion," Jones wrote in her diary. Even as her daughter lay in the pains of childbirth, the yard was full of Yankees. Although Mrs. Jones was unable to prevent them from setting foot in her house, they did make one concession: they removed their spurs before entering! The men helped themselves to family provisions, ransacked the house, and stole or killed livestock. When it was finally over, Mrs. Jones raged, "Do the annals of civilized, & I may add, savage warfare, afford any record of brutality equaled in extent and duration to that which we have suffered." Yet though she admitted to desolation, she remained hopeful that God would see her family through the ordeal, and that it would emerge "purged & purified in this furnace of affliction."[31]

White women were not the only ones to suffer, nor were they the only people to show courage. In the slave quarters of the Jones household, for instance, blacks employed various ruses to protect themselves and their belongings. The young cook disguised herself as a sick old woman. Another dissuaded soldiers from entering his cabin by telling them that there was "yellow fever" inside. One female slave stopped the theft of her clothes by claiming that they were "dead people [sic] clothes."[32] Union soldiers commonly helped themselves to the goods of blacks and whites alike. In Liberty County, many slaves had been able to acquire some personal property. This area had been settled by Puritan Congregationalists, and "under the aegis of this Christian paternalism, many blacks as carpenters, blacksmiths, drivers and mangers had been able to accumulate modest amounts of livestock and crops."[33] In the immediate postwar period, ex-slaves filed eighty-nine of the ninety-two settled claims for wartime damages. In one such deposition, a freedwoman explained that her husband had accumulated his modest wealth by "buying, raising [livestock] and trading."[34] It is possible, therefore, that on the Jones's plantation, blacks had more reason to fear the Yankee troops than to welcome them.

The nature of encounters between slaves and the Union army depended on both the character of master-slave relations and the racial attitudes of Northern soldiers. Though many Georgia slaves did seize the opportunity to claim their freedom, others remained behind. Their reasons varied, including loyalty to benign owners, a desire to protect their own property, or distrust of Yankee troops.[35]

Black distrust of Union soldiers was not unwarranted. Never had Mary Jones heard "expressions of hatred & contempt" for blacks as severe as she heard from the mouths of Yankees. One soldier told her that he wished he could "blow their [the slaves'] brains out." Another, less vindictive than his brother-in-arms, said that he did not approve of a war for abolitionism. Yet Mrs. Jones, like so many of her race and class, displayed concern for blacks in her own racist terms. She envisioned only "extermination" for black people as a result of emancipation. "Facts prove that [only] in a state of Slavery such as exists in the Southern states, have the negro race increased and thriven most." Once free of the "interference of Northern abolitionism," Southerners would be able to make the necessary reforms to ensure the continuation of a "benevolent" slavery.[36] Such feelings were common in antebellum Georgia. In fact, Mary Jones's words echoed a sermon preached in Savannah just two months earlier, in which Reverend Stephen Elliot had described the war as a "conflict involving the future of a race." Even if subjugated the white race would continue to exist, but "the black race perishes with its freedom."[37]

Northern soldiers expressed their own ambivalence regarding fleeing slaves. "It must be excruciatingly painful for the slaveholders to see their property walk off thus, thousands of dollars at a time!" rejoiced one Union soldier. At the same time, he found "these wretched children of Ham present a repulsive appearance as they trudge along in their miserable rags, seeking their freedom."[38] Fleeing slaves were generally seen as an encumbrance to marching ranks. "Despite all discouragements we have a large following," wrote an Indiana soldier. "General Sherman has tried in evry [sic] way to explain to them that we do not want them, that they had better stay on the plantations till the war is ended." A captain from the same state reported that guards were posted to "prevent all colored females and children from following the army."[39] Other Union soldiers welcomed the presence of young black women in their ranks, treating them as "dark houries [whores]" and even gave them horses to ride.[40] On the Jones's property, black men were forced to rescue their wives from "infamous" Yankees.[41]

Nevertheless, many slaves did follow the Union army into Savannah. When the city streets "resounded with the tread of the Yankee hosts" followed by a retinue of liberated slaves, reactions of Georgians spanned a gamut of emotions.[42] The spirits of many blacks, and some whites with Unionist sympathies, no doubt soared to the jubilant notes of regimental bands. Those who were war weary, or were struggling to find food and shelter in impoverished conditions, welcomed the thought of the material relief the Union forces could provide. Those people probably made up the citizens who crowded streets and balconies, causing one soldier to note that "the wildest enthusiasm prevailed"; another thought that residents were joyful to be under "the care of the 'blue coats.'"[43] But not all inhabitants were so demonstrative. Captain George Pepper recalled seeing women at the windows of mansions "casting significant and scornful smiles." Others, who had homes and possessions at risk, or whose thoughts dwelled on loved ones fighting in the ranks or languishing in prisoner-of-war camps, no doubt remained indoors, wrestling with feelings ranging from resentment to despondency, from fear to rank hatred. One white woman grudgingly complimented the Yankees on the "orderly way" in which they entered the city. "Of course," she added, "there were many robberies committed, the lower classes and the negroes, whom they came to befriend, being the greatest sufferers."[44]

There was no questioning the mood of Union soldiers, however, as they made their triumphant entry into the city. Major General Alpheus Williams described to his daughter a "series of military reviews down the broad streets of Savannah." He was especially proud of the spectacle that his corps made as the troops marched to the music of "three of four of the best bands in the army." Another soldier described the reviews as "emphatically" great—"great in numbers, great in enthusiasm, great in devotion, great in character, sublime in object."[45]

The apparent order in Savannah was in direct contrast to the confusion and chaos in the countryside. Under the upright administration of Major General John White Geary, commanding the Second Division, Twentieth Corps, increasing numbers of citizens appeared on the streets, "surprised and gratified to find that no insults were offered."[46] Sherman informed his superior, General Ulysses S. Grant, that the people of Savannah "seem to be well content, as they have reason to be, for our troops have behaved magnificently; you would think it Sunday, so quiet is everything in the city day and night."[47]

Exhilarated by their part in this triumph, Union soldiers did not hesitate to share their feelings and took this time to catch up with personal journals and correspondence. One soldier felt that Christmas in Savannah was "more like civilization than we have seen before for a long time." An Indiana soldier, hearing the news of General John Bell Hood's defeat in Tennessee, appreciated the fact that marching with Sherman had "let [him] out of a nice scrape."[48] Others wrote to their families of their pride in being part of Sherman's "glorious war" or of the "poetry of campaigning."[49] The North felt a similar satisfaction. An Illinois editor, responding to a soldier in Savannah, wrote, "I am so lost in wonder and admiration of that great March through Ga. & its glorious termination in Gen. Sherman's 'Christmas Present,' that even to be known and remembered by one of the participators in it is a very valuable thing to me."[50]

The broad streets and grand houses on squares surrounding parks, where trees drooped with Spanish moss, made Savannah a welcome sight to weary, yet triumphant soldiers. Major James A. Connolly told his wife that Savannah was "the finest [city] I have seen in the south." Here, instead of his tent, he took up private rooms in a grand residence where he had "gas light, coal fires, sofas, fine beds, bath room with hot and cold water and all such luxuries."[51] But while soldiers reveled in their victory and enjoyed their new surroundings, the mood in Savannah was not one of uniform acquiescence. A deep gulf separated the two sides, even as both longed for an end to the war. Whereas a private from Indiana envisioned spending next year's holidays "at home, enjoying the fruits of our labor," a Savannah woman warded off her despondency by looking forward to her next Christmas in the Confederacy.[52]

The common ground of war weariness and youthful ardor sometimes brought these two groups together. Some young women were clearly captivated by Yankee soldiers. Colonel Jackson thought the Savannah ladies the "tastiest 'secesh'" he had seen. "Don't look like war now," commented an Indiana captain as he watched officers and men riding about the city with Savannah women.[53] Another soldier told his sister that he had found "the sweetest girl here that ever man looked at. She is just your size & Form, with large very deep brown eyes, almost black that sparkle like Stars. I swear I was never so bewitched before."[54] Of course, some of these young women used their charms to further their own agendas. In her diary a young Savannah woman described her friend who regularly entertained Federal troops, "buttering them well all for her own ends." She had little doubt that her friend "will get all that she wants out of these Yankees."[55]

Southern women displayed a variety of reactions to Union soldiers, ranging from curiosity to apathy to outright hostility. They could freeze Yankees with a look or ignore them with an aura of disdain. Fanny Cohen's father was fearful that his headstrong daughter would lose her composure and endanger the family with "an open avowal of hatred." She herself admitted that when confronted with a Yankee officer, she struggled to keep her inner passions intact. "The contending feelings were more than I could control," she confessed in her journal. Another woman privately expressed the wish that "a thousand papers of pins" were stuck in General Sherman's bed and that "he was strapped down on them." She later related the story of one of her braver friends who dared a Union soldier to arrest her for refusing to walk under a Union flag. "I know you have the power, if not the right," she exclaimed. "See if you can shake my resolution."[56]

Privileged white women used a variety of measures to ensure their physical and economic survival. Frances Howard, a particularly enterprising planter's daughter, was quick to see an opportunity to deal with the enemy on her own terms. As she realized that Yankees were about to occupy the city, Howard did not cower in a corner or rage in frustration; instead, she immediately purchased three pumpkins and some tobacco that she later exchanged for sugar. As she stood in her kitchen baking pumpkin pies, the words of a nursery rhyme taught to her by her old "nurse" rang in her ears—"'Ingin pudden an' pumpkin pie, Make dem Yankees jump sky high." Howard sold all of her pies to Union soldiers and cleared "fifteen dollars in greenbacks." Of course, she did not venture into the streets to ply her trade but sent her "servants" to sell them. Other women proved equally enterprising traders. Elizabeth Stiles, whose husband had been killed on the eve of Savannah's fall, wrote to her son in the Virginia trenches that she had raised money by making "ribbon bows and nets." Another family member sold her jewelry and then went into the flower business. Eschewing direct contact with the enemy, she sent her slave into the streets to sell her bouquets.[57]

No such compunction was involved when it came to feeding a tired, hungry group of Confederate prisoners, whom Frances Howard saw halted opposite her home. Yet how was she to protect this food from Yankee soldiers? Setting a careful plan, she and her sister invited the captain of the guard to dinner. After politely entertaining him, they disabused the Northern officer of the illusion that he was a welcome guest. On the contrary, they told him, "We hate you as all good Confederates should." Now that they had fed their enemy, however, they persuaded the captain that he had a moral obligation not only to allow them to feed the Confederate prisoners, but also to provide a guard to protect that food from Yankee "paws." These enterprising women got their way. Another woman, eager to protect her carriage from being taken by the Yankees, was also able to strike up a bargain. She removed one wheel from the vehicle and hid it four flights up in her attic. Each time an officer sent for it, she refused to comply. Eventually a compromise was reached—she handed over the wheel in return for a supply of fresh meat.[58]

Outward compliance did not always fool Northerners. A Yankee civilian writing to a friend in Boston felt that genuine Union sympathies were scarce. "The people look upon the Confederate cause as lost, and therefore come forward and take the oath of allegiance to the United States; but they still retain their Southern sympathies and have no love for the Union." During a church service, he noted that the minister omitted the prayer for the president of the United States and preached a sermon "calculated to inspire the people with the hope that 'right truth' and rebellion will finally succeed against 'persecution.' " He also witnessed more blatant resistance. At a dinner party he attended with the family of General Hardee, he found the women to be "great secessionists." One of them even suggested that Secretary of State William Henry Seward had been responsible for starting the war after a Southern lady had jilted him.[59]

It is difficult to tell whether civilian attitudes toward enemy soldiers changed during the period of occupation. Perhaps once white civilians realized that they were going to survive relatively unscathed, they felt more confident and engaged in more blatant acts of resistance. A Cincinnati newspaper reported in January 1865 that Savannah displayed "none of the rank bitterness" found in other cities. Six weeks later another newspaper from the same town wrote that, if able, "the majority of the people would cut all our throats tomorrow."[60]

At first blush, however, most Northern soldiers viewed Savannah as completely subjugated, suggesting that it was the beginning of the end of the Confederacy. Northern officials immediately noted that they had a hungry population to feed, and the influx of a large number of refugees only exacerbated this problem. At first Sherman refused to take on this responsibility: "No provision has been made for the families in Savannah, and many of them will suffer from want," he wrote to Major General Wheeler, adding, "I will not undertake to feed them." Nevertheless, when the mayor of the city called a meeting in which resolutions were passed to submit to Federal authority, Sherman relented. Given the shortages of both food and fuel, the mayor's actions may have represented pragmatism rather than Unionism. Sherman was encouraged by Mayor Arnold's compliance and ordered that "citizens destitute of provisions make application at the city store, where they would be supplied upon the order of the mayor."[61]

Sherman's change of heart provides an excellent opportunity to look more closely at the overall strategy of this complex man. His drive for an efficient end to the war was inextricably linked to his desire for a conciliatory peace and complicated by his ongoing concern about his reputation. The Northern general was no stranger to this part of the country. He had been stationed in the South for six years during the 1840s and was living in Louisiana when the war broke out. He thus believed that he understood the Southern psyche and planned his campaign accordingly. In March 1864 he had admitted to his wife that he could not help feeling a reluctant admiration for Southerners' determination. "No amount of poverty or adversity seems to shake their faith," he wrote. By the summer he expressed regret that he was gaining a monstrous reputation, for he had been "more kindly disposed to the People of the South than any general officer of the whole army." If only the South would admit the error of its ways and return voluntarily to the Union, Sherman would extend the hand of a benign patriarch and welcome the quondam rebels back into the bosom of the American family.[62]

Sherman thus struggled to maintain a precarious balance between harsh warfare and a harmonious peace—a goal that he had made clear before commencing his March to the Sea. Addressing the Atlanta City Council in September 1864, he had explained that the only way to reach his ultimate goal of peace was "through Union and war," which he would wage with a view to "perfect an early success." Yet, he assured the officials, once peace was established, "you may call on me for anything. Then will I share with you the last cracker, and watch with you to shield your homes and families against danger from every quarter." In private conversation with a Confederate chaplain who was traveling across enemy lines, Sherman displayed a characteristic concern about his reputation. Chaplain Henry Lay noted that the general was highly sensitive to charges that he was either "brutal or inhuman." Indeed, Sherman insisted that once the war was over, "the past would be quickly forgotten and both parties would love and respect each other."[63]

In Savannah, Sherman continued to navigate his chosen path between harshness and benevolence. In December he ordered that "where there is no conflict, every encouragement should be given to well disposed and peaceful inhabitants to resume their usual pursuits." In private correspondence, he berated the Southern press for characterizing him as a "savage monster" and reiterated his long-term goal to "make all sunshine and happiness where gloom and misery reigns supreme."[64] He found it ironic that although his army had gained a reputation for burning, raping, and murdering, he had received requests from two Confederate generals to care for their families who remained in Savannah. "These officers knew well that these reports were exaggerated in the extreme," he wrote to his wife, "and yet tacitly assented to these false publications to arouse the drooping energies of the people of the South."[65] Bringing relief to Savannah's compliant population gave Sherman the opportunity to play the part of the "Military Santa Claus"—as the Northern press had dubbed him—a role entirely consistent with his long-term strategy. At the same time he could demonstrate to Georgia, and the Confederacy, the advantages of a voluntary return to the Union.

The Savannah relief program serves as a prism through which we can view not only the nature of William T. Sherman, but also the conflicting sentiments that Yankees and Confederates held for each other. For Union men in Savannah, the distribution of food to suffering people elicited both sympathy and condescension. Many needy inhabitants welcomed the benevolence of their enemies; many more raged in frustration and humiliation. On the other hand, the request for relief provided the North with a powerful tool of propaganda—one that reinforced the picture of a subjugated South eager to return to the Union. At the same time it allowed Northerners to indulge in an image of themselves as merciful conquerors.

On December 30, 1864, as a gesture of goodwill, Sherman turned over to the Savannah City Council fifty thousand bushels of confiscated rice in order that the city might negotiate a trade with the North for much-needed supplies. At this time Union colonel Julian Allen made a timely appearance on the scene to offer his services as a "special agent" to negotiate the trade. Colonel Allen had never seen active service but had been abroad recruiting immigrants to serve as substitutes for Bostonians. On his return to New York, he heard of the capture of Savannah. In the spirit of his prewar career as a salesman and crusader for a variety of political causes, he immediately recognized an entrepreneurial opportunity.[66]

Although Allen was charged with negotiating a trade agreement between New York and Savannah, he took it upon himself to turn an economic exchange into a moral crusade. In an emotionally charged speech before the New York Chamber of Commerce, he called for "noble charity for a fallen and repentant foe—charity for the weak and starving women and children who raised themselves from their pallets to cheer, weakly but fervently, the old flag as it passed."[67] The Northern press eagerly took up this crusade, urging New Yorkers to sympathize with citizens whose pride had been crushed by an "almost bloodless victory." Surely this was a sign that the South had "learned wisdom from bitter experience." Let the North take this opportunity to demonstrate to the Southern people "the brotherhood we would extend to all of them if they would but cease resistance to the constitution and the laws."[68] New Yorkers responded enthusiastically, raising over thirty thousand dollars in three days.

The appeal to Bostonians to extend charity to a "prodigal son" enjoyed even greater success. Aided by the oratory of a local minister, Allen stressed that what was accomplished in Savannah might influence other parts of the South. For good measure, he emphasized images of women and children in the city with "haggard looks, wasted frames, and careworn countenances."[69]

On January 9, 1865, Boston residents were called to a public meeting to "consider measures for the relief of the suffering people of Savannah." Five hundred copies of the proceedings and resolutions passed at the meeting were sent for distribution to the mayor and citizens of Savannah. Boston congratulated the citizens of Savannah on their "deliverance from the irresponsible power of the Rebel Government" and considered it "a privilege to extend assistance to the suffering poor."[70]

This report of the proceedings of the relief program in Boston provides not just an account of the events, but a window into resistance in Savannah, for undoubtedly the wording of this document would have sounded more than a little condescending to proud Southerners. The situation was exacerbated by the fact that Boston was congratulating itself on its refusal to take Southern rice in exchange for goods. Rubbing salt into wounds of humiliation, the final speaker of the day emphasized this point. "New York and Boston don't want their rice," he exclaimed. "Savannah wants our pork, beef and flour; and I say, in the name of Heaven, let us send it to them without money . . . let us show that we are glad of a chance to minister to the wants of our fellow-citizens in the South, when we are under no moral obligation to do so."[71]

One month later, a committee sent to Savannah to oversee the distribution of provisions reported back to the Boston City Council. The method of distribution, it explained, was to send "a number of responsible gentlemen" from door-to-door to establish each family's needs. Those qualifying for relief received a ticket that was renewable each week. The committee expressed its belief that "expressions of gratitude" were "sincere and heartfelt." Unfortunately, it added, the condition of the people of Savannah "prevented them from showing us more hospitality."[72]

Apparently the committee felt obligated to establish whether there was a "true state of Union sentiment" among these recipients of Boston's bounty and decided to investigate the matter further. By visiting residents known to have opposed the Federal government and by surreptitiously attending meetings of leading citizens of a more "private character," they concluded that "there have always been in Savannah *few* and *thoroughly* loyal Union men." But nearly all of the male residents were now "convinced of the *hopelessness* of the *rebel cause*. Exhausted in the face of the 'power and determination' of the North, they were ready to cease the struggle and 'renew their allegiance' to the Union." If there remained any "ardent advocates of the rebel cause," it was the women of the city. The explanation for this distinction was that women's more passionate and impulsive natures had not afforded them the opportunity to give the matter "calm and sober consideration." The committee trusted that eventually female opinions would become more reasonable. Meanwhile, it was of the opinion that, with few exceptions, women—"and the clergy"—remained firmly on the side of the Confederacy.[73]

Perhaps some of these women had heard the sermon given by Reverend Stephen Elliot just two months earlier. In an uncanny prophesy of the "benign" occupation of Savannah, Elliot warned that what Georgians had to fear most in their exhausted condition was "an administration which would come with kindness on its lips." What they needed was "such fury as Grant's, such cruelty as Butler's, such fanaticism as Sherman's." "It is men like these" he continued, "who revive our courage and reanimate our efforts." Sherman himself may well have anticipated such a reaction. After all, he had intended to allow Savannah to trade with the North, thus permitting its citizens to retain some sense of their autonomy and dignity. Even if his plan had been carried out, however, he may not have been trusted. Despite his best efforts outside Atlanta, Sherman had been unable to convince Chaplain Lay of his humanity. The minister was left with the abiding conviction that the South must "at whatever cost, win our independence. There is no other alternative open to us which can be for one moment considered."[74]

Sailing on a tide of Christian benevolence, Union ships docked at Savannah harbor laden with flour, meat, and vegetables. A crowd of "all ages, all sizes, all complexions—with a variety of costumes such as was never seen at a masquerade or fancy dress ball," greeted the cargoes. The scene would have "rejoiced the heart of every one of the philanthropists who aided in piling up those barrels of food," declared the Savannah Daily Herald.[75]

But the Northern bounty was not received with the Christian humility that had been expected. A letter to the editor of the Savannah Republican remonstrated that "no appeal has been sent to any place for aid . . . and none is needed in the manner proposed." "The people of Savannah," the writer claimed, "never intended to be placed in such an abject condition before the world." Certainly many inhabitants, especially those who populated the more elite classes, must have felt a great sense of humiliation as they were forced to line up for handouts from their sworn enemies. A New York Times correspondent described the relief line as "a motley crowd . . . both sexes, all ages, sizes, complexions, costumes, gray haired old men . . . well-dressed women wearing crepe for their husbands and sons . . . demi-white women wearing negro cloth, negro women dressed in gunny cloth; men with Confederate uniforms."[76] One white woman allowed her pent-up resentment to spill onto the pages of her journal. "They think they are so liberal, giving us food," she wrote, "and they stole more from one plantation than the whole of New York subscribed." Similar sentiments could be found in public and private correspondence. "If there is one sink lower than any other in the abyss of degradation the people of Savannah have reached it," wrote an Augusta editor. A South Carolina refugee expressed skepticism about this "conciliatory" policy, laying the blame squarely on Sherman's shoulders. "He is patting them with his cushioned paw, but the claws will soon appear," was her scathing remark.[77]

In Savannah, Sherman found the resilience and stubbornness of the women remarkable given their increasing impoverishment. As early as 1863, he had determined that there was no parallel to the "deep & bitter enmity of the women of the South." Now he wrote that "the girls remain, bright and proud as ever." Despite the fact that he had cut a path through the very heart of their state, "they talk as defiant as ever." Mary Jones, who had been caught up in that path for so long, reassured herself that she had "never failed" to let the enemy know that she believed her cause was "just & right." Despite the fact that she had occasionally been compelled to "use entreaties," her greatest achievement was that she had never appeared cowardly. As she gazed upon the devastation of her home and the desecration of her personal belongings, she became ever more resolute. "Every development of the enemy," she wrote in her journal, "but confirms my desire for a separate and distinct nation." In Milledgeville, a young woman wrote of the degradation she felt when she saw the Yankee flag flying from the capitol. But, she reported, people were now singing "We shall live and Die with [President] Davis . . . the people are firmer than ever before."[78]

In a similar vein, a Savannah woman refused to be intimidated even when faced with expulsion from the city for writing "imprudent letters." Regardless of the danger of finding herself and her four little children homeless in freezing weather, she stood up to Federal authorities and insisted on her rights as "a southern woman" to hold such sentiments. Although she admitted that, under the circumstances, it may have been unwise to express such attitudes in writing, "there was nothing treasonable or criminal in those letters, I had only spoken the truth . . . that the South had been wronged; that the North had been the aggressor." She did eventually gain permission to remain in the city.[79]

Reports of women's reactions to the enemy traveled far from the Georgian city. In the Virginia trenches, a Confederate soldier expressed satisfaction that women in Savannah had treated Union soldiers with "undying hostility, in peace as well as war, in defeat as well as in success."[80] Not surprisingly, the Northern press adopted a more derisive tone. One article remarked on the number of pastry shops that had opened in Savannah during the Yankee occupation. "How are the mighty fallen," it exclaimed. It invited readers to imagine the irony of elite Northern families, such as the Astors or Belmonts, "turning cake vendors here to gain a little Confederate script."[81]

William T. Sherman was growing tired of "the importunities of rebel women" and was eager to begin a new, more daring campaign. He also expressed distaste for the "civilians from the North who were coming to Savannah for cotton and all sorts of profit." Other soldiers were more ambivalent. "Our whole army has fallen in love with this city," wrote Major Connolly, "and we leave it with regret." Still, he was eager to move on. "Ever since I left you I've been marching from you," he told his wife, "but tomorrow I start to march toward you."[82]

Many Union soldiers sensed that this was a turning point in the war. Nonetheless, the tenacity of the rebel spirit was not lost on them, and mingled with confidence was an awareness that the Confederacy would "not die an easy death." In a letter to his sister in New Hampshire, George Balloch said he believed that the South "will fight on as long as a single man can be found to fight with." Yet he and his comrades had an abiding faith in their leader, who seemed to them a "genius." "Let the rebels brag," wrote Sherman's military secretary to his wife, with such a man leading the army and the soldiers' "increased moral strength," a Northern victory was assured.[83]

Sherman also felt this sense of inevitability. "Every step I take from this point northward," he wrote to General H. W. Halleck, "is as much a direct attack upon Lee's army as though we were operating within the sound of his Artillery." In a more intimate message to his wife, he revealed the pressures of leadership. "I dread the elevation to which they have got me," he wrote. "A single mistake or accident, and my pile, though well founded, would tumble."[84]

Sherman's men, however, had indomitable faith in their leader and in the tangible manifestation of power that was his army. "Let the South build as many aircastles as people please," asserted Reverend Bradley. "One fact stands out apparent to every one who has been where we have, that the rebellion is fast tumbling to ruins. Sherman is knocking the bottom out."[85] As the news of the general's victory in Georgia reached Lieutenant Samuel Byers, a Union prisoner of war in Columbia, South Carolina, he inscribed it in a poem that he would later present to Sherman:

Proud proud was our army that morning,
That stood 'neath the cypress and Pine,
When Sherman said "boys you are weary,
This day fair Savannah is thine."
Then sang we a song for our chieftain,
That echoes in river and Sea,
And the stars in our banner shone brighter.
When Sherman marched down to the Sea.[86]

So Sherman's soldiers turned northward, toward South Carolina, the "cradle of secession," and toward home. As they left, they proposed three cheers for Savannah, a sound that generated "groans" from inside Frances Howard's household. These soft groans were just the seedlings of a bitter rancor that would be nurtured by the sting of defeat and the humiliation of Reconstruction.[87]

2 : ROCKING THE CRADLE OF SECESSION

On January 17, 1865, the statehouse in Columbia, South Carolina, housed a grand bazaar to raise funds for the Confederate cause. In a spirit that combined denial with arrogant confidence, a crowd of 3,800 jammed the halls. Leaving war cares at the door, people "jostled each other, laughed and made fun and forgot for the hour that the battle for home and fireside was soon to commence."[1] Banners covered the walls with slogans such as "Don't Give Up the Ship" and "Contribute to the Comfort of Our Sick and Wounded Soldiers." Tables and booths were set up to represent each of the Confederate states, displaying such a variety of articles that it was difficult to imagine that a war was going on. At the same that a young girl bemoaned the fact that her family was living on meager meals of "a very small piece of meat, . . . a few potatoes . . . a dish of hominey and a pone of corn bread," the tables at the bazaar groaned under the weight of "ducks, turkey, chickens [and] every kind of meat that could be found in the Confederacy."[2]

The daily rhythm of life was often played to the beat of Sherman's drum, even for Southerners who would never encounter the dreaded general. Two decades after the war had ended, a Virginia lady wrote an account of how the progress of Sherman had affected her dinner table. Each morning the family read the newspapers. If the news was bad, she "ordered sorghum pudding, with a reckless amount of butter." On the other hand, if things seemed hopeful she would "eschew sorghum pudding, *in toto*." The reasoning behind this menu choice was perfectly logical. If the enemy threat was imminent, her family wished to eat all the delicacies it had. On the other hand, if the war was to continue indefinitely, "who could contemplate the dreariness of existence . . . without the sweet solace of sorghum?" In Richmond, these desserts were named "Sherman puddings."[3]

South Carolinians had, of course, heard of Sherman's exploits in Georgia; in fact, Grace Elmore believed that Georgians were "greatly incensed against the government for evacuating Savannah." What could it mean for her state? she wondered. The rumor was that Sherman had announced that although he had handled Savannah with his "gloves on," he promised that "in Carolina I will take them off."[4]

Such was the paradox of life in Columbia that the citizens dreaded the possibility of Yankee rule at one moment and the next indulged themselves in the pleasures of a bazaar. "No one but those who have lived in times like ours can understand," wrote Elmore, "the gay and the tragic so closely intertwined." But it was impossible to shut out the impending horror indefinitely and, as January turned into February, Sherman *fever* grew. With every new rumor a feeling of inevitability settled on the city. When she joined other women in closing down the bazaar, Elmore described it as "a Tribute to our sick and wounded soldiers" paid with "loving hands and loving hearts, even with Sherman knocking at our door." As the winter winds intensified and the rains lashed down, nature reflected the mood of Columbia.[5]

Torrential rains, mud, and intense cold were the primary enemies of Union troops in the first months of 1865. Although the first troops left Savannah in early January, Sherman reported that the weather was "villainous, and all the country is under water, and retards me much." These adverse conditions delayed the main thrust of the army into South Carolina until early February.[6] It was immediately clear to Union major general Alpheus S. Williams that the campaign of the Carolinas would be "a decided contrast" to the Georgia march. South Carolina presented a landscape of "mud, swamps, treacherous quicksand and quagmires—cursed cold, rainy weather, hard work, much swearing . . . and altogether a more irksome and laborious campaign." Other soldiers felt that these new demands "threw the Georgia campaign far in the shade" or even made it seem like a "joke" in comparison.[7]

This hostile environment fueled a desire for revenge against the state that Northern troops regarded as the "cradle of secession," and disparaging remarks about the countryside were soon extended to embrace Southern culture as a whole. Judging the South and its people as culturally inferior helped ease misgivings about bringing destruction into the homes of civilians and manifested itself in a resolve to impose Northern standards of efficiency on a seemingly backward South. But when Sherman's men set foot in South Carolina, they crossed both a geographic and a cultural fault line. Residents and invading armies conceptualized their environments differently, and these perceptions influenced their decisions.[8]

The confrontation between Sherman's troops and Southern civilians involved a clash of ideological as well as physical space. When the invasion and punishment of South Carolina became an invasion of homes populated for the most part by women and children, many soldiers struggled with a series of conflicting emotions. When white civilians faced the demons of their worst nightmares, fear frequently turned to anger as they saw the enemy destroying their homes and belongings. African Americans' guarded anticipation was often replaced with a sense of betrayal as they suffered along with their owners, complicating their decision of whether to flee with or from Union troops.

The various historical actors thrown together in this encounter interpreted their surroundings through cultural lenses that influenced both their actions and their options. Only by grasping the anticipatory elements of the campaign can we fully understand the confrontations themselves and especially the cultural determinants of invasion.[9]

WHEN THE WIND BLOWS

As Federal troops prepared to leave Georgia in January 1865, Major Henry Hitchcock, Sherman's military secretary, wrote to his wife, "When or where we shall come out, nobody seems to have any idea, only that Sherman knows what he is about as usual."[10] Other soldiers also voiced uncertainty about what route the South Carolina campaign would take. "I hope to write to you by and by from Branchville, Charleston, Columbia, or Augusta," a Union captain told a friend. "Can't tell which or how many as Bill has not laid his plans before me yet."[11] Another officer who wondered which city would be their next target trusted that "the rebels know as little as we do which one is in the most immediate danger of a visit." Commissary Officer George Balloch observed that "Sherman's moves are a puzzle to everybody, friends as well as foes." Yet he urged his wife to be confident, for the general's army was composed of veterans who had never been defeated. One soldier felt that Sherman was the "profoundest man in the world," the originator of "deep plans and brilliant combinations and movements which surprise and startle mankind."[12] The resounding confidence that Sherman inspired in his men was carefully nurtured by the leader himself. "My men believe I know everything," he declared in private, adding, "They are much mistaken, but it gives them confidence in me." This confidence, he believed, made his army "almost invincible."[13]

In addition to boosting the confidence of his soldiers, Sherman claimed a second weapon: creating confusion and uncertainty in the minds of his enemies. He would use the two wings of his army to feint on both Augusta, Georgia, and Charleston, South Carolina. Once his actual objective, Columbia, became clear, it would be too late for the Confederacy to rally any meaningful resistance.[14] He did divulge the next stage in his plan to his wife, yet exhorted her silence, "for the walls have ears and foreknowledge published by some mischievous fool might cost many lives."[15] The general's strategy was based on both sound preparations and an understanding of the nature of Southern society. The years he had been stationed in various parts of the South during the 1840s now proved "providential." "Every bit of knowledge thus acquired is returned ten fold," he told his family. Moreover, the maps and statistics at his disposal ensured that "no military expedition was ever based on sounder or surer data."[16]

Union maps drawn up for invasion served both practical and psychological purposes. Civilians found the Northern army's knowledge of the landscape disconcerting. One Confederate woman commented on how well Union soldiers knew the area—"every house, or well, or mark of any kind." Another woman in South Carolina reported seeing Sherman holding a "complete diagram of all the farms, roads, and rivers in the Orangeburg county."[17] These maps were a source of pride to Union soldiers, who frequently sent copies to their families as souvenirs. "Just look at that pocket map of mine," wrote a corporal to his sister in Ohio, "and you can see how far we have marched." Major Hitchcock enclosed a map of the Georgia campaign in a letter to his wife. He promised her that in due time he would send her copies of the maps being prepared for the next stage, which would be "equally valued mementoes of a more important, probably more tedious march."[18]

Buoyed by increasing self-confidence and faith in their leader, Sherman's troops manifested a burning desire to seek revenge on the Southern state that had instigated four years of bloody warfare. These men were hardened veterans who had been seasoned by physical and emotional adversity. Now South Carolina was to pay the price of keeping them away from home for so long.[19] Sherman was aware of his army's "insatiable desire to wreak vengeance" on the Palmetto State. He felt sure that his troops would show less restraint in the next phase of the campaign:

> Somehow, our men had got the idea that South Carolina was the cause of all our troubles . . . and therefore on them should fall the scourge of war in its worst form. Taunting messages had also come to us, when in Georgia, to the effect that, when we should reach South Carolina, we would find a people less passive, who would fight us to the bitter end, daring us to come over etc., some that I saw felt that we would no longer be able to restrain our men as we had done in Georgia.[20]

Soldiers' private correspondence revealed just such a mind-set, predicting that once the men crossed the state line, bringing to South Carolina the "restitution she richly deserved," their cries would become "burn and destroy" and "ruin and desolation."[21] Union commander William Scofield, now "in the best of health," felt ready to "stand the hardship of another campaign" through "that detested State." In an impassioned letter to his father, he warned South Carolina that "the Hell Hounds of Yankeedom are on your track to burn your Cotton and destroy your crops. . . . We will be Wild Tigers let loose."[22] Major Connolly was also anxious to begin a "chastisement" by fire. "If we don't purify South Carolina, it will be because we can't get a light," he told his wife.[23] Another soldier wrote in his journal that "South Carolina has commenced to pay an installment long overdue on her debt of justice and humanity." He relished the thought that the "ground trembles beneath the tramp of thousands of brave Northmen, who know their mission and will perform it to the end."[24] Captain John Herr observed that nearly every soldier was "for disstroying [sic] everything in South Carolina." He expected the army to sweep through the state like a "hurricane."[25]

Armed with weapons of destruction, detailed maps, and a yearning to put an end to this bitter war, Yankee soldiers set their feet firmly on the terrain of South Carolina. Major Hitchcock expressed emotions shared by many of his comrades: "This campaign cannot but be even more important in its bearings on the war than the last; it will very likely not be as much of a mere picnic . . . [b]ut we have the same genius to guide us, [and] an even more demoralized enemy to meet." Captain George Pepper reported that the "very hope of treading the soil of the wretched state that inaugurated secession, fired every [soldier's] heart, and brightened every eye." He contrasted the exultation of the Union soldiers with an image of "panic stricken" Southerners, "so without counsel, so confounded, and so despondent."[26]

Emma Holmes, a young Confederate woman in Camden, South Carolina, could not repress a shudder when she heard that Union soldiers had left Savannah with "fearful denunciations of fiendish revenge." Women in particular felt increasingly anxious as they heard accounts of the "violent and unscrupulous acts of the soldiery in Georgia." In Charleston, Eliza Fludd suffered "intense distress" on learning that Union troops in Savannah had forewarned Southern women of the treatment they could expect. Rumors of "outrages and horrors" caused one woman to think "long and intently upon the righteousness of suicide should that worst of all happen." Exaggerated and unsubstantiated stories of Yankee depravities had circulated in the South for several years, and many women feared for more than the loss of their property.[27]

Southerners may have been vulnerable to fluctuating fears and emotions, but they were not lacking in their own geographic or strategic knowledge. Senator Warren Akin's wife, from her refuge in Elberton, Georgia, knew of the current Yankee position and expected the army to move on to Augusta. Later she heard of the fall of Fort Fisher in North Carolina and surmised that Wilmington would fall soon after. In that case she projected the evacuation of Richmond and advised her husband not to linger there. Ella Thomas in Augusta knew that if Sherman reached Branchville, he would cut off South Carolina's communications with Richmond.[28] Emma Holmes, in Camden, made detailed entries in her diary on the movement of Sherman's troops and the Confederate defeat at Franklin, Tennessee. She was aware that there might be strategic advantages in abandoning coastal cities such as Savannah or Charleston. The need to protect the interior was more important for both the state and the Confederacy, "for if all our railroads are cut & communications, cut off, how is the Army of [Northern] Virginia to be maintained with supplies?" she asked.[29] One member of a group of young women who had taken refuge in North Carolina wrote home to Columbia to tell a friend of the "safe arrival of the retreating column," as they dubbed themselves. The author of this letter parodied the exact strategy that General Sherman used. "The right wing of my force being placed under the command of General Conversation, the left under General Circumspection, the center being led by General Indifference," read her facetious report.[30]

Such a grasp of the larger picture of war belies the notion that women focused only on the survival of their own families. Civilians' knowledge of the progress of the war probably exceeded that of many ordinary soldiers who were involved in day-to-day military maneuvers. Emma Holmes's military map was shaped by the "40 blood relations who were or had been in the service, several being dead."[31] While soldiers were commonly enmeshed in the web of their own front, civilians at home followed news from the battlefield and thought of their loved ones far away.[32] When a soldier was called upon to build a road through the swamps of South Carolina, it was hard to see beyond the muck. When a family read accounts of Sherman's campaigns and traced his route on newspaper maps, their broader geographic vision of the war may have actually encouraged them to think nationally.[33]

Civilians' geographic knowledge was a mixed blessing as they studied their maps and realized that so much depended on "the whim or caprice of Gen. Sherman." This uncertainty kept morale in a constant state of flux and created an atmosphere of chaos and confusion.[34] Many Southern families now faced a difficult decision. Should they stay and meet the invader or pack their belongings and flee? And where were they to go? "Where shall we find safety, where can we lay our weary heads and rest our sickened hearts?" asked one young woman, adding, "There is not a spot to which we can flee with an assurance of safety."[35]

The vagaries of Sherman's policies in Georgia cities confused civilians and military authorities alike. In Atlanta, the civilian population had been forcibly removed; in Savannah, no evacuation was ordered. This lack of consistency created a dilemma over which many families agonized. "Flying is contagious," commented one woman. Another took the time to weigh her decision: "To go, meant horrible discomfort—[to] stay meant—we did not quite know what," wrote Mrs. Harriett Ravenel. It was almost comforting for her to believe that all places were equally vulnerable, and she decided to remain at home. "It is better to be taken in a city by the regular army, than in a lonely place by scouts or raiders," she told a friend. A Confederate soldier gave similar advice to his family, adding that if the Yankees came, it would be better to be among friends "than in a strange place among strangers."[36] Some families had faced the decision of whether or not to refugee before. Mrs. Emily Goodlett fled from Midway and arrived in Columbia only two weeks before Sherman threatened that city. Members of the Hamilton family acted as a "sort of avant courier" of the Yankee army. "By incessant hurrying [and] scurrying from pillar to post" over a five-week period, they ran from Columbia as far as Fayetteville, North Carolina, unable to escape the ominous shadow of Sherman's forces.[37]

African Americans were also in a quandary as rumors circulated of the Union army's approach.[38] One Confederate soldier advised his wife that "as the danger approaches," she would find some of their slaves "true," whereas others would be "carried away with the false promises of freedom." If she could identify those who would be loyal, she should "let them harness up all the mules and horses and load up the wagons with provisions and drive out of the track of the enemy and camp out until he passes and then come back home."[39] In Columbia, Grace Elmore decided to discuss with her more "intelligent servants" whether or not the whole family should flee. She explained that if they were to become refugees, life would be hard. On the other hand, she warned them "how wicked the Yankees had been in their conduct to the negro, how women and children had been abused just so soon as they had ceased to be an amusement and excitement."[40] Elmore eventually decided to remain in the city but escorted her slaves to the railroad depot to secure them safe passage. There they stood in the rain "huddled together under one umbrella, looking so cold and comfortless" that her heart went out to them. The trains were too full, however, and they "formed a mournful procession" back home. The Heywards decided that it was the white family members who should flee to safety. They told their "maid" to move into the main house and protect it as best she could. If they did not return, the faithful servant would have the house as her own.[41]

How these slaves interpreted their mistresses' messages we do not know. Certainly the Union soldiers were the vanguards of freedom, yet blacks had no reason to trust any white men, and as sexually vulnerable beings, African American women were in a particularly precarious situation.[42] Even if the Yankees brought freedom, what would their new role be? They could not join the army; most had family ties, and some felt loyalty to the white women with whom they had spent their entire lives. In Columbia, Emma LeConte's household slaves "dressed in their Sunday best" in preparation for flight, with the exception of her maid, Mary Ann. This young woman wept in front of her mistress, fearing that the Yankees might force her husband to go with them, in which case she would have to accompany him. "She seemed greatly distressed at the thought of leaving the master and mistress who had supplied the place of father and mother to her, an orphan," wrote LeConte.[43]

Yet one thing was clear. White masters and mistresses were losing power and becoming vulnerable in ways that were all too familiar to the slaves. Privation, separation from beloved family members, and fear of the future may have been new experiences for elite whites, but they were common in slaves' daily lives. When African Americans saw their owners suffering the same types of personal tragedies that they had inflicted on others, their reactions spanned a spectrum from delight to ambivalence and sometimes compassion. But for the most part, they kept their feelings hidden. Mary Chesnut was aware that her slaves must be contemplating freedom, yet outwardly they remained "more obedient and more considerate than ever," giving no inclination that they knew "Sherman and freedom was at hand."[44]

The minds of Union troops were not, however, on emancipating slaves but on the immediate physical obstacles to their new campaign. South Carolina was experiencing the worst precipitation in over a decade. This deluge flooded roads, destroyed bridges, and created swamps in the lowlands. One soldier remarked that "it began to rain as if the very heavens were coming down." Quartermaster William Schaum complained that the persistent rain kept sleep at bay and left him "wet threw [sic] to the skin." A lieutenant from Iowa told his family that soldiers often became sick after such a soaking: "disease—diarhea [sic]." The mud and water were so deep that another soldier supposed that "the way So. Ca. got out of the Union was by swimming."[45] Roads became impassable, and troops were often "mud bound" with water "two & three feet deep." "I thought I had seen mud before but this beats everything I imagined," wrote Sergeant Rufus Meade. Private Charles Brown described himself "stuck in the swamps, in the sand knee deep, [and] cold as a dog."[46]

In such harsh conditions the thoughts of many soldiers wandered to the comforts of their far-off homes. Had it not been for the actions of South Carolina in instigating this war, Captain Dexter Horton might have been in his quiet "little home on the banks of Shiawasee" instead of "knee deep in mud." Lieutenant John Cooper could not help but compare winter conditions in South Carolina with those in his native Ohio. In the North, sufficient warm clothing protected one from the elements, but in the South, regardless of the many layers one wore, "the cold dampness strikes through and chills your very bones."[47]

The sodden ground created obstacles in the countryside that would have stopped a less determined group in their tracks. Here soldiers encountered roads bordered by "dense woods full of almost impenetrable underbrush" and had to cross rivers whose "sedgy, oozy banks were covered for miles with dismal swamps." As temperatures plummeted, "ice froze on hats and trees." It was so cold that Sergeant Rufus Meade found "ice from one-quarter to one-half inch thick every morning"; soldiers had to wade through water so bitterly cold that many "became almost paralyzed." So ubiquitous were soldiers' complaints about the hostile environment that their feelings toward the state would doubtless have been inflamed by having to struggle through such treacherous conditions. An army chaplain was convinced that there could be "no worse punishment than to be obliged to march just one day through South Carolina swamp and mud."[48]

Yet the buoyant confidence of Sherman's men, both in themselves and their leader, allowed them to accomplish the unthinkable.[49] Confederate generals William J. Hardee and Joseph E. Johnston felt certain that the combination of geographic obstacles and inclement weather would impede the Union forces. Years later Johnston admitted to Sherman that Confederate engineers had predicted that "it was absolutely impossible for any army to march across the lower portions of the state in winter." Civilians, too, hoped that the swollen swamps and rivers and Northerners' unfamiliarity with their surroundings might prove advantageous to the Confederacy. In March 1865 South Carolina author William Simms criticized Confederate leadership for insisting on lines of defense "chosen without any regard to the topography of the country." According to Simms, there were many places of "dense swamp . . . and almost impenetrable thicket, where soldiers and officers who were familiar with the geography could have overcome a much superior force."[50] A Union officer concurred with Simms's evaluation, noting that his map showed places ideal for the concentration of troops. Lack of enemy resistance and unprecedented feats of engineering enabled Sherman's forces to conquer the Southern elements and increased their confidence. "The roads have been awful, and the obstacles in the shape of rivers, streams, and swamps, most numerous," wrote one Northern officer, "but we have conquered them as we have everything else."[51]

Union soldiers saw not only a hostile territory, but also one that was vastly inferior by their standards. As they slogged through swamps and mud, the troops conflated the physical and ideological geography of the rural South in a way that convinced them of their own moral and cultural superiority. It was not long until their contempt embraced the entire state. A Connecticut soldier wrote that South Carolina was unfit for "man or beast to inhabit," adding, "I wouldn't actually take all I've seen of SC [as] a present if I had to live in it." Corporal Eli Ricker looked forward to the day he could "depart from this land of alligators and pestiferous swamps."[52] Others commented on the poverty they encountered and what they judged to be sloth. In South Carolina, observed a Michigan officer, "respectable houses are very rare and superior ones rarer." Major Thomas Osborn remarked on the lack of plantations and the "few poor houses," as well as the paucity of good roads. Lieutenant Colonel Charles Fessenden was a little kinder, finding that planters' homes were slightly superior to those in Georgia, yet "none of them were what we should call more than second or third class houses in the North."[53] In fact, soldiers were inclined to compare the landscape with their own back home. Many of Sherman's infantry came from the Western states of Ohio, Illinois, and Indiana where new towns had been designed to impose a man-made order over nature. Professional surveyors laid out straight roads and neat towns, in which squares and courthouses regulated the landscape. Now in the rural South, Northern soldiers found small towns, poor roads, and inferior housing, all indications that their preconception of Southern inferiority had been correct.[54]

Northern soldiers might have tempered their harsh judgments had they considered two factors. First, the war had been raging for almost four years, and almost all Southerners had felt the effects of shortages of goods, inflated prices, and other economic hardships. They could hardly be expected to look prosperous. Second, Southerners had different attitudes about consumption and wealth. In many parts of the rural South, plantation houses were "commodious in a rambling way, with no pretense to distinction without nor to luxury within."[55] Due to soil erosion, many smaller planters were prepared to move frequently. Wealth was thus more conveniently displayed through movable items such as livestock, food, and slaves. A Northern teacher visiting the South reported seeing many plantation houses without doors between rooms and without glass in the windows. Yet tables were loaded "with an almost endless variety of the richest delicacies," fields were full of slaves, and yards teemed with livestock. Despite all of this, the plantation house "was a mere shell, and could all be taken down and removed in a few hours."[56]

A young New York woman who had married a North Carolinian explained to her family that those things Northerners considered essential were of no importance to Southerners. Although her husband was a wealthy planter, she found their house "very unassuming." "Ambition is satisfied here by numbering its thousands of dollars, acres of land and hundreds of negroes," she observed. "Houses, furniture, [and] dress are nothing." She also noted a lack of any systematic organization within the household—"wash, bake or iron, just as the fit takes." She desperately missed the "order and neatness which pervades a Northern home."[57]

In the Northern mind, ideas of cultural superiority were often reinforced by geography. When Henry Adams made his first trip to the South in 1850, he decided that "slave states were dirty, unkempt, poverty stricken, ignorant, [and] vicious." At the same time, he claimed, "bad roads meant bad morals."[58] This was obviously the mind-set of Major General Alpheus Williams, who found evidence of "decay and retrogation" everywhere he looked. "How even the politicians of South Carolina can boast a superiority over our hardy industrious northern people is more than I can imagine," he wrote.[59] Despite the inhospitableness of the land, many soldiers agreed that Northern farmers would have more efficiently taken advantage of whatever resources the countryside had to offer. As he passed a plantation owned by an allegedly "rich widow," Major Hitchcock commented that the owner had realized only "half the comfort out of her money that many a Northern farmer on 80 or 160 acres has. Rough rail fences, except just around the house—unthrifty looking yard, cabins and out buildings, and general air of slovenliness, dirt and waste."[60]

Union soldiers' contempt for South Carolina soon became evident in both words and deeds. Commander William Scofield vowed that in that "detested" state, a "conquering Army of true Americans" would "drive the demons before it like the wind." Major Osborn considered it to be a "contemptible country," a sentiment he extended to the inhabitants. "Treat the people here kindly and they are impudent and disgusting," he wrote. "Treat them . . . without consideration and they become reasonable beings." Captain Pepper concluded that "the soil is treacherous, like the people who own it."[61]

The Union army constructed an image of rural space in terms of power, control, and cultural superiority. Furthermore, in the language of the period, Federal soldiers commonly referred to South Carolina as feminine. "We will make her [S.C.] suffer . . . we will let her know it isn't so sweet to secede as she thought it would be," wrote one soldier. Lieutenant Samuel Mahon explained to his family in Iowa that as "she [S.C.] sowed the Wind [so] she will soon reap the Whirlwind." "She will yet weep tears of blood for her folly in firing at our glorious old flag," was his dire warning.[62] A Union chaplain expressed similar sentiments: "The thousand of homes she has filled with mourning, the unnumbered hearts *she* has wrung with anguish, are all witnesses of the justice of *her* punishment. Let *her* drink the cup *she* has brewed, and lie on the bed *she* has made."[63]

Such gendered rhetoric may have been used unconsciously, but, nonetheless, it must have resonated in the minds of those who penned such words, especially among men who had already determined that Confederate women were the staunchest supporters of the rebellion. Feminist scholars have argued that men see both women and nature as resources; this model seems especially applicable to an army of invasion and its female targets, linking images of aggressive masculinity and female vulnerability.[64] The problem with interpreting this language as indicative of male aggression and female passivity is that it tends to essentialize men as inherently violent and women as peace loving. Neither is an accurate picture.[65]

Although soldiers knew that their duty was to conquer a hostile territory that was metaphorically female, they soon discovered they were invading a land that was also literally female. The constraints of gender ideology prevented most soldiers from physically assaulting white women, and many expressed misgivings about invading female domestic space. By the same token, the emotional ties that bound Southern women to their homeland often led them, not to passivity, but rather to a fierce defense of hearth and home.[66]

When Sherman's men invaded the Confederate heartland, Southern households became strategic targets of war. Demoralizing white families and freeing slaves would destroy the integrity of the institutions on which Confederate identity was based. As home front became battlefront, however, strategic targets became living human beings, and confrontations frequently turned out in a different manner than anyone could have anticipated.

WHEN THE BOUGH BREAKS

In early February 1865 a Union officer in South Carolina observed that the countryside was "alive with men who made foraging their sole business." Squads of soldiers were sent in advance of Sherman's army, "mounted on scraggy old mules, or cast off horses," to return at night with "strings of chicken, bacon, turkeys, and geese" pillaged from farms and plantations whose occupants were for the most part women and children.[67] Despite the fact that men were deployed in organized units under the supervision of officers, "hundreds were constantly out, independent of all control. Many roamed through the country solely to plunder, and in their nefarious work threw off all restraint—fearing neither God nor man—nor his mythical majesty the Devil."[68]

Bands of foragers, whom one Union soldier described as unequaled in "scientific and authorized stealing," ransacked homes and ravaged the landscape, exacting a devastating toll on civilians both materially and psychologically. These men came to be infamous as "Sherman's bummers."[69] Captain Pepper described bummers as "stragglers—not in the rear, but in front of the army." In fact, with the exception of Columbia, "every town in South Carolina through which the army passed was first entered by the bummers." By the time the last of the columns passed, houses were "entirely gutted." Colonel Oscar Jackson recognized that the bummers were becoming "a distinct part" of the army; they were generally in front to carry out their main objective, "pillage and plunder."[70] In many cases all that was left was "a heap of smoldering ashes." So many houses fell victim to the Yankee torch that one officer characterized his surroundings as a landscape of chimneys. Another soldier overheard Sherman comment on the strange way that South Carolinians built their houses: "They put up their chimneys first" was his sardonic remark.[71]

Black families who had longed for freedom soon realized that few Union soldiers harbored true abolitionist sympathies. The majority of Sherman's men regarded the slave population as a tool with which to strike at the economic foundation of Southern society, thus ignoring the humanity of individual African Americans. The sight of their homes being despoiled or destroyed by white men struck at the heart of what little security slave families had. A slave cabin had often been a place where black people might attain some degree of autonomy beyond the scrutiny of white eyes.[72] But whereas white owners frequently left African Americans to their own devices within the confines of their quarters, Sherman's "rough riders" would "go through a Negro cabin . . . with just as much freedom and vivacity as they 'loot' the dwelling of a wealthy planter."[73]

Union officers were aware of the mistreatment of blacks, especially assaults on black women. At the start of the Carolina campaign, Major

General O. O. Howard expressed concern over the "many depredations . . . that would disgrace us even in the enemy's country, e.g. the robbing of some negroes and abusing their women."[74] An ex-slave from Winnsboro, South Carolina, echoed these sentiments many years later, when she remembered the Yankees as "a bad lot dat disgrace Mr. Lincoln dat sent them here. They insult women both white and black."[75]

Many white soldiers viewed black women as the "legitimate prey of lust." Some officers even believed that "colored women are proud to have illicit intercourse with white men." A Northern missionary based in South Carolina reported that "no colored woman or girl was safe from the brutal lusts of the [white] soldiers—and by soldiers I mean both officers and men." She complained that offenders were seldom punished.[76] One historian has found sufficient evidence of sexual victimization to argue that "the abuse of black women by Union soldiers at Beaufort [S.C.] was endemic."[77] Few black women have left a record of such treatment. Illiteracy and a sense of powerlessness were major factors in this dearth of evidence. Many of them may also have been reluctant to open up that area of vulnerability to the scrutiny of outsiders. A white woman in Camden indicated that she had heard about abuses of black women but gathered little concrete information. "Negroes were so ashamed they could not bear to tell," she wrote. Another told her sister that Yankees had stripped black women and "spanked them round the room" in front of their mistress. "They violated all the women servants publicly and left them almost dead, unable to move."[78]

Although evidence from Southern whites regarding Yankee depredations against blacks might be self-serving, one might well surmise that Union soldiers in the South, starved for female company and shunned by white Southern women, were likely to turn to African American women, both willing and unwilling. One such soldier wrote that there were no white women available, "nothing but these damn negro wenches," complaining, "I can't get it hard to go to them." Although he subsequently overcame his revulsion, he maintained that he only went with black women because the white prostitutes who came to the area were diseased.[79]

Northern soldiers' attitudes toward race varied, of course, depending on both individual background and experiences in the field.[80] In a letter to his wife, one soldier involved in the campaign asserted that his abolitionist sympathies were weakening, "for it is first a nigar, then a mual, & then a soldier, & the soldier is used worse than any of them." Others were impressed by the determination and bravery of blacks. Despite the fact that the soldiers frequently mistreated them, many African Americans fell in behind Sherman's lines, inspired by the possibility of freedom and viewing the soldiers as their deliverers.[81] Lieutenant C. C. Platter, of the Ohio Infantry Volunteers, thought South Carolina "beat all the places for contrabands" that he had ever seen. Another soldier credited blacks with a "large degree of shrewdness . . . [they] take a more just view of the present struggle than we generally give them credit for."[82] Colonel Jackson wrote that many black refugees suffered "the most painful privation" as they struggled to keep up with marching troops. In his view, "the silly prejudice of color is as deeply rooted among Northern as among Southern men." He bitterly condemned those "degraded" soldiers who "plunder the houses of the blacks of the last mouthful of food and every valuable, and take pleasure in insulting and molesting them."[83]

African Americans, too, had mixed responses to Union soldiers. Many slaves who once regarded the Yankees as their deliverers quickly became disillusioned. "Us looked for the Yankees . . . like us look now for de Savior," wrote an ex-slave. "Dey come one day in February. Dey took everything carryable off the plantation." Violet Guntharpe maintained that "all us had to thank them [the Yankees] for was a hungry belly, and freedom."[84] Freedom was of little benefit to her without the wherewithal to survive, and food shortages hurt slaves as much as their white owners. Black people frequently remembered a barren countryside and "hungry bellies." Amy Perry recalled that in the wake of the army, "de white folk hab to live wherebber dey kin', and dey didn't hab enough to eat . . . de cullered people didn't hab nuttin' to eat neider." Another ex-slave condemned the Yankees for both "things they ought not to have done" and leaving undone "things they ought to have done." The war, it seemed to him, had been more "bout stealin" than a "Holy War for de liberation of de poor african slave people."[85]

Slaves frequently found Union soldiers as capricious as white Southerners, complicating their decision of whether or not to flee.

Though most white owners chose to believe that their slaves remained with them out of loyalty, clearly blacks' motivations were more diverse. The army correspondent of the *New York Herald* reported that, although in the majority of cases "the slaves betrayed their masters, revealing their property and joining in its destruction," he had also observed cases in which slaves showed an obstinate loyalty. "Cruel masters reaped the fruits of their tyranny now, while the property of kind ones was in many instances saved by the tact and discretion of their slaves," he wrote.[86]

Many African Americans became angry and perplexed when Northern troops destroyed their property, stole their goods, and assaulted black women. Despite repeated orders to curb the indiscriminate pillaging of black homes, these infamous practices continued.[87] One ex-slave remembered the coming of the Yankees as "scandalous days." Heddie Davis thought that they "was de worst people dere ever was." "Every Yankee I see had de stamp of poor white trash on them," recalled another. "They trolled round big ike [sic] fashion, a bustin' in rooms widout knockin', talkin' free to de white ladies, and familiar to de slave gals, ransackin' drawers, and runnnin' deir bayonets into feather beds, and into de flower beds in de yards."[88] The ingenuity of one slave simultaneously saved his own possessions and protected the female house servants. When he saw Yankees carrying off his blankets along with those from the main house, this slave begged the soldiers in a terrified tone "not to mix them [the blankets] with his as all the house girls had some catching disease."[89]

The majority of firsthand evidence from African Americans comes from reminiscences collected in the 1930s. Most of the witnesses who contributed to these narratives were children during the war and so offered their own unique perspective.[90] Unlike their parents, who may have suffered the worst barbarities under slavery, many black children had valid reasons to distrust a band of ferocious white soldiers. Slaveowners frequently terrified these children with stories of Yankee atrocities. Sometimes these fears were allayed; Captain Conyngham heard one black child say, "Mamma, the Yanks have good feet; not like de debbil as massa says." Another was so frightened that she hid in a tree until a Union soldier coaxed her down with the offer of money. Others found their suspicions validated. Nancy Washington recalled seeing "uh big blue cloud comin' down dat road en we chillun was scared uv em . . . in some uv de places dey jes ruint eve't'ing."[91] One child saw the Yankees take her mother's moss mattress that had been a gift from her mistress, rip it open, empty out the moss, and fill it with meat. One soldier took her mother's "red stripe shawl" and put it on his horse as a saddle cloth. After choking this child's mother to find out where the whites' valuables were, the Yankees took her mother away, although she subsequently escaped and returned to her daughter.[92]

Even black children who were not exposed to such cruel acts frequently viewed the Yankees as disrupters of the only life they had ever known. Children, of course, might have been spared the real atrocities of slavery, as they were too young for heavy labor or even to catch the eye of a lascivious master. Sara Brown, for example, could not understand why some slaves kicked up their heels and shouted in joy. She thought she had been "free all de time."[93] Others felt a genuine attachment to their white owners. When her mistress told her she was free, Hester Hunter sobbed, "I ain' gwin to leave you!" "Dat was my white mammy," she explained, "an' I stay dere as long as she live too." Jimmie Johnson vowed never to let any soldier hurt his mistress. When he heard that he was free, he vowed to remain and protect her until his dying day.[94]

In fact, many slaves, both children and adults, showed a reluctance to leave the places where they had lived and worked.[95] They felt a love of the land that had been their home, even though they detested the oppression they had suffered there. Major General Carl Schurz, who was appointed by President Andrew Johnson to report on the social and economic conditions of the South immediately after the war, noted that in South Carolina, "the large majority of the freedmen remained on the old plantation." Another Northern traveler commented on the numerous freedmen he saw returning "to the region with which they were familiar."[96] That ex-slaves chose to remain was sometimes frustrating to whites. Catherine Hammond, widow of South Carolina planter James Henry Hammond, wrote in September 1865 that she had lost few negroes. "I wish we could get clear of many of the useless ones," she complained.[97] Ex-slave George Briggs still lived in Union County, South Carolina, when he was interviewed in the

1930s. He had left only once and vowed: "If de Lawd see fitten, I ain't gwin to leave it no mo', cept to reach de Promis' Land. . . . I loves it, and I is fit throughout and enduring the time dem Yankees tried to get de country, to save it." In a similar vein, Genia Woodberry said that she had never desired any other home: "[I] ne'er wanna hunt to better libin' den we hab dere."[98]

Attachment to the land, a characteristic closely associated with Southern distinctiveness, affected the war experience of both blacks and whites.[99] Southern blacks in Sherman's path occupied a liminal space between two racist forces; for many of them the sensible decision may have been to remain with the devil they knew. On the other hand, the white women who experienced an army of invaders tearing up their homeland and destroying their possessions suffered no such dilemma.

Sherman's men frequently complained that Southern whites refused to recognize either the cultural or military superiority of the North and expressed astonishment at the intensity with which Confederate women fought to maintain both their dignity and their property.[100] A female refugee from Atlanta, for example, faced Sherman again in South Carolina. Mrs. H. J. B. "prayed fervently" for courage that she might not forget that she was "a true Southern soldier's wife." When she overheard a Union officer blaming Southern women for "egging on the men to fight," she faltered yet still demanded protection. Although personally unmolested, her house and larder were ransacked. When she later gained an interview with General Sherman himself, he inquired whether she was the wife of a "rebel soldier." This woman surprised herself at the intensity with which she replied in the affirmative, adding, "and [I] glory in the thought."[101] Sarah Jane Sams, a resident of Barnwell, South Carolina, determined to "remain as firm as possible" when Union cavalry invaded her home. In no uncertain terms she told a soldier that she "expected civil and polite treatment from gentlemen." Although the soldier tried to intimidate her by claiming that the Union army had no "gentlemen" but was rather composed of convicts "released for the purposes of subjugating the rebellion," she refused to be shaken. "My strength had been given to me by an Almighty Power," she wrote, "and could not be taken from me by a Yankee's venomous tongue."[102]

It was their own venomous tongues that many white women used as their primary weapon against the Yankee invaders, eliciting responses of both reluctant admiration and moral castigation. A New Jersey lieutenant remarked on how "determined" and "resolute" he found the white women of the Palmetto State. One of his comrades commented that this so-called tender sex was the match of "the roughest and most brutal" soldier when it came to the use of "obscene words."[103] Emma Holmes wrote of the heart-throbbing excitement of facing the enemy. In fact, she found it almost cathartic when she was at last able to "relieve her bottled wrath and show [the Yankees] the spirit which animates the Southern women." In the case of soldiers, this "insensibility to fear" has been attributed to what we now recognize as a rush of adrenalin.[104] This surely worked similarly for women on the home front who faced the enemy so bravely. One Confederate woman explained just such a scenario when she heard a Union officer boasting that the Union forces would soon turn the "proud women of Carolina" into beggars. "You women keep up this war," he shouted. "We are fighting you!" At this point the young woman's terror "gave way to indignation." She demanded that as a representative of a "civilized country" it was this officer's duty to protect her family from insult and robbery. Another Southern lady bragged that many of her female friends vented their wrath against Union troops to such an extent that soldiers claimed the women talked too "damn strong" and were not worthy of protection.[105] On the other hand, Mrs. A. E. Steele, who headed a household of "three generations of white women" in Barnwell, bit her tongue when "the dirtiest, most villainous set of men" she had ever seen ransacked her house. Although the incendiary actions of the troops led to their renaming the town "Burnwell," one of "the most decent looking officers" told Mrs. Steele they would spare her house as she "had not 'sassed' them." Nevertheless, soldiers could not resist taunting this proud woman and told her she would soon get over her "d——d pride" if her house did burn. Steele refused to give them any satisfaction and left her dwelling in silence. Maria Haynsworth kept her eyes on her Bible when the Yankees entered her home. She prided herself on maintaining her dignity, which she believed had "kept them [the Yankees] in check." Discretion may have proved to be the better part of valor, as women's sharp tongues were sometimes their undoing. Captain Horton lost patience with a young woman who, after seeking his protection, proceeded to condemn those Southern ladies who consorted with the enemy. This sorely "vexed" him, and he decided to leave her to the mercy of "cruel straggling soldiers."[106]

It was relatively easy for Northern soldiers to define Southern women who eschewed the role of passive victim as aberrant. On one occasion the Union army had officially equated Southern women's patriotism with prostitution. Exasperated by women who took every opportunity to insult or humiliate Federal soldiers, General Benjamin Butler, commander of occupied New Orleans, ordered that any woman displaying such behavior would be "regarded and held liable to be treated as a woman of the town plying her avocation." The widespread Confederate outrage at this decree suggests that, in Southern minds, the behavior of these women fell within the limits of gentility—one could be rude and insulting and still be a lady.[107]

No one expressed this sentiment more clearly than the Confederate soldier who spelled out the following instructions to his wife: "Be cautious not to expose yourself more than necessary to intercourse with the enemy, but there must be no cringing, no timidity. Modest resolution is respected everywhere. Do not allow [yourself] to be irritated or intimidated, but keep cool control of [yourself] and be punctiliously polite. Give no expression of your sentiments unless there is necessity for it. If it should be necessary, speak the truth and the whole truth if you die for it."[108]

Many Northern soldiers were deeply perturbed by Southern white women who refused to be cowed and humiliated but instead lashed out with vitriolic tongues. One officer expressed sympathy for those women who sat "with grief depicted on their countenances, or the tears rolling down their cheeks," but women who "vent[ed] their feelings in curses and rude epithets" made it difficult for him to overlook "what the women of the South have done to keep up this war."[109] Not only had Confederate women stepped beyond the pale of appropriate female behavior, but they had also failed in their duties as Republican Mothers. This role, which channeled women's moral superiority into the production of patriotic citizens, had clearly gone awry in the South.[110] Major Hitchcock rationalized the situation to his wife:

"Even in the case of women, what they received was but a just retribution for the large share they personally had in bringing on and keeping up this war."[111]

As there was no sustained attack in the North, we cannot tell whether representations and realities would have been equally contradictory had Yankee women been called upon to confront an invading army. Nevertheless, while Union soldiers blamed Southern women for their part in supporting the Confederate war effort, they continued to seek support and validation from their own families. Although they believed that South Carolina deserved punishment for instigating a conflict that had kept them away from their families for four long years, contact with the civilian population raised a certain amount of ambivalence regarding the suffering of women and children. Major General Alpheus Williams described the army's sweep through South Carolina, the "fountain-head of rebellion." Convinced that the entire state consisted of rebels, the troops spared nothing. "All materials, all vacant houses, factories, cotton gins and presses, everything that makes the wealth of a people, everything edible and wearable, was swept away," he wrote to his daughter. Yet he found the sights "often terribly sublime and grand; often intensely painful from the distressed and frightened condition of the old men and women and children left behind."[112] An even more sympathetic officer tried to imagine how a "lone woman with a family of small children" would feel when an enemy soldier "pryed open . . . chests with his bayonet or knocked to pieces . . . tables, pianos and chairs; tore . . . bed clothing in three inch strips, and scattered the strips about the yard."[113]

Corporal Eli Ricker asked his sister how she would like to have "troops passing your house constantly for two days, dozens within it all the time, ransacking and plundering, and carrying off everything that could be of any use to them?"[114] Concerned that he might be judged "unfeeling," Major Samuel Duncan of the 14th New Hampshire Volunteers justified the "fearful destruction" as one of the "legitimate fruits of the rebellion." His words conveyed the feeling shared by many of his comrades that South Carolina was paying just retribution for its sins. Although he acknowledged some sadness, his overriding feeling was one of triumph when he saw a planter's house going up in flames. "Is *rebel* property more sacred than the lives of our loyal soldiers?" he asked his future wife.[115] Another soldier felt some regret at the level of destruction and wondered how he would feel if this war was on his own doorstep. Still, he viewed the campaign as a "military necessity" and believed that South Carolinians must "reap the reward of their evil doings." Private Charles Brown thought that South Carolina had suffered an "awful punishment" and was grateful that this war was on Southern soil. "You never can imagine a pillaged house, never—unless an army passes through your town," he wrote to his wife.[116]

The desire to punish the Palmetto State encouraged Union soldiers to cross the bounds of legitimate foraging practices. Captain George Pepper chronicled another form of "devastation" practiced by troops, namely "the deliberate and systematic robbery for the sake of gain." Pepper reported that soldiers stole not only money but also "plate and silver spoons, silk dresses, elegant articles of the toilet, pistols, indeed whatever the soldier can take away and hopes to sell."[117] An army chaplain wrote that house robbing was "universal," explaining, "I do not mean all the men rob houses, but all the houses are robbed." George Balloch asked his wife if she had received the stolen items he had shipped to her. What had she thought of a particular statuette? "I suppose if I send much more plunder you will need a larger house to hold it," he remarked. Corporal John Herr sent home rice and clothing, and Private Charles Brown, sheet music and jewelry. Surgeon Charles Tompkins had a predilection for fine books.[118] Sherman acknowledged that, although he personally "refrained," many soldiers sent "trophies" home. Immediately after the war a Northern journalist reported that on several occasions "gentlemen of respectability" had proudly shown him a variety of "trinkets that they *picked up when they were in the army*."[119] One Union officer who found this behavior reprehensible wrote that, rather than have property "seized and sent North by any of the sharks who follow in the rear of a conquering army," he would prefer to see it destroyed.[120]

Men who cherished their own domestic values now found themselves in a situation where the virtues of manhood were being redefined and their sense of morality was being stretched.[121] Union soldiers understood that the success of their campaign necessitated behavior that would have been unacceptable at home, and many shared

Southerners' revulsion for the military depredations. Charles Brown, of Michigan, declared that the extent of the destruction sickened him, "& that, for me to say in S.C. is considerable." One army chaplain felt that such outrages were enough to "make a soldier blush with indignation." His primary concern was nevertheless directed at the tendency toward demoralization among Union troops rather than the suffering of Southern civilians. "The army must be fed and the Bummers must feed us," he reasoned. "Some [foragers] would discriminate, others would not, and thus the few have caused a great deal of unnecessary suffering." Major Thomas Osborn doubted whether such "scientific and authorized stealing" had ever been seen before. He recognized "a strong demoralizing tendency connected with this work." Sergeant Rufus Meade told his family that foragers "cleaned the country" and "committed much private depredation." But, he explained, "it was the only way we had of living . . . even if it left poor women and children to starve as I fear it did in some cases."[122]

A recent study of Union policy toward civilians argues that Sherman did not conduct a "total war" but one that was limited by an underlying sense of morality. It was this "combination of severity and restraint" that was the innovative aspect of Sherman's campaign, while his strategy was a rediscovery of an older form of European warfare—namely, the *chevauchée*.[123] The chevauchée dates back to the late medieval period, when "massive raiding expeditions . . . systematically pillaged or destroyed everything in their path." Their purpose was to demoralize and consequently subjugate the inhabitants of enemy territory. Sherman's strategy showed a similar logic, "as systematic and extensive as anything Europe had seen, yet also more enlightened, because it was conducted not by brutes but by men from good families, with strong moral values that stayed their hands as often as they impelled retribution."[124] This moral calculus of Union men was, however, a double-edged sword. If the majority of Northern troops were indeed moral men, an attack on women may not have seemed the most heroic part of warfare. Soldiers needed to rationalize their discomfort in violating—even if only symbolically—Southern white womanhood.[125]

Although behavior might have been stretched to the limits in the aberration of wartime, Sherman's campaign was shaped according to prevailing ideologies of acceptable conduct that illuminated nineteenth-century social values. In the face of the increased levels of destruction in South Carolina, moral castigation of Southern womanhood proved an insufficient rationalization. In these circumstances many soldiers eased their consciences by differentiating their own roles as legitimate foragers from those who indulged in immoral pillaging. Captain George Fleharty of Illinois believed that those who pillaged "show no compunction or conscience." Lieutenant Colonel John Cooper asserted that although "there seems to be some justice and rightful retribution in the wholesale destruction of property in this state, I do not wish to be the agent." A Connecticut soldier could not "countenance" the actions of some soldiers who seemed to "have no regard for anything that is gentlemanly." He personally did not intend to indulge in such behavior. "I have my certain duty to do, and that I intend to perform as faithfully as I know how and let plundering alone," he reassured his family. A soldier from Massachusetts thought that the army was justified in taking necessities but drew the line at "overhauling everything even ripping open beds, and emptying them in search of money & plate," which seemed to him "a little too much like plundering." Corporal Ricker experienced mixed emotions of excitement and guilt when entering homes and taking provisions but consoled himself in the knowledge that he "never went beyond [his] duty to pillage."[126]

The struggle of essentially moral men to come to terms with the violence and terror they were bringing into Southern homes suggests that although Sherman's strategy may have had historical precedent in military terms, in ideological terms it was understood differently. If we examine Sherman's campaign through the lens of gender, other factors come to light that clarify soldiers' restraint and ambivalence. During the period of the chevauchée, no separate sphere ideology existed. Furthermore, women were a normal part of these early armies, performing essential support roles; thus warfare on a civilian population was less stratified by gender.[127] In the eighteenth century the military increasingly took control of the army, and within one hundred years women's vital military roles had become obscured. At the same time as the armies were becoming exclusively military—and exclusively masculine—military history was emerging as a field designed to educate young men in the art of warfare. The ensuing focus on battlefield tactics and strategy contributed to the invisibility of women as an essential part of military efforts. These changes coincided with the development of a separate sphere ideology that was rapidly becoming a paradigm for gender roles in the North. Thus models that masculinized politics and the military reinforced the exclusion of women from both.[128]

The enforcement of gender boundaries in both social and military practice changed the face of the culturally sanctioned limits of war. It was relatively easy for armed men to cross physical boundaries. Crossing the conceptual boundaries constructed to fix both home front/ battlefront and gender demarcations proved more problematic. A Union chaplain questioned the veracity of the modern myth of war that made the army the essence of masculinity. "Men will always persist in foolishly imagining that there is some way of making war simply on armed men," he wrote. "It cannot be done successfully. The fields and houses, the women and children always suffer."[129]

The track of desolation through the South Carolina countryside provided Southerners fertile ground for the seeds of bitterness and recrimination, while it led Northern troops onward to the heart of the "cradle of secession." Union soldiers cleansed their misgivings in a tidal wave of anticipation as they approached the state capital. The city of Columbia represented the epitome of South Carolina "chivalry," a word that Federal soldiers used with contempt to describe the "boasting, whining and poltroonery" of the Palmetto State's elite.[130] Corporal Ricker saw Columbia's inviting streets as a temptation to "many a 'vandal' to tread their 'hallowed pavements.'" Major S. S. Farwell looked down upon that "beautiful but doomed city" and thought it "one of the finest sights" he had ever seen. Still, he imagined how its citizens might feel as "the shots from our batteries told them but too plainly that they were at our mercy." A schoolteacher in that town concurred as she looked up at the gathering troops and, in fearful anticipation, trembled under the scrutiny of the "malicious eye of the enemy."[131]

3 : THE MOST DIABOLICAL ACT
OF ALL THE BARBAROUS WAR

By mid-February 1865 Columbia's prewar population of eight thousand had tripled. The city contained a larger number of refugees than anywhere else in the state, including over one hundred female employees of the Treasury Note Department and numerous wealthy planter families from Charleston and the Carolina Low Country. They had been attracted by the city's "excellent transportation and communication facilities, hotels, boardinghouses, government ordnance plants, and laboratories."[1] Refugees who fled before Sherman's forces poured in daily. William Simms described roads lined with "wives and children, and horses and stock and cattle, seeking refuge from the pursuers."[2] Yet even as these fugitives spread tales of atrocities and the relentless progress of Sherman's men, the residents of Columbia believed that their strategic city would be defended to the hilt and "the inhabitants cherished their delusion, until it was dispelled by the sound of the Federal cannon at their gates."[3]

When Sherman's arrival was imminent, mass confusion erupted in the capital city as government officials, military personnel, and civilians all fought to get their respective goods and persons out of town. At the railway station "car windows were smashed in, women and children pushed through, some head foremost, others feet foremost." Others witnessed "surging pleading masses" of women and children begging to be taken aboard trains "jammed to suffocation." So great was the chaos that by February 15 martial law was declared, and the last available transport out of the city was assigned to government property. From her haven in Lincolnton, North Carolina, Mary Chesnut heard that she had been one of the last refugees from Columbia who entered a train by the door. After that "women could only be smuggled in by the windows. Stout ones stuck and had to be pushed, pulled, and hauled in by main force."[4]

In Columbia, Emma LeConte dared not venture into the bedlam of the streets, although she desperately needed firewood to keep out the bitter cold. But she was unable to stop the outside noises from infiltrating her home. All day she heard the noises of trains and wagons, followed by the rumble of distant cannon. By nightfall she was alarmed at the sound of shelling. "I do not know why," she wrote in her journal, "but in all my list of anticipated horrors I somehow had not thought of bombardment." Shivering from the outer chill and inner dread, she braced herself as best she could for the events of the next day.

The assignment of blame for the burning of Columbia has been debated by many scholars, although they generally concur that approximately one-third of the city was demolished through a combination of carelessness on the part of Confederate authorities in destroying cotton, a preponderance of alcohol that encouraged incendiarism by some Union soldiers, and violent winds.[5] But underneath the flames can be found a host of voices that offer a more kaleidoscopic view. As a case study, the destruction of Columbia gives us a deeper insight into the complex interactions between civilians and soldiers, blacks and whites. It also challenges the conventional wisdom that elite Southern women's relationship to the Confederate cause was so fragile that Sherman's invasion caused a downward spiral from demoralization to disaffection. Rather, it suggests that initial feelings of despondency were, in fact, only the first stage in a process of rededication to Confederate rebellion.[6]

An almighty blast jolted the residents of Columbia awake in the early hours of February 17. "The house shook," wrote Emma LeConte, "broken windowpanes clattered down, and we all sat up in bed, for a few seconds mute with terror." This was not the Yankee invaders, but an accidental explosion of gunpowder stored in a warehouse at the South Carolina Railroad depot. The explosion had been caused by pillagers making the most of the confusion as Confederate troops withdrew from the city. Simms reported many "females and negroes" among the looters, claiming that they were following the example of

General Wheeler's cavalrymen, who "systematically, as if they had been bred to the business, proceeded to break into the stores along Main Street." General Sherman observed the smoldering ruins of the railroad depot from across the Congaree River, where he awaited the official surrender of the city. From there he could see the confusion of citizens and cavalry in the streets as well as "quite a number of negroes [who] were seemingly busy in carrying off bags of grain or meal, which were piled up near the burned depot."[7]

White residents, who feared to venture into the streets, sent their slaves out to salvage what provisions they could and to bring back news. Many loyal slaves returned with supplies of "sugar & bagging, tools, flour, salt, tobacco, &c." Emma LeConte noted the irony of the situation. "Those whom we have so long fed and cared for now help us," she wrote. "We are intensely eager for every item of news but of course can only hear through the negroes."[8]

The cacophony of the streets etched itself vividly on the memories of many citizens. Grace Elmore heard "a steady roar . . . mingled with the trampling of horses . . . accompanied with yells, and screams as from drunken men." Another resident was struck by the "bellowing" of cows led by Yankees through Main Street. At the same time bands were playing "Yankee Doodle," and "Hail Columbia," the lyrics of which Northern troops corrupted to, "Hail Columbia, Happy land, If I don't burn you, I'll be damned." William Simms recalled groups of soldiers on street corners, "drinking, roaring, revelling—while the fiddle and accordeon [sic] were playing their popular airs among them."[9]

One Union soldier, however, remembered the sounds of music as the background to flirtations with Southern women. In a letter to his family in Iowa, Sergeant Henry Wright conveyed the spectrum of his war experiences. The period in Columbia was "the awfulest time I ever seen," he wrote; yet he had also been introduced to some dozen young ladies "who played piano and guitar." "Miss Mollie was my favorite," he continued. "I almost fell in love with her and she declared she would marry a Hawk Eye or never marry." After the war this sergeant did, in fact, return to Columbia to claim his "secesh" bride.[10] Sergeant Robert Hoadley also indicated a particular liking for the women of the Carolinas, whom he found "much better educated and more enlightened than they wer' in Ala. & Georgia, they do not use quite so much tobacco &tc."[11]

The stories told by these two soldiers seem even more incongruous when one considers that both were in the Fifteenth Corps, a group of predominantly Western men whose infamy had reached the ears of South Carolina residents. A Northern soldier told Grace Elmore that when the Fifteenth was put in front, "we know it means fire and pillage."[12] Another woman related that Sherman had sent his "tigers" in first. "Whenever he sends these men ahead he intends to do his worst. He says he would not be afraid to go to the lower regions with this regiment in the lead."[13] Sherman was aware of the corps' deserved reputation as he planned his Carolina campaign in which it would take the lead. Writing to General Halleck, he said, "If you have watched the history of that corps, you will have remarked that they generally do their work pretty well." A Union colonel shared this opinion, commenting that these men "have an independence about them that shows to a good advantage on a campaign, but is decidedly out of place in civilized society."[14]

Yet the juxtaposition of the Fifteenth Corps' infamy with Sergeant Wright's apparently innocuous story of flirtation offers an excellent example of how individual encounters between Southern civilians and Northern soldiers often played out very differently from the grand narrative of pillage and destruction. This is not to deny the terror, suffering, and extreme losses of many civilians. Yet a gamut of emotions engulfed the city, ranging from terror to respect, from tears to laughter, and from sympathy to disdain.

Those who experienced terror most often expressed it through hellish images of devils against a backdrop of flame. "The wind was raging," wrote Mrs. Bachman to her daughter. "The elements conspired with man to remind us of the scenes in which demons delight." A crowd of soldiers in Lily Logan's yard filled the night air with "fierce yells of demoniac delight," while "their forms shone out hideously in numbers on all sides in the light of our flaming home." By midnight it seemed that "Sherman's Hellhounds" had turned the sky into a "quivering molten ocean." William Simms continued this analogy, describing "volcanic torrents of sulphurous cloud" that engulfed buildings and brought them down in "great billow showers of glowing fiery members."[15]

Throughout this saturnalia, soldiers broke into houses, threatened the residents, destroyed their possessions, and made off with valuables. Yankees ransacked the Elmore household, all the while "laughing, and saying coarse things, or talking in loud rough tones." "A roaring stream of drunkards" poured into Mrs. Ravenel's home. They tore up her carpets, burst open her trunks, and took her goods. Yet, although "plundering and raging," they seemed "curiously civil and abstaining from personal insult." Both Elmore and Ravenel became convinced that these marauders were more interested in stealing goods than in abusing the white women with whom they came into contact. This realization conjured up "abhorrence and disgust" in Grace Elmore. "If I were but a man how firm would be my arm to strike," she raged.[16]

Although these women may have lacked the physical strength of their menfolk, they were able to call upon other weapons to defend their homes and persons. Many used the moral authority commonly ascribed to women of their race and class to stop soldiers in their tracks. Two women knelt and loudly sang a psalm, which "strange incantation" had an immediate influence on the soldiers in question. Another managed to make soldiers feel "sheepish" by her unflinching stare as she stood on her piazza.[17] Mrs. Ravenel gave a more detailed account of this behavior. "If a number of men were fighting over a trunk or a closet, spoiling more than they took, I would go and stand by, not saying a word, but looking on, they would become quiet, would cease plundering, and would sometimes stop to tell me that they 'were sorry for the women and children, but South Carolina must be destroyed.' "[18]

William Simms later praised the women of Columbia for their "almost masculine firmness," displayed in a spirit of "inflexible endurance." Many succeeded in facing the taunts and insults of their assailants "in silence and with unblenching cheeks," answering only in "monosyllables" or in "brief stern language."[19] And these taunts were many. Two officers allegedly called out to a group of women shivering outside their burning home, "Ladies, it is a cold night. Why don't you go into your burning town and warm yourselves?" Another took the blankets under which a group of children were huddling, telling them that there was fire enough to keep them warm. Others shouted, "Here they come, women and children rebels—let them suffer—who cares!"[20] Yet women strove to show "no signs of regret or faltering" in the face of such indignities. A schoolteacher, confronting more than twenty soldiers who were destroying her barn, demanded to know if they were "thiefs [sic] or soldiers" and called them "a disgrace to the military profession." When a Yankee officer asked an elderly woman why she did not appear frightened, she retorted, "Because I do not feel so." Others concealed insults behind a dissembling ladylike demeanor. The Yankees "received the most nauseous doses of truth gilded with smiles," boasted Harriott Middleton.[21]

Laughter sometimes managed to find its way into this night of fire and destruction. One soldier expressed amusement at the quick-witted response of a woman who, when asked whether she had ever seen a Yankee before, replied, "Oh yes, we have often seen your fellows with a pack on their back, or with a monkey and organ!" When an enterprising young woman hid her carriage wheels to prevent soldiers from stealing the conveyance, they told her that it was "such a d——d good Yankee trick" that she deserved to keep it. Although Grace Elmore was unable to save her pony carriage, she could not resist "entering in the spirit of the fun" at the absurdity of the ensuing scene. Inside the stolen vehicle, fastened among bags of flour, she saw "half a dozen or more turkey cocks . . . stretching their necks outside of the carriage, and all gobbling and trying to spread their tails and resent[ing] the indignities to which they were subjected."[22]

Although elite white women in Columbia described the Yankees as a group in the most vituperative terms, many soldiers and civilians touched each other on a very human level. In the accounts of the destruction of the city, written by civilians during or immediately after the event, a notable feature is the sympathy and kindness of individual guards, acts that became obscured in publications of later years. A woman who had described Sherman's men as "tigers" noted that she was protected by a Yankee captain from Iowa. Lily Logan, who called the Northern soldiers "demons in human shape," went on to praise a "Yankee on horseback" who had escorted her to a safe place and then salvaged some of her belongings from her burning home. "His name was Charles Lamar," she informed her brother. "Do not forget him, for I owe a great deal to his protection and kindness." Mrs. Pringle Smith befriended her Union guard, who "stayed during the night & came off & on during the day, & always took supper & conversation, & became to our surprise quite one of the family." Another guard openly wept at the condition of the city. "The kindhearted man was appalled by the fate he believed was in store for us," wrote his Southern charge. The next morning, with tears in his eyes, he told the family, "If I saw any rebels burning down my home as all of you are seeing us burning down yours, I would hate them all my lifetime."[23]

Whereas Mrs. W. K. Bachman described a night of terror in which "women in the last stages of consumption, some with infants two weeks old, [took] refuge in the damp, chill woods and [were] taunted by their enemies," her personal experience proved very different. So grateful was she to her guard that she presented him with a silver cup when he departed. "I never thought I could feel toward an enemy as I did toward him," she told her daughter. Mrs. Bachman commended the actions of Private Davis to the Confederate military, and the reply brought a gasp of astonishment to her lips. "The man you mentioned as having protected your house . . . was an enlisted man of the . . . Fifteenth Army Corps," it read. "I can only say that so far as this man was concerned that had he been captured by our men . . . and had the badge of the Fifteenth Army Corps located him, he would have been shot and left lying in the woods as were so many of his comrades." And so the kind Private Davis came from the dreaded Fifteenth Corps, whose very name made the people of Columbia tremble. What makes this even more remarkable is that the guards who assisted Lily Logan and the Pringle Smith family were also from the Fifteenth Corps, as was the soldier who wept over the fate of the residents of Columbia.[24]

Although these predominantly Western soldiers had assumed a specter of evil in the minds of white Southerners, their behavior frequently belied their infamy. William Simms stated that the guards who most often betrayed their trust were "chiefly Eastern men." The troops from the Western states "were frequently faithful and respectful; and, perhaps it would be safe to assert that many of the houses which escaped the sack and fire, owed their safety to the presence of . . . some of these men."[25]

On the other hand, when Simms compared the treatment of African Americans at the hands of men from the East and the West, that respect shifted. The Westerners seemed to despise blacks, whom they "used as drudges . . . and rewarded with kicks, cuffs and curses, frequently without provocation." Easterners' relationship with blacks appeared to be of a totally different nature: "They hob-a-nobbed with the negro, walked with him, and smoked and joked with him; filled his ears with all sorts of blarney; lured him, not only with hopes of freedom, but all manner of license." According to Simms, when Eastern soldiers failed to "seduce" blacks to run off, they "resorted to violence." Other Southerners also commented on the contempt Westerners displayed toward African Americans. A woman heard one of these soldiers say that he would "rather put a bullet through an abolitionist than through a Confederate soldier."[26]

Although no detailed studies exist of regional differences in racial attitudes, there are reasonable grounds to suspect, at best, an ambivalence among Westerners toward black emancipation and even more evidence to suggest extreme racial prejudice against Native Americans that shaped attitudes toward blacks. The sympathetic Private Davis admitted to his charge that he harbored an intense hatred of Indians, who had murdered his sister and her children in Minnesota. Furthermore, many inhabitants of those Western states that bordered the slave South dreaded emancipated blacks crossing their borders without the strict controls of slavery. Thus, although they may have professed antislavery sentiments, Westerners were often extremely racist. In a "stump speech" in Columbia, one Western officer declared that to keep the country "only for the white man . . . the Indian, as well as the Negro had to be . . . exterminated." Personally, he would wish to have the "entire Negro race [placed] on an immense platform, and powder sufficient to blow them all to atoms."[27]

Many black residents of Columbia had, in fact, greeted the Yankees with "demonstrations of delight," and several "piloted the men to the best places for plunder." But the arrival of the army of "emancipation" fell far short of its promise. As a group, blacks were robbed of their goods in the same way as whites. Soldiers "stole the servants' clothes, ripped open their trunks and boxes, especially ones which they declared contained clothes too fine for any negro." By the night of February 18, Emma LeConte felt that blacks were becoming "somewhat disgusted with their *friends*."[28]

William Simms found Yankees' racial attitudes particularly abhorrent when it came to the fate of black women. "We should grossly err," he wrote, "if, while showing the forebearance in respect to our *white* women, we should convey to any innocent reader the notion that they exhibited a like forebearance in the case of the *black*."[29] African American women, who were unable to call upon weapons of moral authority, did not escape with mere insults and rough words. Assaults on black women were so common that "at last, the Negroes themselves became thoroughly disgusted, and . . . vowed vengeance for the base treatment their women had been subjected too [sic]."[30] On the morning of February 18, black women's naked bodies "bearing the marks of detestable sex crimes" were found in the streets of Columbia. One female slave was raped in the presence of her white mistress, and another "old negro woman" was "subjected to the most brutal indecency from seven of the Yankees." With the encouragement of the group to "finish the old Bitch," she was "put into the ditch and held under water until life was extinct."[31]

In the wake of attacks by Union soldiers, black and white Southerners were often forced into a mutual dependency. Those slaves who remained and helped their owners may have felt a sincere loyalty, but in protecting their owners, slaves were also helping to protect themselves. After all, white Southerners were their main shield against the depredations of Northern soldiers.

Despite her appreciation for the "faithful and considerate" behavior of her slaves, Grace Elmore's sense of racial superiority allowed her gratitude to go only so far. Her slaves quenched the fire that Yankee soldiers set in her home and in the aftermath of the invasion assumed a protective role toward her. One slave refused to let her into the downstairs billiard room until he had wiped off the coarse message soldiers had written on the walls. Yet only two weeks later, Elmore wrote in her diary that "those [slaves] who remain must understand they belong to me now as ever." A Union soldier commented with derision that, regardless of the privations rich white South Carolinians would suffer in the wake of Sherman's forces, "there is one thing they invariably do, no matter how great the cost; they cling to the niggers as the visible proof of their respectability and chivalry."[32]

Although Union soldiers generally held the elite of Columbia in contempt, many had misgivings about attacking Southern homes and terrorizing civilians. Several took the time to rationalize both guilt and pride over the once "beautiful and wealthy city" that was now "a blackened mass of smoking ruins." The devastation "sickened" Major James Connolly, who had not envisioned "how frightful the reality would be." Similarly, a Union chaplain found the sight of "crying & despondent" women and children "too bad to be endured." Captain George Pepper reported tears on "many a soldier's cheek" at the sight of "refined and cultivated ladies . . . in beseeching attitudes, calling for help." Nonetheless, he believed that this terrible punishment had shown an arrogant people the falseness of "all their pretensions of superiority." Captain David Conyngham was moved by a scene of "desolation heightened by the agonized misery of human suffering." He hoped never to see such a sight again. Yet, he insisted, the city's inhabitants had reaped the reward for their "Spartan State's treachery."[33] Many soldiers believed that Columbia, "wherein rebellion commenced," had now "received her just rewards for the evil deeds she did" and "tasted some of the legitimate fruits of nullification and secession."[34]

Other soldiers eased their consciences either by blaming the devastation on the effects of alcohol or by exercising selective memory. Lieutenant C. C. Platter thought the burning of the city "a very disgraceful affair" that did not reflect much "credit" on the army. "But whiskey done it, and not the soldiers," he rationalized. Another officer had never in his life seen "such a wild set of people" as the intoxicated soldiers in Columbia. "I saw men who never drank before in their lives drunk that day," he maintained.[35] Major Thomas Osborn, on the other hand, decided that he would leave the scenes of "pillaging, the suffering and terror of the citizens, the arresting of and shooting negroes, and our frantic and drunken soldiers" for those who "choose to dwell upon it." "I have," he determined, "seen too much suffering by far, and choose rather to remember the magnificent splendor of this burning city." In a similar vein, despite earlier expressions of compassion,

Major Connolly decided that he "wouldn't have missed it for anything." Chief Commissary Officer George Balloch also struggled to
come to terms with his emotions. By the time he reached North Carolina, however, he focused on his admiration for General Sherman.
"My heart fairly swells with honest pride within me when I think of the
results of his operations," he wrote. "All the other movements of the
war sink into insignificance when viewed beside his."[36]

Citizens of Columbia also shifted their attention to the leadership
of William T. Sherman, holding him directly responsible for their
plight. After all, remarked Simms, Sherman's troops were renowned
for their discipline. "They were as an army, completely in the hands
of the officers. Never was discipline more complete—never authority
more absolute," he wrote. One woman remarked that once Sherman
ordered guards into the streets, "the effect was instantaneous. Order
reigned everywhere."[37]

How uncanny it seemed to Grace Elmore to watch the Yankees leave
Columbia in such a disciplined fashion. When the ranks stopped to
draw some water from her well, she found it hard to believe that "these
quiet, well behaved" soldiers, who carefully threaded their way along
the garden paths, could be the same men who, just two days ago, had
"thronged the same spot, and made the garden hideous by their ram-
paging over every portion." She could not suppress her rage at the
passing of this band of "insulters of women and children." Reverend
Peter Shand's opinion was that, even if Sherman had not actually
ordered the burning of the city, he had "winked and connived at it"
and "could have prevented it with a word." Mrs. Ravenel insisted
that one could never overestimate the "admirable discipline of General Sherman's army. They greatly mistake who attribute the horrors of
that night to accident or insubordination," she continued. "The skill-
ful commander held his men in the hollow of his hand, and said
to them so far shall thou go and no further."[38] Sherman's troops
left the city with the sound of "hisses and boos" echoing in their
ears. A Union soldier recalled that some of his comrades were spat
upon and "not a few of the women undertook to lay violent hands
upon . . . them."[39]

In the wake of the army an "awful sadness and stillness" filled the
air, broken only by the whispers of friends exchanging tales of their

experiences. Emma LeConte noted the contrast to the conflagration of the previous two days. "The destruction and desolation around us which we could not feel while under such excitement and fear now exerts its full sway," she wrote. "The few noises that break the stillness seem melancholy and the sun does not seem to shine as brightly, seeming to be dimmed by the sight of so much misery."[40]

A devastated home front was Sherman's most immediate goal. He trusted that an invasion of both geographic and psychological space would leave in its wake a population focused on the need for food and shelter rather on supporting further political and military conflict. South Carolinians were both materially and spiritually exhausted and concerned over shortages of food. However, initial disillusionment and war weariness were not enduring emotions for all citizens, but frequently just the first stage in a process of rededication to Southern independence.

As James McPherson has demonstrated in his study of the tenacity of Civil War soldiers, morale is a dynamic entity.[41] But such a nuanced model has never been applied to the women of the Confederacy. The prevailing argument for slaveholding women, set out by Drew Faust, is that the war burdened them emotionally and materially in ways they were not prepared to handle. Thus, Confederate women became increasingly disillusioned and disaffected by all things military.[42] Yet, as Gary Gallagher and William Blair have suggested, we cannot assume a direct link between disillusionment and disloyalty. For example, Blair has argued that in war-torn Virginia enduring and surviving the depredations of an army of invasion might actually have stimulated commitment to the cause by "solidifying the picture of an enemy."[43] The city of Columbia, where Southern women had firsthand experience facing the enemy, provides an ideal arena to test a hypothesis that elite white women could see themselves as viable political actors with interests that extended beyond the immediate concerns of home and family. Their initial despondency might have been channeled into a demonization of the enemy, a renewed embrace of the Confederate cause, and identification with the Army of Northern Virginia.[44]

In Columbia, a community of sufferers forged new bonds in response to deprivations. "We have things in common," wrote one citizen, "drawing rations from the free market, and living on the charity of those who have more than we."[45] Governor Andrew Magrath personally responded to the mayor's request for relief. He felt duty bound "to minister actively in the relief from the starvation of those, who are of our own State; who are of our blood; who have the same cause to advance; and who now stand before us, the victims of devotion to that cause."[46] Many families reaped the benefits of such public assistance. "Seven thousand are drawing rations free, two thousand paying for their rations," noted Mrs. Bachman. Mary Leverette told a friend that "everybody is drawing rations, and we pay—some do not." "You can send and buy rations every day," wrote Harriott Middleton, "or draw them gratis if you have been burnt out." Lily Logan, who had lost her home, reported that a neighbor had offered to share hers. The mayor took in several homeless families that shared rations of "beef, rice and corn" on a daily basis.[47] In March a concert was held for the benefit of the "Columbia sufferers," and the Greenville Ladies Relief Association, which worked in conjunction with a similar organization in the city, enjoyed a new lease on life. In the month before the attack on Columbia, its total expenditure had been $182. In the next month relief efforts exceeded $1,100 and the association was still adding new members to its roster.[48]

As mutual assistance filled empty bellies, the smoldering ruins of the city revived waning spirits, and the "pallid mourners" began working through their despair. Julia Gott realized that, despite the terrible suffering she saw around her, "people cannot die from fear." Although she had "nothing left to eat but sorghum molasses and black shortbread," Mrs. Poppenheim rejoiced that she had survived with her life intact. Mrs. Emily Ellis, who met the "vile wretches" alone, showing them only a spirit of "independence," was not only relieved to have "escaped their vengeance," but also satisfied that she had attained their "respect." Another young woman advised a friend that, if confronted by a Yankee gun, she should not be frightened: "'Tis only done to alarm," she wrote. Mrs. Ravenel felt that the women of Columbia had escaped "better than we could have hoped," and that now they knew "just how much could be borne." Although a Union captain had hoped that the charred city would serve as a reminder to South Carolinians of their terrible crimes, the city, "wrapped in her own shroud, the tall chimneys and blackened trunks of trees looking like so many sepulchral monuments," facilitated recommitment by providing a constant reminder of the depredations of the enemy.[49]

The smoldering ruins and the lines of homeless families waiting for rations gave a "concrete, visceral form" to the "abstract" concept of Southern nationalism. In his analysis of combat motivation, James McPherson uses these terms to explain how soldiers' defense of "home and hearth" transforms ideological tenets into rank hatred. This would seem an even more appropriate argument for civilians who defended a literal home and hearth rather than the far-off home that was in a soldier's mind. Grace Elmore, for example, had always known the Yankees were "wicked," but she had never realized "the extent of their malice until their occupation of Columbia." Mrs. Poppenheim railed against the "brutal wretches" who insulted them and stole their food. Emma LeConte thought that she had hated the enemy as much as was possible before their arrival. Now she knew that there were "no limits to the feelings of hatred" she harbored for men whose name had become "a synonym for all that is mean, despicable and abhorrent."[50]

With the enemy on their doorstep, many Confederate women could see a direct link between the survival of their families and the survival of the nation; thus they could defend one in the name of both.[51] These women understood that, together with their menfolk, they had a vital role in defending the institutions on which Southern society and its way of life depended. "The right to govern ourselves," wrote Grace Elmore, "that is what we desire, for which we suffer, and for which we are willing to die." Women filled their correspondence with vows to continue the struggle, disabusing Yankees of the notion that they had been subdued. Harriott Middleton suggested to her cousin that it would be better to "form an army of women" rather than live under Yankee rule. Emma LeConte determined that "the more we suffer the more we should be willing to undergo rather than submit" and bitterly attacked the manhood of Union soldiers. Could this be "civilized warfare"? she asked. "One expects their people to lie and steal," she continued, "but it does seem an outrage even upon degraded humanity that those who practice such wanton and useless cruelty should call themselves men."[52]

Drawing on the same sense of honor that was so vital to keeping

Southern soldiers in the field, many white women in Columbia took pride in the fact that they had faced Sherman's army of "demons" unflinchingly, declared their enduring support for cause and country, and earned a reputation as virulent rebels. Mrs. Bachman reveled in the way she had shown the enemy that she "suffered willingly for [her] country." Emma LeConte was proud of the fact that the Yankees called South Carolina women "the most firm, obstinate, and ultra-rebel set of women they had encountered." Similarly, Harriott Middleton felt gratified when she overheard Northern soldiers lauding women of her state as the "pluckiest, the bravest, [and] the most outspoken they had met in the South."[53]

It has been argued elsewhere that Confederate women's commitment to the cause waned in the final months of the war, as their many sacrifices seemed increasingly useless. But, having survived an army of invasion without the protection of Southern soldiers, many women of Columbia now exhorted their men to remain at their posts and exact vengeance on the enemy.[54] "Let me entreat you not to seek a place here, with a view to give us security," wrote one such woman to her husband, ending her letter with the words "Don't Come!" Susan Cheves similarly assured her husband that there was no reason for him to be "uneasy" about her well-being. Emma Holmes called upon all Southern soldiers to "die in defense of their country [rather] than live under Yankee rule."[55] Lily Logan urged her soldier brother to keep up his spirits and "let us whip Sherman." She assured him of her own enduring confidence in an early victory, claiming that they should all be "ready to bear even more for our glorious cause." Such tactics obviously had the desired effect on one Confederate soldier, who thanked God for such a "brave mother and sisters. With such a spirit emanating from you[,] how could we do else but perform our duty nobly and manfully."[56]

Elite women of South Carolina renewed their faith by focusing on the Army of Northern Virginia and, more specifically, its leader, General Robert E. Lee, the personification of Confederate manhood. Against this image they created his nemesis in the shape of Union general William T. Sherman and his army of demons. Even had they momentarily questioned the ability of the Southern system and Southern manhood to meet their needs, it was much more comforting to blame their ills on Yankee soldiers than on the inadequacies of their own people and government. Having met Sherman's soldiers face-to-face, they now had an enemy on which to vent their wrath. "The people are undemoralized and more determined than ever," wrote Emma LeConte. Another young woman had heard that the spirit of the people in Columbia was even better after the Union attack. "Now that they have experienced their [the Yankees'] tender mercies, they are resolved to persevere unto the bitter end." A Palmetto State soldier wrote home from the ranks that he had heard "the people who have suffered are very patriotic, but those who were not molested are badly whipt."[57]

Hope refused to die as long as their armies stood. Even before Sherman's arrival, Emma LeConte had looked to "Lee's noble army." Once again she placed her faith in the general and "his poor little half starved army," yet "an army that has never suffered defeat." "God be with our men," prayed Grace Elmore, "and give them strength for victory." Elite women in Savannah expressed similar sentiments. "With General Lee at our head . . . we shall not be made slaves to these wretches," a mother told her son.[58] These women identified with President Jefferson Davis's proclamation of November 1864 in which he stated that the Confederacy did not depend on points on a map, nor on bricks and mortar, but on the "indomitable valor of its troops, [and] in the unquenchable spirit of its people."[59]

It may well have been that the arrogance of this group of South Carolina elites, and the fact that they had suffered the wrath of Sherman's men at its most extreme, provided a unique set of circumstances. In February 1865 Columbia was home to a disproportionate number of wealthy whites who had both strong material and ideological reasons for identifying with the Confederate cause. Bracing for, enduring, and responding to this harrowing experience with others surely encouraged a unity that did not exist in more isolated areas.[60]

But there may be another explanation for elite white women's tenacity that has implications for other contexts where Confederate civilians and enemy soldiers came face-to-face. Analyses of areas where home front became battlefront suggest that men and women did not have two different and oppositional sets of values, but rather shared many of the components that comprised the will to fight. James Mc-Pherson's 1997 investigation of Civil War soldiers provides a helpful model. McPherson argues that the will to fight was a function of "war aims and positive cultural values shared by soldiers and the society for which they fought." A further motivation, he argues, was hatred and a desire for revenge.[61] The evidence presented here strongly supports the argument that many women could easily identity with these values and desires. They recognized the broader goals of war, they saw themselves as political actors, and they shared the cultural mores of the men of their own race and class. They certainly had reason enough to hate the Yankee soldiers who wrought such devastation on their homes and region. Confronting the enemy face-to-face allowed these women to share in a sense of responsibility for actively defending the Confederacy, with a consequent upsurge in patriotism.

Sherman's continuing campaign into North Carolina would bring his troops into contact with a much poorer and more beleaguered population. An examination of the confrontations in this state will allow us to test this model of civilian resiliency in very different circumstances.

4 : GOD SAVE US FROM THE RETREATING
FRIEND AND ADVANCING FOE

As Union major Thomas Osborn crossed the border into North Carolina in the early hours of March 8, 1865, he expressed relief in leaving behind the most "contemptible" state, which "had but one element of which it can boast, and that is treason."[1] North Carolina, on the other hand, was expected to contain a strong element of Unionist sympathy, and Union troops prepared themselves accordingly. As Sherman planned for the next stage in his campaign through the Confederate heartland, he modified his tactics, reminding his troops that North Carolina had been one of the last states to secede and that "from the commencement of the war there has been in this State a strong Union party." In these circumstances, "marked difference should be made in the manner in which we treat the people and the manner in which those of South Carolina were treated." Soldiers received instructions to take only what was necessary and not to enter private homes; officers would be held accountable for the behavior of their men.[2]

At the same time, Sherman received news that would draw him into a more traditional campaign against the military forces of the enemy. The general was furious when he saw a copy of the *New York Tribune* that revealed his destination as Goldsboro, North Carolina. He knew that his Confederate counterparts would have obtained the same information, and it was no longer possible for him to keep them confused as to his next move. Moreover, he also learned that his "special antagonist," General Joseph Johnston, had been reinstated as commander of the Confederate forces in the Carolinas. Johnston was no rival to be dismissed. Sherman was aware that he would not be easily misled by "feints and false reports." In fact, the Union general concluded that he must be prepared to meet a concentrated force and thus "exercise more caution than I had hitherto done."[3]

Despite the fact that Sherman's men expected to find considerable Unionist sympathy in North Carolina, they knew that the war was not yet won. Major Osborn reflected on the past few months, which had been "occupied in maneuver, more than fighting," and in the "destruction of property, impoverishing the enemy's country, taking cities and military depots," all of which had been accomplished with little loss of life. Now, as a direct consequence of Sherman's March, Confederate forces had been driven together. "They will be able to compel one more campaign, at least, of severe fighting," he wrote. It had become a question of "who can endure the draught of blood the longest."[4]

To be sure, time and geography had rendered North Carolina the ideal state for Sherman to bring his plans to fruition. Here a war-weary populace—beleaguered by four years of internal disorder, social banditry, deserters, and fear of slave insurrections—was now being pressed by enemy forces on all sides. It seemed logical, therefore, that the arrival of Sherman's troops would sound the death knell of a state already weakened by inner turmoil.[5] But what Sherman and his men anticipated as Unionism was not an accurate definition of the spirit of most North Carolinians. For many of these proud people, rooted in cultural values of independence and autonomy, discontent with their government did not equate to lack of faith in the Confederate nation. Dissension and resistance were frequently attempts to negotiate an equitable distribution of the burdens of war rather than expressions of disloyalty.

In North Carolina, battlefront and home front truly became one. Although Sherman's troops curtailed the destruction they had wrought in South Carolina, plunder of homes and malicious damage to treasured possessions remained ubiquitous acts. Furthermore, the citizens of this state were now eyewitnesses to battlefield carnage, as private homes were transformed into makeshift hospitals in the wake of remarkably fierce Confederate resistance. Ironically, civilians did not protest the loss of life on the battlefield. But Union depredations and wanton destruction of personal possessions and livestock seemed reprehensible acts that breached the accepted ethics of traditional warfare. Sherman's arrival thus served as a catalyst to redirect antagonisms from the Confederate government toward the enemy.

As Sherman's men crossed the state line, their outward appearance belied their good health and excellent spirits. The ardors of the journey had worn out uniforms and shoes, and smoke from the fires set in North Carolina's vast pine forests and rosin factories had blackened their faces. In a letter to his wife, the general described men "with smoke-black faces, dirty and ragged, many with feet bare or wrapped in cloth." One Union soldier reported that a "dense, dark smoke, black as if sent up from the heart of the bottomless pit," heralded their arrival. Another found the column of smoke that rose in the sky "beautiful beyond description," adding that although he was "ragged as a beggar," he was also "ten pounds heavier" than when he left Savannah.[6] Major S. S. Farwell wrote to his home newspaper in Iowa that although soldiers were "barefooted, with their feet chapped and swollen, their clothes all ragged and torn from the long march through the swamps and brush," their disheveled condition could not quell their fine spirits. Lieutenant Robert Finley observed that despite the fact that many were "barefoot and their clothing was ragged & dirty, yet they were willing to follow their leader wherever he went." Sherman reported that his army was "as united and cheerful as ever, and as full of confidence in itself and its leaders."[7]

Clearly, Union soldiers did not feel the same degree of alienation in their new surroundings or the raging animosity that had fueled their destruction of the Palmetto State. As he crossed the state line, an Illinois soldier was struck by the "Northern like" appearance of his surroundings, especially the number of "small farms and nice white, tidy dwellings." Major George Nichols saw an "air of thrift" around him that was a marked improvement on what he had seen in South Carolina. He believed that North Carolina farmers were a "vastly different class of men . . . who work with their own hands, and do not think themselves degraded thereby."[8]

Perhaps this sense of familiarity encouraged the belief that here the people "would gladly embrace the old flag again, if they have the opportunity." Captain George Pepper was of the opinion—shared by many of his comrades—that "North Carolina could be made a thoroughly loyal State with a little persuasion." This conviction may have motivated the marked change in the conduct of the Union troops, as numerous soldiers observed. "There is a great difference in the behavior of the men since we got into NC.," Captain Snow informed his family, "there being less pillaging & burning." Michigan private Charles Brown thought that "the men seem by instinct to treat NC as well as possible." Despite the fact that many soldiers had their "feet tied up with cloths and old socks instead of shoes," Colonel Jackson noted that they were "not destroying property in this state like we did in South Carolina." Yet he added—almost as an aside—"we have more forage than we need."[9]

Although soldiers may have been more restrained, they were clearly helping themselves liberally to all that North Carolina had to offer. "You wanted to know if we had plenty to eat," wrote corporal John Herr to his sister. "We have more than we know what to do with." One month after crossing into North Carolina an Iowan officer informed his cousin that in only three of the last thirty-six days had he drawn army rations: "Most of the time we lived first rate . . . Sweet Potatoes, Ham, Bacon, Fresh Pork, Corn Meal, Honey, Chickens, Turkeys, Geese &tc."[10] On March 19 a soldier noted in his diary the return of a squad that, after a five-day excursion, had amassed "a good abundance of forage." Another particularly compassionate soldier told his family of the extreme poverty of the people, many of whom were left destitute after the army had passed. He regretted that his ranks contained men so lacking in "feelings of humanity" that they would rob poor women and children of "the last morsel of bread they had on earth." An Illinois officer explained that whereas sympathetic soldiers would leave needy families with some means of subsistence, less humane troops would take everything so that the majority of citizens were left "utterly destitute." Despite his orders to the contrary, Sherman acknowledged in private correspondence that his men were "sweep[ing] the country like a swarm of locusts." Soldiers engaged in such practices were apparently less loquacious than their more sympathetic comrades, though an Indiana infantryman boasted in his diary that the men had "stripped the country so clean that there is little left for any one."[11]

Sherman's men were only the most recent group to rob civilians of their provisions. North Carolinians had been complaining for some time about bands of "Confederate raiders," who "laid waist [sic] the countryside." Confederate officials, both political and military, also voiced concerns regarding "depredations or outrages" that were being "committed indiscriminately" by men who were worse than any "plague" inflicted on the Egyptians.[12] A Confederate officer sent from Virginia to round up deserters in the Piedmont area reported that in North Carolina he was able to "supply the men with more and better provisions." Lee's army had become increasingly dependent on supplies from its Southern neighbor, especially at the end of 1864, when Union raids through Virginia ravaged its landscape. Now the newly reinstated General Joseph Johnston learned that food supplies stored in depots across North Carolina were earmarked for the Army of Northern Virginia, and he would have to feed his own troops "by collecting subsistence through the country."[13]

Among all these groups, the long-suffering folk of North Carolina found one especially troublesome. Bands of deserters who regularly raided homes had been an ongoing problem for some time; when news came of the advance Yankee army, the people felt that they "were being swallowed up." Nowhere seemed safe, wrote one citizen; people in his community were "trying to hide their provisions expecting the enemy or deserters." When the renegade bands attacked North Carolina homes, they left behind scenes of confusion and devastation curiously similar to those wrought by Sherman's men. "Everything is torn to pieces," read one description of a recent raid. "My dear father's safe is broken and a large amount of money taken, besides so many other things it is impossible to enumerate."[14] Nor did these raiders satisfy themselves with robbery. In one young woman's neighborhood, they had been "taking a wide swath for some weeks, robbing, beating, plundering, &c." A man who signed himself "A Quaker" was horrified at the "hundreds of robberys [sic] and thefts, to say nothing of the numerous murders committed by the deserters." Although he had originally supposed that deserters shared his pacifist sympathies, he now condemned their actions. Others reported that these "perfect outlaws" were becoming increasingly "bold and defiant," creating a "deplorable condition."[15]

General Robert E. Lee, commander of the Army of Northern Virginia, also expressed concern over the number of desertions among

North Carolina troops. Lee's belief that many desertions were "occasioned to a considerable extent by letters written to the soldiers by their friends at home" has been used as evidence of the waning loyalty of the Tar Heel State.[16] Extant correspondence between battlefront and home front, however, consists mainly of letters written by soldiers to their families, and from these it is difficult to ascertain that requests from increasingly disaffected civilians motivated desertions. Furthermore, recent scholarship has challenged the view that North Carolina led the Confederate states in the number of desertions, arguing that these figures were based on erroneous War Department records.[17]

Men in the ranks were always aware that desertion was an option, and one group of North Carolina soldiers, who sent a petition to their governor, used this as a negotiation tool. "It is not in the power of Yankee armies to cause us to wish ourselves at home," they wrote, but "we cannot bear the cries of our little ones and stand." Had these soldiers wished to desert, they would have already fled the ranks; instead, they urged Governor Zebulon Vance to assist those on the home front, and "there will be less desertion, and men will go into battle with heartier goodwill."[18]

From the other side of the line came letters from Confederate civilians who also warned authorities about the dangers of desertion. One woman asked the governor to put a stop to speculators who were keeping supplies from soldiers' families. "I never had tried to discourage my husband any at all—I try to encourage him all I can," she assured him. But her letter also indicated that unless things improved, soldiers would become "disheartened." "I don't want them to have to come home without an honorable peace," she wrote, "and if they will find me plenty to eat my husband will fight through this war." Another woman expressed similar sentiments, bitterly resenting the deserters who were "robbing, an' taking, an' stealing everything they want, an' threatening the lives of our loyal citizens." She urged the governor to provide her community with "home defense." Were soldiers to hear of the vulnerability of their families, "it will almost cause them to desert the camp an' come home." Above all, "I don't want no more deserters." In a final plea, she declared, "I have seen my native land run over as long as I can bear"; yet she wanted everything "for the best" and hoped to "have an independent Confederacy before another year runs round." Harriet McMasters also urged the governor to take harsher measures against deserters. Her only brother was in the army, and she would "ten times rather he would die there than he should run away."[19]

We cannot assume that the civilians and soldiers who alerted Confederate authorities about the potential of increased desertions were disloyal. The truly disaffected would surely not have drawn attention to themselves. This was especially true of Confederate women, for whom desertion posed a multitude of problems; not only were their homes subjected to the raids of these marauders, but also when their menfolk did desert, women found themselves burdened with the extra responsibility of hiding and feeding outlaws.[20] By the end of January 1865, officials and citizens alike were demanding that harsher measures be taken against deserters and those who protected them. Brigadier General Theophilus Holmes requested reinforcements to apprehend deserters, fearing that "the disaffection among those of our people who harbor or protect them will react unfavorably on the troops in the fields." A woman in Randolph County asked the governor to instruct the home guard to "take no prisoners," urging that those who harbored deserters also be "arrested and punished severely."[21] Many families with men in the army resented others who shirked their duties and called for harsher reprisals against both the men themselves and their families on whom they depended for support.[22]

The female kin of deserters were frequently the targets of reprisals by the home guard and state militia, suffering greater extremes of violence at the hands of Southern men than they experienced under Sherman and his hardened veterans. Confederate authorities were well aware that deserters required the support of their families to ensure their survival. Assistant Secretary of War Campbell recognized that these men were "everywhere shielded by their families."[23] A late-nineteenth-century commentator maintained that the burden of the deserter's wife was even greater than that of a soldier's wife. Not only did she share the anxiety that her husband might be captured or killed, but she had the added responsibility of smuggling food to him and keeping his presence a secret. The writer claimed that these women "proved quite as true and sacrificing as their more refined sisters who sent their husbands, sons, and brothers to the field instead of the woods."[24] That this observer characterized these women as less "refined" was a concept shared by those units who sought out deserters, and their wrath was most often directed at women of the poorer classes.

It was their class as well as their gender that made these women targets. The poorer classes of North Carolina were traditionally viewed by elites as a potential threat to the social order. Gender provided no protection to the wives and mothers of deserters when Confederate authorities sought to flush out renegades.[25] Governor Vance received disturbing reports of women tortured by state militia. Soldiers had slapped one woman, tied her thumbs together behind her back, and suspended her from a tree limb so her toes barely touched the ground. Over fifty women in each of Chatham, Randolph, and Davidson Counties had been "dragged from their homes and put under close guard." Five of these women were in a state of "advanced pregnancy."[26] In one of the most severe incidents, women were whipped and hanged until near death. A young mother was dragged outside in the snow and tied to a tree while her baby was left exposed in the doorway of her home. There, she was told, the infant would remain until she decided to cooperate.[27] Thus women often suffered violence at the hands of both deserters and Confederate authorities.

Violence was not a new phenomenon to ordinary men *and* women of North Carolina. The yeomanry of the state has been described as a "self directed, stubborn and independent group," who would fight "fiercely and on occasions violently to maintain their traditions and their autonomy." Further, recent studies have pointed out that there was historical precedent for disorderly female behavior. North Carolina women were neither shielded from nor unwilling to use violence on their own behalf. Poor white women in the antebellum period were quite prepared to be violent; even across class, "white women could be as brutal as their menfolk."[28]

Women were most likely to display an aggressive posture in retaliation for apparent economic injustices. In March 1863, for example, Greensboro newspapers described "A Female Raid" in which approximately fifty soldiers' wives attacked a merchant whom they identified as a speculator. The women demanded to buy provisions at a fair price. When the merchant refused to sell them flour at a subsidized cost, the women seized the goods and made certain that they were distributed in an equitable manner. In the wake of similar riots across the state, both newspapers and government officials urged North Carolina women not to take the law into their own hands. The fact that these appeals were directed to women reveals a recognition of their political actions and assumes a literate audience, indicating that these actions were not confined to the least educated classes.[29]

These women were explicit in their actions and did not consider them disloyal to the Confederate cause. Instead, they pursued social justice with the support of their respective communities.[30] In other words, their actions represented a quest for a "moral economy" to which even poor citizens thought they were entitled, one that would preserve the social order on which Southern society was based.[31] The women in North Carolina were driven by a sense of legitimation; their purpose was not destruction or theft but setting a fair price. We cannot read these riots simply as evidence that women put the needs of family before the needs of state or nation. As has been argued for Confederate Virginia, "it was possible to be discouraged by one's government, and mad at the rich, while still pulling for the Confederacy."[32]

In letters to Governor Vance, long-suffering wives and mothers extended their quest for social justice beyond the marketplace into the political and military arenas and sought a moral economy of war.[33] A poor widow with two sons in the army complained of the "numberless frauds practiced upon civilians by Government officials." Still, she did not object to her sons' military service: "Had I more," she wrote, "they should all go." Her objection was to the "young able-bodied men here at home with nothing to keep them out of the army but some petty office that might be filled better by older men unfit for service." Whereas, she assured the governor, she was motivated by "nothing but a sincere desire to serve my country," these young men, possessed of "neither age nor judgment . . . render the government of which they are the representatives exceedingly trivial and tyrannical in the eyes of those who have neither ability nor opportunity to rightly understand our glorious nationality." A women who signed herself "Nina" told Vance that she had lost her oldest son and had three others in service. "I just want to say to you," she wrote, "if you have one particle of respect of the Ladys in our country take the men at 55 . . . and no exemptions." The men in her town who held government offices were abusing their positions, and those were the very ones she wanted to see in the army. Despite her frustration at the injustices of the system, she declared that "my sons are for you no matter what you ever offer—for I have six." Another woman asserted that "the people would pay with cheerfulness five times the amount [of taxes] if the wants of the government required it" if only the system was not so "unequal and unjust in its operation."[34]

Many letters reveal a political logic through which women expressed their discontent with the conduct of the war, yet simultaneously stressed their loyalty. When they asked that a male family member be discharged or furloughed, women truly believed that this would be beneficial to the greater cause. A woman from Alexander County emphasized that her entire community had need for her father's mechanical skills. In fact, there was such a demand for his work that "3 or 4 Petitions [were] sent to the secretary of war all assigned [sic] by the county seal." She assumed that it was "by negligence" that they had received no response. She had often heard it said that her father "would do more good to be at home an' work for the people than 20 good soldiers would do in the field." Harriet S. Briley requested either a discharge or a furlough for a member of her community, asserting that "he will do more good at home than he will in the army." Mrs. Briley believed that she had earned the right to ask for such a favor; when Vance was running for election, she had given him "the praise of being a fine man and . . . don' all I could to reelect you again." Although without a vote of her own, this woman obviously was aware of her political influence.[35]

Women protested social inequities by claiming moral justification and inherent rights, demanding a response from the government.[36] At the same time, the personal nature of these letters suggests an intimate connection with the Confederate cause and an enduring confidence in Governor Vance. General Lee encouraged the North Carolina chief executive to make every effort to raise the spirits of the home front by holding public meetings. State regimental commanders also recommended going to the people "with words of cheer, encouraging the timid, satisfying the discontented, and suppressing party discord." In fact, the personal influence of Governor Vance remained an important rallying point. Even in the final days of the war, one Southerner reported that citizens frequently called at the governor's office for "advice and comfort," and "none left him without greater courage to meet what was coming."[37]

In public speeches, Vance stressed the need for social harmony and attempted to redirect the discontent of North Carolinians by vilifying the Yankee enemy. Many citizens responded with renewed determination.[38] One woman who had been anxiously contemplating the arrival of Sherman's troops heard her governor's rousing words. She trusted his assurance of "ultimate success" and determined to follow his advice to "be of good cheer & to stand by one another & vigorously to prosecute the war." A member of the home guard urged that the organization be made more efficient and thus "show to Sherman that his late 'strategic movement' through Georgia could not be repeated." And a woman who had bitterly complained about the infamous acts of deserters determined that the Yankees be stopped in North Carolina and that her people should "whip them worse than they ever have been whipt."[39] Even those who felt overwhelmed by problems might regroup when they became eyewitnesses to Yankee invasion. As William Blair argues for Virginia, the arrival of the Yankees served to "solidify the portrait of an enemy." Thus war rhetoric might fuel the heart even while the stomach was growling.[40]

Ironically, as white North Carolinians faced multiple enemies in the early months of 1865, blacks in the state felt similarly threatened. In its aftermath, one ex-slave described the war through the metaphor of two venomous snakes, "one lying' wid his head pintin' north, de other wid his head pintin' south. . . . Both bit de nigger, an' dey wus both bad."[41] Racial fears ran high in North Carolina as the patterns of paternalism under which slavery had functioned broke down. Some planters from the East Coast moved their slaves inland, away from the Union lines; as refugees, black and white, flooded the cities, residents began to fear social unrest. Concerns were voiced of towns "fill[ed] with strangers." In Charlotte, one diarist noted that "everything was in confusion [with] refugees and fleeing negroes."[42] Sherman's arrival in North Carolina with several thousand fugitive slaves in tow only exacerbated the growing tension. Rumors of slave insurrections were rife. From across the state the governor received reports of blacks charged with "conspiracy and plotting and persuading other slaves to insurrection." One man wrote that a plot had been uncovered of a "general massacre . . . of all white persons, regardless of age, sex or condition, except such as they might choose & select for wives or concubines." One of the alleged conspirators had been hanged and forty more awaited trial. There were similar reports of plans to murder white men and "have the young white Ladys for their companions." A Confederate soldier wrote that he had heard of "numerous arrests of slaves . . . & several hung by the incensed citizens." A news correspondent in the Union army thought it was a "barbarous business" when informed that a group of fugitive slaves had been "captured, and after a kind of mock trial, twenty five were hung."[43]

Into this seething cauldron of racial anxieties General William T. Sherman rid his army of its "encumbrance" of "20,000 to 30,000 useless mouths," whom he complained had "clung to our skirts, impeded our movements and consumed our food." A Union major echoed these sentiments, writing that Sherman's March had been a "marvel of military operations," especially "with twenty five thousand useless, helpless human beings, devouring food and clogging every step onward." As the refugees left camp, a Union officer described them as a "flock of black sheep." This ragged group, the majority of whom were women and children, took three hours to pass by the camp gate.[44]

The black refugees who were taken by boat to the North Carolina coast no doubt fared better than their counterparts who resided in the area where Sherman and his men continued their pattern of plunder. As in South Carolina, many white owners had warned their slaves that the Yankees would treat them harshly, and many slaves were frightened by this hoard of blue-coated soldiers who swarmed into their homes. It seemed to one slave that the air was "dark wid Yankees." He had never seen as many "mans, hosses, an' mules" in his life. Parker Pool saw enough Yankees to "whup anything on God's earth."[45] Slaves complained that Sherman's men stole their clothes, possessions, and in one case even their shoes. Fannie Dunn's recollection that "one Yankee would come along an' give us sumptin' and' another would come on behind him an' tak it," was a common remonstration.[46] A young white Southern woman wrote to a friend that, in her opinion, "Mr. Sherman . . . is pursuing the wrong policy to accomplish his designs. . . . The Negroes are bitterly prejudiced to his minions. They were treated, if possible, worse than the white folks, all their provisions taken and their clothes destroyed."[47] It soon became apparent to the slaves that the Northern soldiers' primary concern was not the welfare of African Americans. Lila Nichols described them as a "pack o'robbers" . . . [who] stold ever'thing they could lay hand's on an' tored up ever'thing scand'lous." She and others concluded that Yankees "doan ker' bout de Niggers, but day ain't wanted our white folks ter be rich."[48]

Although the testimony of ex-slaves transcribed years later reflected the bitterness of dashed expectations, both blacks and whites joined in condemning Sherman's men for malicious damage, especially for the indiscriminate slaughtering of livestock. "A Yankee wus pisen to a yard full of cows," recalled freedwoman Kitty Hill. "Somctimes dey would shoot a hog an' just take de hams an' leave de rest dere to spill." Others remembered seeing Yankees "cut de hams off'n a live pig or ox an' go off leavin' de animal groanin' . . . it wuz awful."[49]

The empty stomachs of blacks and whites alike turned queasy at the overpowering stench of dead animals, slaughtered by the Yankees, that littered the streets of city and countryside. Across the Carolinas civilians bitterly resented this wanton waste. In one of the most even-handed accounts to come from South Carolina, William Simms reported that the city of Columbia had been well off for provisions and would have gladly handed a fair share of these to feed the Union soldiers had they so requested. In fact, he did not even complain that Sherman fed his men on the provisions of the countryside—what infuriated him was destruction of livestock that left behind a famished people. "On all the farms and plantations, and along the road sides everywhere, for many miles, horses, mules and cattle strew the face of the country," he wrote. When Esther Alden returned to her North Carolina home, she inhaled a "sickening stench" from carcasses that littered the roads. "There being only women and children at home, the dead creatures are buried nowhere," she reported. Ex-slaves also remembered the "de awfulest stink" and "the sky black with turkey buzzards." Years later one young woman remembered that the most blood-curdling sound of the war was "the scream of a mortally wounded horse." In a particularly gruesome incident, wire was tied around the legs and necks of calves in such a way that, when they tried to walk, "the jagged end of the wire would penetrate the throat."[50]

By the time Sherman crossed the state line, violence had become almost a daily affair in North Carolina and the disorder only increased with the invasion of Yankee troops. Women alone in their homes prepared themselves as best they could. One ex-slave recalled that her mistress "set her mouf[mouth]," claiming she would "fix" the Yankees when they came. "When she done dat I ran an hid," she continued, "kaze I done seed Mis' Virgini set her mouf befo' an' I knowed she meant biznes.' " When Sherman's men arrived, Miss Virginia refused to be intimidated, declaring that she would not be scared by "no ugly braggin' Yankee." Another slave remembered her mistress looking at Yankee marauders "wid her black eyes snapping." Lila Nichols's mistress tried to lock her door against the invaders, but they kicked it in and "insult[ed] de white wimmen an' de blacks alike."[51] Nellie Worth was one white woman who turned the tables on the soldiers who invaded her home. Although their arrival surprised her, she was not afraid. "It seemed as though my very soul had turned to stone," she wrote, "and I knew, felt, nor cared for anything." When the soldiers compelled her to play the piano for their amusement, she vowed to play nothing but Southern songs. She recalled with pride that she breathed "all the fire in my soul" into her rendition of "The Bonnie Blue Flag" and "Dixie." Forcing Southern women to play for them was a favorite pastime of soldiers. Annie Jones recalled a "perfect saturnalia" as the black women of her household were compelled to dance to her musical accompaniment. When another young woman refused to perform, the soldiers played for themselves, although their choice was "Yankee Doodle & other pieces of the same character."[52] These rites of humiliation were bitterly resented by Southern women, but there were other forms of "mischief" that hit them even harder.

In private homes and public buildings, Sherman's men also destroyed items that were closely connected with identity and heritage.[53] In courthouses, soldiers were seen "defacing large account books and scattering the papers" and leaving archival records "in confusion amongst the dirt." Private John Metzgar confessed stealing historical papers from the state capitol in Raleigh.[54] But when, in the privacy of Southern homes, the invaders put their "vile touch" on personal mementos and pictures, they left wounds that would fester for generations.[55]

Evidence of such malicious damage can be found in the testimony of combatants and noncombatants alike. A Michigan private told his family that "time & again," he saw soldiers "pounding piano keys with their hatchets to see who could make the most noise, or pile up a pile of plates to see who could break the most." It seemed to a Union army surgeon that almost "every house was torn up & the clothing scattered." It was common to see "elegant sofas broken and the fragments scattered about the ground, paintings and engravings pierced with bayonets or slashed with swords, rosewood center-table, chairs, &c., broken to pieces and burned for fuel."[56] In some homes family Bibles were destroyed or desecrated. Josephine Worth was appalled that "even the family Bible was not sacred," as a soldier spread it over his horse's back for a saddle.[57]

Stripping families of the necessities of life caused immediate hardships, but the destruction of items that were an integral part of social relationships struck a blow to the very heart of Southern identity.[58] Perhaps no one personified this process more than a young planter woman who took a preemptive strike against such an atrocity by destroying her personal papers. In mid-April 1865 she wrote, "I find myself without a record of my life." Her moving account continues:

> Every letter I possessed, letters which I had cherished as my heart's blood, mementos of those I had loved & lost years ago, literary memoranda, excerpts, abstracts, records of my own private examination, poetry—all destroyed & as I look at my empty cabinets & desks & feel the void that their emptiness causes within my heart a hatred more bitter than ever rises within me as I think of the 'loathed Yankee' whose vulgar curiosity & unbounded barbarity has rendered the destruction of these private papers a matter of self preservation.

It had been especially heartbreaking to burn her husband's love letters, and she could hardly refrain from snatching them from the flames. Only the thought of seeing them "in Yankee hands, or hearing them read in vile Yankee drawl amidst peals of vulgar Yankee laughter, or worse still, of knowing them heralded abroad in Yankee sensational newspapers" had restrained her. She had heard that private papers, stolen from Southern households, had been published in Northern newspapers "to a vulgar curious world as specimens of Southern thought, Southern feeling, & Southern composition."[59]

Such acts were not unique to North Carolina, for similar horror was expressed in the other states where Sherman tread. In South Carolina, a woman described Yankees scattering and trampling upon "pictures, old letters, locks of hair, pressed flowers and other hallowed mementos of the dead." A Georgian woman wrote of how wretched she felt when Yankees pried into "sacred" items, "even into father's papers and relics of the dead." She declared, "If I live a thousand years I shall never forget the enemies of our country."[60] But in North Carolina this malicious destruction took on a particular poignancy as civilians were also witness to more traditional types of warfare.

Confederate forces engaged Sherman's men in two last desperate efforts to prevent his sweep across North Carolina, exposing citizens to the carnage of battle.[61] Janie Smith was witness to both the pillaging of her home by Union troops and the broken bodies of soldiers when her home was used as a makeshift hospital. In a lengthy letter to a friend, she complained bitterly about Union soldiers breaking her furniture, stealing clothes, and killing animals. They were "fiends incarnate" compared with the Confederate "army of patriots fighting for their hearthstone." Sherman's men made her "too angry to eat or sleep," and if any of these "scoundrels" had the "impudence" to speak to her, she only acknowledged them with "the haughtiest nod." Within days her ransacked home was filled with wounded Confederate soldiers, and "every barn and outhouse was filled and under every shed and tree tables were carried for amputating the limbs." Her words convey powerful images of broken bodies and human suffering. "Blood lay in puddles in the grove," she wrote. "The groans of the dying and the complaints of those undergoing amputation was horrible." A Confederate soldier remembered wounded men left with townspeople who "lay stretched upon the hard floor, many of them still weltering in their blood, and some of them with broken limbs that had not been attended to." Although Janie Smith was heartbroken to see the mutilated bodies of her countrymen, the only accusations she made against the Yankees were for behaving like "hyenas" when they plundered her home.[62]

Other white Southern women's accounts similarly emphasize the miscreant behavior of the Yankees over the wounded men struck down in battle. Sally Hawthorne complained at length that in a church in Fayetteville Bibles were "mutilated and defaced." Almost as an aside she mentioned that the hospitals in town were "full of sick and wounded soldiers" and the streets "strewn with dead and wounded men." In a similar vein, Alice Campbell wrote pages describing Yankee soldiers ransacking her trunks and bureaus, damaging family portraits, and pouring flour and molasses onto fine carpets. Her final words mention that "hospitals . . . were filled to overflowing." Elizabeth Hinsdale worked in the Fayetteville hospital, where wounded men were strewed on the floor. Her condemnation of the Yankee "fiends" was not, however, for killing men, but for killing animals and tearing to shreds "all the clothing of women and children."[63]

It was a soldier's duty to give his life for his country, and, as painful as it was to see bleeding bodies and amputated limbs, civilians accepted this as part of the moral economy of warfare. What was not acceptable, however, was the reprehensible conduct of Yankees in civilian homes. Catherine Edmondston wrote that such "works of pillage" were a "breach in the courtesies of war." Even a Union soldier believed that it was the "wanton destruction of property" that would burn the longest in Southern memory. He was convinced that "all other causes of estrangement will pass away and be forgotten before this one is forgiven . . . because it has neither justification nor palliation." A Michigan private expressed similar sentiments when he wrote that, in the light of such depredations, he would not blame the South "if they do go to guerrilla warfare." In her account of the last days of the Confederacy, author Cornelia Spencer of North Carolina wrote that the hatred of Southerners had been aroused, not by their fallen heroes, but by acts of "indiscriminate and licensed pillage," which were "more to be deprecated than any consequence of the blood shed in fair and open fight during the war."[64]

The clash of material deprivation and ideological beliefs drew citizens' discontent away from their government and toward the enemy, which had violated their sense of the moral economy of warfare—not in the killing of soldiers on the field, but by the personal indignities to which they had subjected the noncombatants.[65] Although the final confrontation between opposing armies ended with a Confederate retreat, neither side believed the war to be over. Janie Smith ended her letter with vengeance in her heart for the "widows and orphans left naked and starving" and a firm conviction that "desolation" would yet be carried into the North. Elizabeth Hinsdale reported that when Sherman "cursed" Southern women and blamed them for the war, he fueled "the general feeling that the time is not far off when they [the Yankees] will be punished."[66]

Moral outrage in the face of Northern behavior could reunite a fractured population and engender a new commitment to the Confederate cause. Even as the enemy destroyed the inhabitants' material world, the psychic scaffolding held strong.[67] In the wake of Sherman's forces, a Fayetteville woman wrote: "Terrible has been the storm that has swept over us. After destroying everything we had . . . one of these barbarians had to add insult to injury by asking me 'what I would live upon now?' I replied 'upon patriotism: I will exist upon the love of my country as long as it will last, and then I will die as firm in that love as the everlasting hills.' "[68] This moral economy of war would soon shape the social responses to peace and the memories of causes lost and won.

5 : WITH GRIEF, BUT NOT WITH SHAME

otwithstanding the Confederate retreat, the bold and aggressive action taken by General Johnston at the Battle of Bentonville had raised the morale of his troops and left Sherman's forces believing that they still had a formidable enemy.[1] Confederate treasury secretary Jonathan Worth reported that "from the humblest soldier to the highest officer the most undoubting confidence is reposed in Johnston."[2] Union soldiers also commended Southern efforts at Bentonville, noting that "the rebels fought with splendid gallantry" under the leadership of "the ablest general in the Confederate service, not even excepting General Lee."[3] In mid-April 1865 a Union army surgeon commented on the "stubbornness" of the Confederate forces, and an Ohio private wished they had Johnston "where he could do us no harm."[4] Yet even as these two soldiers wrote, General Robert E. Lee had surrendered the Army of Northern Virginia. So commanding a presence was Lee in the minds of both the North and the South that there was no doubt his demise meant the end of the Confederacy; within one week Johnston and Sherman met under a flag of truce.[5]

On April 18, 1865, two men who shared a mutual respect and a similar desire for a peace with honor negotiated the terms that would formally end four years of bloody warfare. Union major George Nichols marked the date in his journal: "Two great men came together in the heart of the state of North Carolina, intent, with true nobility of soul and in the highest interest of humanity, upon putting a stop to the needless sacrifice of life."[6] Both generals understood that the alternative to peace could only be a protracted partisan war, an idea that was abhorrent to both. By suing for peace with troops in the field, Johnston retained some negotiating power and avoided creating a culture of terror in the South.[7] Thus when the Confederate general proposed a permanent peace whereby the troops in Georgia, the Carolinas, and Florida would surrender in return for more generous terms, Sherman was delighted. Here was an opportunity to reprise the role he had attempted in Savannah, where he had promised to extend a hand of friendship to the vanquished South, thus ensuring his place in history as a maker of hard war and honorable peace.[8]

Sherman's reading of the political climate of the Confederacy proved more accurate than his understanding of the mood of the North. In an ironic twist, it was the North that condemned the general for the leniency of his terms and insisted on an unconditional surrender. As Sherman anticipated, the price of vindictiveness was an embittered and truculent South. What he could not predict was that he would become the focal point of that rancor, particularly at the hands of elite Southern women. This hardening of hearts and consecration of cherished memories manifested itself in a rededication to the Confederate cause, a deification of General Robert E. Lee, and a demonization of William T. Sherman.[9]

When Confederate women learned of Lee's surrender, they mourned his defeat as they would mourn the loss of a family member. "It was a crushing blow," wrote Emma Holmes, "and I wept as if I had lost a dearly loved friend." Grace Elmore envisioned that "grand old man" forced to yield his "starved and ragged" men to an enemy "three times their number." In her succinct fashion Mary Chesnut expressed both grief and humiliation: "Lee's tears—outsider's sneers—Yankee's jeers." Still, hope refused to die. "What is it that sustains me?" wondered Catherine Edmondston. "I believe it is faith in the *country*. Faith in the *Cause*, an earnest belief that we will yet conquer! We cannot be defeated." Elizabeth Collier admitted that Southerners may have been "overpowered—outnumbered, but thank God we have not been whipped." Emma LeConte retained a "deeply rooted" conviction that "the South cannot be conquered, that it can never be reunited with the North."[10]

Soldiers, on the other hand, displayed very different sentiments as a growing disparity of reactions manifested itself along gender lines. A camaraderie sprang up among war-weary veterans as they waited outside the farmhouse in which their leaders were negotiating for peace. The "friendly feeling that appeared to spring up between the Union and Confederate soldiers" seemed to Union colonel Jackson quite "remarkable." "How strange and how mysterious is the human heart," observed another Yankee officer, that erstwhile enemies, who had been prepared to kill each other, were now "brothers." Captain David Conyngham observed soldiers "grouped together around the fires, trading coffee, whiskey, meat and tobacco. Some of them were fighting their battles over again." Yet Conyngham remarked that civilians, especially women, were not as eager to extend a hand of friendship. "I have seen ladies who would treat you to two moral hours' bitter invective against the Yanks," he commented.[11]

As Confederate women struggled to come to terms with the loss of their beloved leader, grief turned to anger. "How I do hate the very name Yankie [sic]," wrote Nellie Worth as she sought divine retribution, praying that the North be rendered "one vast scene of ruin and desolation." Emma Holmes determined that reunion was too high a price for peace—"peace on such terms, is war for the rising generations." In Georgia, Eliza Andrews pronounced herself "more of a rebel today" than she had ever been. One Union soldier encountered an especially bitter North Carolina woman who declared that she would not give a cup of water to a Yankee, even if he was dying. After some conversation with him, she relented. "I would give you a cup of water to soothe your dying agonies," she told him, adding "and, as you are a Yankee I wish I had the opportunity to do so." Ella Thomas was more pragmatic. The question of unification will "depend upon the treatment we receive from the hands of the North," she wrote. "It will prove to their interest to be very discrete, for the South will prove a smouldering volcano requiring but little to again burst forth." If the terms were generous, she was determined to "cultivate friendly feelings." But if the South were humiliated, her "soul" would remain "as hard as iron."[12]

Sherman was in full accord with Thomas's sentiments, understanding that Southern culture, based on concepts of honor and shame, demanded outside recognition of the region's noble effort and a sense of dignity, even in defeat.[13] The peace terms that he and his Confederate counterpart signed on April 19 all but reinstated the status quo in the Southern states. Confederate forces were to be disbanded, disarmed, and paroled; the North would recognize existing state governments; the Southern people were guaranteed rights of person and property; and on the condition of troops resuming "peaceful pursuits," a general amnesty would be granted.[14] On his return from the meeting, Sherman told his wife that he could "see no slip"; the terms appeared to him to be "all on our side." He forwarded the document to Washington for ratification, informing his superiors that it ensured what was most important, namely the "disbandment of these armies . . . in such a manner as to prevent their breaking up into guerrilla bands." As far as slavery was concerned, as General Johnston had admitted that it was "dead," Sherman did not see the necessity of including emancipation as a term of surrender. Rather, he believed that it could be negotiated directly with the states.[15]

The Confederacy held its breath while it awaited Northern ratification of the peace treaty, hopeful that the promise of an honorable discharge would prevent Johnston's army from being "dissolved by desertion." Secretary Jonathan Worth had heard that the terms were "favorable," and if this was actually the case, the South was "indebted to the clemency of the enemy for them." Meanwhile, the residents of Chapel Hill, North Carolina, appealed to Sherman's goodwill to restrain the actions of his soldiers in that town. Their impression of the general was that he did not wish "to add to the undescribable horror of war," to which Sherman immediately agreed. Catherine Edmondston, on the other hand, was dubious of the liberal terms of the peace treaty, which she copied in its entirety in her journal. She suspected "a vile Yankee trick" designed to lure Southerners into submission after which Sherman would destroy the remainder of the Confederacy on his continuing march to Washington.[16]

Sherman may have found Southern suspicion to be reasonable, but the recriminations that emanated from the North took him by surprise. In no uncertain terms he was disabused of the notion that, in pursuing the twin goals of reunion and friendship with the South, he had complied with the wishes of the late President Lincoln.[17] The New York press hurled accusations against Sherman ranging from incompetency to outright treachery. What angered him most, however, was the publication of Secretary of War Edwin M. Stanton's rejection of the treaty in terms that besmirched Sherman's character and integrity.[18]

Union troops displayed both confusion and defensiveness when they heard of the controversy over their leader's actions. According to Lieutenant Samuel Mahon, the men were "justly indignant at the way the Northern papers are 'coming down' on General Sherman." If Sherman had made any error, it had been "of the head and not the heart." An Indiana soldier warned the New York press that if it persisted in calling his leader "a dangerous man and a worse traitor than Lee or any of the Southern generals," it would have "General Sherman's army to reckon with." Other soldiers expressed confusion over Sherman's actions. "We are very much shocked," wrote one officer. "We all had such confidence in Sherman and thought it almost impossible for him to make a mistake," yet the general "did act very strangely in this thing." An artillery officer could scarcely believe that Sherman would make "terms which leaves the surrender of all the Confederate armies nominally an open question."[19]

A Union chaplain was less sanguine, expressing relief that the terms were repudiated. Although anxious to return home, he feared that political concession would "only smother the fires of civil war." Captain Conyngham attributed Sherman's actions to "an error of political judgement"; a Union surgeon admitted that, despite their best efforts, the only "excuse" Sherman's men could find for their leader's behavior was "to deny that he ever signed any such terms, which nearly every soldier did." Even Sherman's wife, his most trusted confidante, disapproved of his leniency. Yet she was prepared to disregard the public criticism as she was confident that his "motive was pure." "However much I differ from you," she wrote, "I honor and respect you for the heart that could prompt such terms."[20]

Sherman was ordered to demand Johnston's unconditional surrender. Although these terms were still lenient, he knew that Southern pride demanded a return to the prewar status quo; anything less would be interpreted as humiliation and could only breed hatred. Elite white women in Georgia and the Carolinas quickly expressed just the rancor that Sherman had predicted.[21] In Georgia, Ella Thomas raged against Northern duplicity. She believed that the South had been tricked, "led to believe that terms of Treaty had been agreed upon which would secure to us a lasting and honorable peace." Now that the North had refused to ratify such terms, she declared herself "more intensely opposed to the North than at any period of the war." Eliza Andrews felt "the wrong of disrupting the Old Union was nothing to the wrongs that are being done for its restoration." A Southern veteran in Savannah noted that although externally the city seemed the same, "iron has entered its soul." In North Carolina, Elizabeth Collier shuddered at the thought of "the disgrace and degradation in store for us." Catherine Edmondston's correspondence with her niece confirmed that both women shared the same intense bitterness against "the Yankee power & the Yankee brutality." In South Carolina, Eliza Fludd vented her wrath in a letter that took ten days to compose and was so thick that she had to mail it in two envelopes. She trusted that once Southerners had written their history of the war, the North would "blush with shame."[22]

Confederate women's determination to win the peace was born of a unique blend of hatred and nostalgia, and nowhere was this more apparent than in Columbia, where many women moved beyond initial feelings of despondency to a new resolve: although defeated, they would never be subjugated. On returning from her North Carolina refuge, Mary Chesnut could not help weeping "incessantly" at the blackened track left behind by Sherman and his men. Closing her eyes, she vowed that even if they were "a crushed people" she would never be "a whimpering, pining slave." In a similar vein, Emma Holmes exclaimed, "Our Southern blood rose in stronger rebellion than ever, and we all determined that, if obliged to submit, never could they subdue us." The only question now, it seemed to Emma LeConte, was "not 'what hope?' but 'what new bitterness?' "[23]

For two weeks following this entry LeConte felt such anger that she feared to express her sentiments in words. Finally, she steeled herself to walk among the ruins of her once grand city. It was a moonlit night and her mind waxed poetic: "As far as the eye could reach only specter-like chimneys and the shutter walls, all flooded over by the rich moonlight which gave them a mysterious but mellow softness and quite took from them the ghastly air which they wear in the sunlight. They only lacked moss and lichens and tangled vines to make us believe we stood in some ruined city of antiquity."[24] In these romantic images lay the seeds of the Lost Cause ideology that was to flourish in the ensuing years.

In the immediate postwar period Northern travelers incessantly commented on the "virulent animosity" of South Carolinians. They sent home reports of constant abuses of the North and Northerners— "Yankees were stigmatized as cowards, robbers of women and children, vandals, braggarts, low fellows, avaricious, cruel and mean."[25] This reaction was hardly surprising. The state had been spared much exposure to the war until the last months, when Sherman's March northward left a trail of destruction in its wake. Moreover, residents were aware of their designation as the worst rebels and traitors and expected little generosity at the hands of their conquerors. "As [South] Carolinians," wrote Emma Holmes, "we expect to fare worse than other states."[26]

A variety of factors made North Carolina's reaction to defeat different from its neighbor's. North Carolina had suffered throughout the war, and its population was more economically diverse. Furthermore, Sherman was still ensconced in the state when peace was declared. Thus its residents lacked the hiatus during which many South Carolinians had recovered their spirits. Although the voices of common folk were muted, it seems reasonable to assume that many greeted the end of the war with a sigh of relief, turning their attention to planting crops and repairing fences. Nor did the majority of North Carolinians see themselves as rebels but rather as reluctant secessionists who had fought the good fight and now expected a return to their prewar lives.[27] They did not, however, expect to be robbed of their self-sufficiency, and this humiliation combined with an intense racism were powerful obstacles to reunion.

It was on the issue of their newly freed black population that rich and poor white Southerners found common ground. A young planter woman thought it totally "inexplicable" and "suicidal in the last degree" that her father and brother were now freeing their slaves. Although she understood that an Emancipation Act had been passed, she did not believe that it had "the force of Law."[28] Many common folks shared her disbelief that blacks were to enjoy the liberties once reserved for whites. One woman explained that even before the war, "we poor folks was about ekil[equal] to the niggers." Now she wanted to know how they were going to live? Even a nonslaveholder who had reconciled himself to reunion with the North still saw emancipation as

"d——d robbery and nothin' else." A woman who professed Unionist sympathies wanted nothing to do with "black ones." Now that they were free, "niggers is jest gone to ruin," complained a poor South Carolina woman, adding, "I wish old Sherman had taken 'em every one when he freed 'em."[29]

Slaveholding women also expressed new fears of racial violence. In Georgia, Eliza Andrews noted with irony that during the war, when "women [were] left to manage the plantations," they felt perfectly comfortable though there "was often not a white man within three miles." Now she trembled at the thought of a "race war." Laura Boykin wrote that the "negroes are discontented and insubordinate and we poor women are the victims." Catherine Edmondston feared that racial "animosity & antagonism" could only "culminate in rapine & murder" by blacks and in "stern retribution" by whites. By June Ella Thomas confessed in her journal that she now "heartily despise[d] Yankees, Negroes and everything connected with them."[30]

Many black Southerners felt betrayed by the Union, which had given them a nominal freedom without the wherewithal to support themselves, leaving them dependent on humiliated and bitter white Southerners. The first winter after the war many were so hungry that it seemed "'bout every nigger in de world cussed old Abraham Lincoln." One ex-slave reported that they all "'bout starved to death" and were forced "to go ter our ole masters an' ax' 'em fer bread ter keep us alive." Although the Yankees had given them freedom, "they took mos' everything an' lef' us nuthin' to eat, nuthin' to live on," complained another. One particularly eloquent freedman condemned the Union for denying blacks "any chance to live for ourselves," forcing them to "depend on the Southern white man for work, food, and clothing," and leaving them in "a state of servitude but little better than slavery." Where was the "forty acres of land an' de mule what de Yankees done promise us?" asked another. A black barber in Fayetteville, North Carolina, tried to explain their dilemma. There was no "darkey house" that Sherman's men had not "ransacked." And when Yankee troops left the city, white citizens immediately returned to their previous oppression of blacks. Nevertheless, African Americans had learned a valuable lesson: now they "no longer believed that every man

of Northern birth must necessarily be their friend," and they determined to "look to themselves for their own elevation."[31]

Where Northern Republicans sought repentance, they found only bitterness. Southerners seemed "sorry for nothing but their ill success," wrote one observer. Another correspondent described the political situation as "disloyalty subdued." Both writers concluded that although further military resistance was unlikely, there was a great danger of political strife. Echoing Sherman's sentiments, reporters questioned the expediency of black suffrage, which would be "very obnoxious to the prejudices of nearly the whole population." The North should eschew "vindictiveness" and "let peace, founded upon true principles be the only retribution we demand."[32]

When Sherman negotiated his original treaty with Johnston, he realized that he was stepping beyond his military role into the realm of statesmanship; yet to his mind, civil and military matters now seemed "inextricably united." After all, he had had "abundant opportunities to Know these People [Southerners] both before the war, during its existence, and since their public acknowledgement of submission." This knowledge underscored his conviction that only a magnanimous policy would immediately restore the majority of Southerners to the "Condition of good Citizens."[33]

Some Confederate women whose lives had been most directly affected by the enemy agreed with Sherman; they also mistrusted government officials and retained an identification with the military. Ella Thomas believed that the original treaty would have "secure[d] . . . a lasting and honorable peace." In anticipation of the vindictiveness of politicians, she wrote that now the South could "count with certainty upon nothing." Eliza Andrews, who found the "transition state from war to subjugation . . . far worse than was the transition from peace to war," was even more explicit. In her opinion, "the military men, who do the hard cruel things in war, seem to be more merciful in peace than the politicians who stay at home and do the talking." Could she have been referring to General William T. Sherman?[34]

In an attempt to write a dispassionate history of the final months of the conflict, a young woman in North Carolina made explicit reference to Sherman. Although Cornelia Spencer accused him of sweeping through the South "with a besom of destruction," she believed that "equal regard for truth" compelled her to recognize his more "commendable" side, namely, "humanity and a capacity for enlarged and generous statesmanship entirely worthy of a really great general." Had Sherman's terms been ratified by the North, peace and goodwill would have speedily followed. "Hard blows do not necessarily make bad blood between generous foes," she concluded; rather, it was "the ungenerous policy of the exulting conqueror" that caused the bleeding wounds to fester.[35]

Yet Confederate women's identification with the military has been obscured by a remarkably persistent model that assumes men and women hold antithetical values, especially in regard to warfare. Although Civil War scholars now question soldiers' growing alienation from the civilian population, tracing their continuing identification with both domestic and democratic institutions, none have examined this sustained affinity from the noncombatant perspective. This may be one of the reasons why women's will to resist has been excluded from studies of the Civil War in general and Sherman's March in particular.[36]

The legacy of defeat mandated gendered methods of healing. But the growing disparity of reactions between women and men was in sharp contrast to wartime experiences when many women had become central players in the arena of war. In the postwar period, soldiers could identify with comrades, even across enemy lines, by mutual recognition of duty fulfilled; women were denied a similar sense of closure. When defeated, Southern soldiers returned to their families; they looked to their female kin to reassure them of their manhood. But women would not go gently into their more passive roles as rehabilitators of Southern men and guardians of Southern memory.[37] Mary Chesnut believed that women were forced to be realistic when it came to material losses, for men had the option to "die like a patriot." Emma LeConte feared that peace might be "worse than war." How could the South consent to "submit" to such "horrible and contemptible creatures?" "Why does not the President call out the women?" she asked. "We would go and *fight* . . . we would all better die together."[38] One young North Carolinian committed to her journal just such sentiments that she dared not speak aloud. "Men of the South, are you dead to all shame?" she asked. How could they accept their "present subjugated state?" "A thousand times it were better that you had all fallen on your swords," she concluded. Catherine Edmondston also remarked that soldiers appeared to accept the situation, saying "we have done all that men could do." What had happened to their "once high spirits, their stern resolve?" she wondered.[39] Some time later a South Carolinian attempted to explain the gendered nature of the healing process. All women, in her opinion, preferred "death" or "annihilation" over reunion, and she suspected that most men felt the same way. But it was impractical for Southern men to express such opinions, and they therefore associated with Yankees for purely pragmatic reasons. If women were to criticize their menfolk for such actions, it would only "increase their pain." Their duty, then, was to "keep pure the fire of patriotism" on behalf of a "conquered people."[40]

This depoliticization of women's wartime roles also served a political agenda—one in which women themselves were implicated. Despite many examples of white Southern women's stern resistance in the face of invasion, postwar rhetoric made Yankee depredations seem even more outrageous by casting them as attacks on defenseless women and children. In the quest to win a moral victory, Southerners frequently accused Yankees of violating manly codes by attacking an otherwise peaceful home front. Sherman and his men were ideal targets for this accusation.

Despite the general's efforts to the contrary, Sherman became the personification of Yankee atrocities, and women were increasingly portrayed as his long-suffering victims. As the perfect foil to Sherman's behavior, Robert E. Lee was honored as the epitome of Southern chivalry, a valiant and heroic leader who had surrendered only in the face of overwhelming odds. Defeat on the battlefield thus signified Confederate valor, whereas subjugation of the home front merely constituted a display of Yankee moral depravity.[41]

The South constructed memories of war around symbols of Yankee barbarities, Southern cavaliers, and virtuous ladies, obscuring individual strengths and frailties and constructing an image of a united white Confederacy whose honorable mission to preserve their way of life had been thwarted by brute force.[42] The heroic defense of Southern soil was portrayed as a male prerogative, while women were praised for their "feminine" qualities of sentimentality, patience, and endurance. Such rhetoric privileged self-sacrifice over self-assertion. As women took on the responsibility of restoring male honor, they became cultural guardians rather than makers of nations and nationalisms.[43]

EPILOGUE

In 1885 Confederate veteran Colonel Lawrence Allen became embroiled in an argument with a Northern man who accused Southern women of being "no better than the streetwalkers of New York City." This insult enraged Allen, and he challenged the "wanton traducer of the noble women of the South" to a duel. The night before Allen killed the blasphemous Yankee, he composed a letter praising Southern women and vowing to avenge their honor. "God bless the ladies of the South!" he wrote. "I well remember their self denial, their great energy and true devotion to the Southern Cause." Yet twenty years earlier Allen had participated in a massacre of North Carolina Unionist sympathizers, during which white Southern women had been horribly tortured.[1]

Allen's willingness to forget the "traducers" in his own region and to remember, despite his own record of violence, all white Southern women as "ladies" was part of an outpouring of acclaim for Southern womanhood. By the 1870s and 1880s those virulent women who had confronted the enemy, or who had simply struggled for a moral economy of war, had become a classless category. In the words of Confederate general Wade Hampton, they deserved "one virtuous name." Husbands and sons, who once urged their wives and mothers to meet the Yankee invader with defiance and even with firearms, now exhorted them to "honor the brave dead and strew flowers on their graves." White women's new duty was the rehabilitation of Southern men; they were urged to "reanimate their self respect, confirm their resolve and sustain their personal honor."[2] No longer vital players in their own right, Southern women had become the appendages of heroes who had glorified themselves on the battlefield. This image of a dedicated and loyal Southern womanhood fed into a Lost Cause rhetoric, a rhetoric that the North eventually came to embrace.[3]

Several scholars have now challenged this myth of Southern womanhood, applying much more nuanced analyses to Confederate women's roles in the Civil War and to the construction of historical memory. Yet the quest to debunk this mythical image has resulted in the counterclaim that Confederate women became increasingly disillusioned and disaffected by all things military. The preceding chapters have offered an alternative interpretation: that Confederate women responded to war in diverse ways, and that firsthand experience in facing the enemy often reinvigorated waning loyalty to the Confederate cause. Yet given this range of responses, the challenge still remains to explain why such an image of loyal, but largely passive, Southern womanhood has been accepted for so long.[4]

As their strength and determination became abstractions, funneled into symbolic roles of sacrifice, rather than active struggle for nation, white women of the South became icons to be protected by men. This depoliticization of Confederate women's roles served multiple purposes, not least the reinvigoration of Southern manhood. In the Southern mind, Yankee actions, especially Sherman's strategy, became egregious acts of war rather than noble and heroic discharges of duty on the battlefield. Southerners' military efforts, on the other hand, became symbols of courage and fortitude, particularly when they were outnumbered and outgunned. The domestication of white women was not, however, simply about highlighting Southern men's bravery; it was also about reclaiming authority in the postwar South. White Southern men laid the blame for black men's emancipation at the feet of the North and then used the threat of black-on-white rape as a powerful tool to control the behavior of white women and to terrorize the black population. The memory of the Civil War thus glorified the role of the white soldier, occluded the roles of blacks, and rendered white Southern women victims of Northern atrocities and potential victims of black rapists.[5]

Racial and sexual control were, moreover, inextricably entwined with larger military and ideological issues, giving us some intriguing new ways to consider the cultural politics of Reconstruction, the construction of historical memory, and the gendered burden of Southern history. Scholars have noted that war simultaneously reinforces and disrupts women's roles. On the one hand, it offers men the opportunity to prove their manhood by defending a female population waiting passively on the home front; on the other, it immediately presents women with the challenges of new roles and responsibilities in the absence of their men. If this argument is extended to an examination of men's roles, however, we find a similar contradiction.[6]

At its inception the Civil War offered all white men an opportunity to display their heroism and prove their manhood.[7] For Southern men, raised in an honor-bound society that required outside recognition, the war provided an ideal arena in which to prove themselves.[8] War held a similar appeal for Northern men, who found their path to independence increasingly obstructed by a burgeoning commercial capitalism.[9] But the reality of war did not always live up to its promise, as regimentation, drill, and subordination often overshadowed displays of heroism.

Paradoxically, as the currents of war led women, especially those who endured invasion of the home front, into an increasingly political role that required demonstrations of courage and honor, the soldier's daily regimen consisted largely of drills, marching, and fighting, all of which centered on the male body. The most extreme case, of course, was the practice of paying for a substitute to fight in one's place, a system that Reid Mitchell describes as "a sort of grotesque speculation on the part of poor men; if they had nothing else to trade in, they had their own bodies."[10] And just as horrific, it was the body parts of injured soldiers—amputated arms and legs, bandaged heads and injured knees, frostbitten fingers and toes—that increasingly represented the cost of war.

Yet in the postwar years this objectification of men's bodies was reinterpreted as a celebration of masculine valor. Scholars of masculinity have argued that as the horrendous memories of mangled bodies faded, war was increasingly viewed as a vital component in shaping men's characters. The argument that the ideals of a martial masculinity replaced more genteel Victorian notions is, of course, based on a Northern version of gender ideology. However, by the 1880s and 1890s this new ideal aided in the reunion process, as Northerners embraced those warlike qualities they had once identified as characteristic of Southern men.[11]

Could this identification with the martial characteristics of Confederate manhood be interpreted as an inherent reluctance of the North to crush their rebellious Southern brothers? At least one man thought so. In an 1879 best-selling novel, Union veteran Albion Tourgée presented a thinly veiled account of his own postwar career as a transplanted Northerner in North Carolina. Through the voice of his protagonist he attacked congressional Reconstruction as lacking in "virility." White truculence, he argued, was the result of the velvet glove, when an iron fist was called for. He criticized the unwillingness of the North to impose an extended period of military rule. Had the South triumphed, it would have "organized [a] system of provincial government . . . because the people of the South are born rulers—aggressives." The North had failed because "*she* hesitates, palters, shirks" (emphasis added). With uncanny accuracy, he predicted that this weakness would allow for the future glorification of Confederate leadership.[12]

Military leaders were indeed subject to the cultural politics of memory and none more than Robert E. Lee. In 1866 Southern historian E. A. Pollard suggested that the "affection and esteem" inspired by Lee was a result of his "epicene" nature." This mixture of masculine and feminine qualities may have held special appeal for Southern women, particularly those who had confronted his nemesis, William T. Sherman. Moreover, Lee was the only Confederate general who had seemed able to win victories that held the promise of Southern independence. According to Gary Gallagher, "Lee's stunning victories between June 1862 and May 1863 created a mystique that lasted until the final stages of the war." By the turn of the century Southern rhetoric had transformed the general into a symbol of all that was noble about the war.[13]

As a direct antithesis to Lee, Sherman came to represent the lowest levels of barbarism. In 1881 Jefferson Davis published his *Rise and Fall of the Confederate Nation*, a book that Sherman's biographer, John Marszalek, describes as a "literary assault on Sherman's method of warfare" and one that transformed the general into the devil incarnate. This demonization of Sherman, combined with Southerners' continuing quest to win a moral victory, served to obscure women's roles in the shaping of Confederate nationalism.[14]

In a world of emancipated blacks, white Southern women also played an essential, if passive, role in ensuring racial purity and white supremacy. The misogynistic qualities of chivalry that purported to protect white women against rampant black men's sexuality placed them under intense scrutiny. It may well have been that there were now more restraints on elite white women's behavior than in the antebellum period. But although this was a time of cultural transformations, it appeared on the surface as cultural persistence.

White Southern women were not, however, silent victims of the forces of racial and sexual control but assumed active, and vocal, roles in the creation of historical memory. Their voices took on two diametrically opposed tones. The more familiar is exemplified in a 1911 address to the first college chapter of the United Daughters of the Confederacy. Here the speaker informed the young women of Winthrop College, South Carolina, that they could "conceive of no nobler and honored name than a Daughter of the Confederacy." Young Southern women had a special distinction and responsibility to remind the world what their fathers had fought for and "to compel for them respect and reverence for a noble cause and a worthy fight." She reminded them that, "in honoring our sires and their patriotism, we honor our selves."[15]

Other Southern women, possibly those who experienced the war more directly, were often less sentimental. By the time their memoirs were printed, Southern women who had lived through the war had spent years nurturing bitter seeds of resentment. Their voices often projected more rancor and frustration than respect and reverence. The North dominated the publication of women's wartime experiences until the early twentieth century, and the first books praising Northern women's patriotism did not hesitate to compare their virtues with Southern female vices. A volume published in 1867 claimed that history provided few examples of more "fiendish" behavior than that of Confederate women. Their malevolent crimes ranged from displays of "malice" and "petty spite" to demands for the murder of prisoners of war and trophies of "Yankee skulls, scalps, and bones for ornaments." It is little wonder that when Southern women had the opportunity to tell their own stories, any evenhanded portrayals of Yankee soldiers had all but disappeared, and Sherman was fated to live in opprobrium as the scourge of the Confederacy.[16]

No one encapsulates this outlook more accurately than Elizabeth Meriwether, who observed:

In those dark days just after the close of the war hate was a feeling that came into many a Southern woman's breast. The Southern men were too busy trying to retrieve their fallen fortunes, but the women—they had more time to brood over the wrongs that been done them. . . . To this day I cannot truthfully say I love Yankees, but my dear husband who fought four years in the Confederate army, seemed to feel no bitterness in his heart, not even in the years following Lee's surrender. Were he living now, more than fifty years after Appomattox, he would probably be as kindly and as just in his estimate of a Northern, as of a Southern, soldier. I cannot feel that way—at any rate, I cannot feel kindly toward Gen. Sherman. He was a monster and I want the whole world to know it.[17]

The cultural politics of war and memory reflected the interrelationship of race, sex, and the military. Together they linked Sherman and the white women of the South in an eternal war.

NOTES

Abbreviations

AS   George P. Rawick, gen. ed. *The American Slave: A Composite Autobiography.* 19 vols., 12 vols. in supplement. Westport, Conn.: Greenwood Publishing Co., 1972. AS citations take the following form: volume number(part number):page number.

DUL   Perkins Library, Duke University, Durham, North Carolina

GHS   Georgia Historical Society, Savannah

NCDAH   North Carolina Division of Archives and History, Raleigh

OR   U.S. Government, *The War of the Rebellion: A Compilation of the Official Records of the Union and Confederate Armies.* 128 vols. Washington, D.C.: GPO, 1880–1901. OR citations take the following form: volume number:page number. Unless otherwise indicated, all volumes cited throughout notes are from series 1.

SCDAH   South Carolina Division of Archives and History, Columbia

SHC   Southern Historical Collection, University of North Carolina, Chapel Hill

UNCC   Atkins Library, University of North Carolina, Charlotte

USC   Caroliniana Library, University of South Carolina, Columbia

WTS   General William T. Sherman

Introduction

1. Elliot Welch to Mother, February 14, 24, 1865, Welch Papers, DUL; Harriott to Susan, March 2, 1865, Leland, "Middleton Family Correspondence," 104; Hurmence, *Before Freedom,* 96.

2. WTS, *Memoirs,* 2:221. Sherman claims that the march north from Savannah was ten times as important as the march to the sea. Although the general was prone to exaggeration and nothing he did in the Carolinas matched the challenge of his campaign to capture Atlanta, where he faced a powerful Army of Tennessee with Joseph Johnston at its head, still, despite a plethora of studies on Sherman's March, few have given the Carolina campaign its due. Exceptions are Barrett, *Sherman's March through the Carolinas,* and Glatthaar, *March to the Sea.*

3. Stiehm, "The Protected, the Protector"; Nancy Huston, "Tales of War."
4. Lawrence, *A Present for Mr. Lincoln*; Bailey, *War and Ruin*.
5. I am building here on the work of William Blair (*Virginia's Private War*) and Gary W. Gallagher (*Confederate War*), who both argue that common suffering could lead to greater resolve on the home front as well as the battlefront. This modifies the prevailing argument that women of the planter class became increasingly disillusioned and disaffected by all things military; Faust, *Mothers of Invention*. See also George Rable, *Civil Wars*, who finds Confederate women's relationship to Southern nationalism equally fragile. Although this work considers only Sherman's March, a similar approach could equally be applied to other Civil War campaigns to investigate civilian morale, Confederate nationalism, and gender as factors in understanding warfare, as well as the interplay between home front and battlefront.
6. Escott, *Many Excellent People*; Durrill, *War of Another Kind*. Victoria Bynum (*Unruly Women*, 111–50) finds unrest along class, race, and gender lines.
7. Murrell, " 'Of Necessity and Public Benefit,' " offers a similar revisionist argument. See also Gallagher, *Confederate War*, 58.

Chapter One
The chapter title is a quotation from Edward L. Wells to Mrs. Thomas L. Wells, January 12, 1865, in Smith, Smith, and Childs, *Mason Smith Family Letters*, 162.
1. *Chicago Tribune*, December 26, 1864.
2. George Balloch to Sister, December 25, 1864, Balloch Papers, DUL.
3. Bailey, *War and Ruin*; Lawrence, *A Present for Mr. Lincoln*.
4. Connolly, *Three Years*, 372; Captain Divine to Captain J. H. Everett, December 19, 1864, Everett Papers, GHS. See also Private Charles S. Brown to "Mother and Etta," December 16, 1864, Brown Papers, DUL.
5. WTS to Ellen Sherman, October 21, 1864, in Simpson and Berlin, *Sherman's Civil War*, 738–39; Merrit Comfort to "Dear Father and Mother," January 4, 1865, Comfort Letters, DUL; Robert Hoadley to "Cousin Em," December. 18, 1864, Hoadley Papers, DUL. For an almost identical list of available food, see Corporal John Herr to "Dear Sister," December 18, 1864, Herr Papers, DUL; see also John Reid to "Friend William," January 2, 1865, McCreary Papers, DUL.
6. Balloch to Wife, December 16, 1864, Balloch Papers, DUL; Fleharty, *Our Regiment*, 117. See also Edward Allen to Parents, December 17, 1864, Allen Letters, SHC, and Morse, *Letters*, 204.
7. Fleharty, *Our Regiment*, 118, 122.

8. *Georgia Countryman*, January 10, 1865, in Huff, "'A Bitter Draught,'" 326.
9. Bailey, *War and Ruin*. Mark Grimsley (*Hard Hand of War*, 200) notes that in proportion to its length, the March to the Sea was no more destructive than previous raids in Mississippi or the burning of the Shenandoah Valley.
10. Bonner, *Journal of a Milledgeville Girl*, 60–63, and "Sherman at Milledgeville," 280.
11. Chief topographical engineer Captain John Rhiza meticulously mapped out the route through Georgia, quantifying the destruction. In 1955 a historical geographer retraced the march with these maps in hand. To his surprise, he found them to be accurate and that far less private property had been destroyed than was generally claimed. See DeLaubenfels, "Where Sherman Passed"; Grimsley, *Hard Hand of War*, 198–99; and Kennett, *Marching through Georgia*, 276, 321.
12. P. Lawson to Jefferson Davis, December 27, 1864, OR ser. 4, 3:967–68.
13. Letter from "Bertha" to *Georgia Countryman*, January 1865, in Gragg, *Illustrated Confederate Reader*, 338.
14. Conyngham, *Sherman's March*, 295.
15. Harriet Cumming to Sister, January 10, 1865, in Boggs, *Alexander Letters*, 289; Elizabeth Mackay Stiles to William Stiles, March 2, 1865, Mackay-Stiles Family Papers, SHC.
16. Robert Hoadley to "Cousin Em," December 31, 1864, Hoadley Papers, DUL.
17. Ash, *When the Yankees Came*. Ash describes three distinctive zones of geographic occupation: the "garrisoned towns," like Savannah, where citizens lived in the constant presence of Union troops; "no-man's land," or the areas surrounding garrisoned towns, where frequent Yankee raids were the norm, as in Liberty County; and the "Confederate frontier," which remained in Confederate hands with only sporadic penetration by the enemy.
18. Oscar L. Jackson, *Colonel's Diary*, 176.
19. Faust, *Mothers of Invention*, 198. Faust argues that "northerners and southerners shared fundamental cultural assumptions about the prerogatives of white womanhood." I contend that some of these assumptions were open to misunderstanding and conflict. Moreover, a rural/urban division may also have been at work here. Civilians in Pennsylvania acted in a similar way when Robert E. Lee invaded the North in 1863; see Ericson, "'The World Will Little Note.'" Unfortunately, the absence of large-scale Confederate military operations on Northern soil limits the potential for comparative analysis. Nevertheless, the disparaging remarks made by Union

soldiers on this phenomenon, especially when examined in the light of postwar criticisms of Sherman's tactics against Southern womanhood, suggest that gender ideology was an important force at work here. The power of gender ideology is apparent in its use as a judgmental tool to critique both male *and* female behavior even in the face of material constraints that preclude such idealized gender roles.

20. For the classic argument on separate sphere ideology, see Kerber, "Separate Spheres." On the culture of domesticity, see Cott, *Bonds of Womanhood*. For the obfuscation of the economic value of women's labor, see Boydston, *Home & Work*. On the growth of gender as the prime determinant of political power, see Baker, "Domestication of Politics." On the concept of the "passionless" woman, see Cott, "Passionlessness." The paradigm of separate spheres has, of course, been challenged along the lines of race and class; for an overview, see Hewitt, "Beyond the Search for Sisterhood." On the political nature of the Southern household, see Fox-Genovese, *Within the Plantation Household*, 38–39. On patterns of political power in the South, see Ayers, *Vengeance and Justice*, 23. For a critique of the "New Englandization" of Southern women, see Clinton, *Plantation Mistress*, xv–xvi. On Southern women's limited mobility, see Cashin, *Family Venture*. The increased geographic mobility of Northern women might appear to have offered them greater opportunities than afforded women of the South, but this privilege called for strict controls of what was deemed acceptable behavior. A good example of this phenomenon was the proliferation of books on the etiquette of travel that "instructed women to use male protectors and follow strict rules of behavior"; Cohen, "Safety and Danger," 119.

21. I am using Bertram Wyatt-Brown's (*Southern Honor*, xv) definition of honor as "the cluster of ethical rules . . . by which judgments of behavior are ratified by community consensus." When the system requires outside acknowledgment, it renders it both dependent on, and accessible to, all the players. Wyatt-Brown goes on to argue that Southern female honor was manifested in the "exercise of restraint and abstinence" (p. 227). For the argument that honor was a male prerogative, see Ayers, *Vengeance and Justice*, 29, and McPherson, *For Cause and Comrades*.

22. During the war, of course, these periods of sole management were protracted and may have seemed increasingly burdensome, but individual case studies highlight the diverse ways Southern white women reacted to these responsibilities. For two contrasting examples, see Faust, " 'Trying to Do a Man's Business,' " and Inscoe, "Civil War Empowerment of an Appalachian Woman."

23. Bonner, "Plantation Experiences," *North Carolina Historical Review* 33 (July 1956), 391, 410; (October 1956), 529, 532.
24. On Northern women as farm managers, see Ulrich, *Good Wives*, 37. My argument is that this prerevolutionary role of "deputy husband" was still common in the nineteenth-century South. See also Clinton, *Plantation Mistress*, and Fox-Genovese, *Within the Plantation Household*.
25. Louise Caroline Reese Cornwell, November 1864, in Jones, *When Sherman Came*, 20; Sarah Lawton to Sister, September 7, 1864, in Boggs, *Alexander Letters*, 269.
26. Huff, " 'A Bitter Draught,' " 325.
27. "A Few Words in Behalf of the Loyal Women of the United States by One of Themselves" (Loyal Publication, Society No. 10), New York, 1863, in Friedel, *Union Pamphlets*, 766–67, 769, 785.
28. Mitchell, *Vacant Chair*, esp. chap. 6, "She Devils," 89–113.
29. William C. P. Breckinridge to Isa D. Breckinridge, January 25, 1865, in Royster, *Destructive War*, 187.
30. Rev. G. S. Bradley, *Star Corps*, 186, 225.
31. Jones and Mallard, "Yankees A'Coming," 41, 45, 66, 76.
32. Ibid., 63; Mohr, *On the Threshold of Freedom*. For the varied reactions of Sherman's men to Southern blacks, see Glatthaar, *March to the Sea*, 39–65.
33. Drago, "How Sherman's March . . . Affected the Slaves," 371.
34. Paine Papers, box 2, GHS; Morgan, "Ownership of Property by Slaves," 405.
35. Drago, "How Sherman's March . . . Affected the Slaves," 370–71. The decision of whether to stay or flee was never clear-cut, an issue that is discussed more fully in Chapter 2.
36. Jones and Mallard, "Yankees A'Coming," 77, 49. Although as Gary Gallagher ("Blueprint for Victory," 32) has noted, no one has yet made a detailed study of Northern soldiers' response to emancipation, especially comparing the reactions of Midwesterners to Eastern soldiers, many examples can be found of racism among Western soldiers. See also Chapter 3 below.
37. Elliott, *Sermon*, Confederate Pamphlets, DUL. Of course, the testimony of Southern whites to the racism of Union soldiers, even when accurate, was self-serving.
38. Fleharty, *Our Regiment*, 116–17. Approximately 19,000 blacks did flee to Sherman's ranks; unfortunately, many of them did not reach Savannah. The worst atrocity occurred when Union general Jefferson Davis prematurely raised a pontoon bridge before black contrabands had an opportunity to cross. Many fleeing slaves threw themselves to their death in the icy river rather than face the wrath of General Wheeler's cavalry, following

close on their heels. Captain David P. Conyngham (*Sherman's March*, 277) gives a good account of this incident. See also Drago, "How Sherman's March . . . Affected the Slaves."

39. Winther, *With Sherman to the Sea*, 136; Boltz Diary, December 8, 1864, DUL.

40. Conyngham, *Sherman's March*, 277. How the attitude of Union soldiers affected slaves and their decision of whether or not to flee the plantation is discussed more fully in Chapter 2 below.

41. Ibid., 52. Although Mary Jones's testimony may be disingenuous, many blacks were subjected to severe treatment at the hands of the Union troops. Mark Grimsley (*Hard Hand of War*, 96) found that "utter disregard for blacks" was the norm among Sherman's men.

42. John W. Reid to William G. McCreary, January 2, 1865, McCreary Papers, DUL.

43. Fisher Diary, December 21, 1865, DUL.

44. Pepper, *Personal Recollections*, 293; King, "Fanny Cohen's Journal," 410. See also Willey, "I Soldiered for the Union," 227.

45. General Alpheus S. Williams to Daughter, January 6, 1865, in Quaife, *From the Cannon's Mouth*, 355; Pepper, *Personal Recollections*, 289.

46. Conyngham, *Sherman's March* 295

47. OR 44:841.

48. Burton, *Diary*, 49; Willey, "I Soldiered for the Union," 226. In November and December 1864, Confederate forces under the command of General Hood suffered devastating defeats at the Battles of Franklin and Nashville, Tennessee, as a result of which Hood resigned.

49. Connolly, *Three Years*, 369; Hitchcock, *Marching with Sherman*, 193.

50. C. E. Bishop to Levi A. Ross, January 8, 1865, in Royster, *Destructive War*, 365.

51. Connolly, *Three Years*, 368, 374. See also Charles B Tompkins to "Dearest Mollie," January 3, 1865, Tompkins Papers, DUL; Morse, *Letters*, 204; and Pepper, *Personal Recollections*, 283.

52. Willey, "I Soldiered for the Union," 227; King, "Fanny Cohen's Journal," 412.

53. Oscar L. Jackson, *Colonel's Diary*, 174; Diary of Captain Eli Sherlock, 100th Indiana Regiment, January 8, 1865, in Wiley, "Southern Reaction to Federal Invasion," 502. See also Merrit Comfort to "Dear Father and Mother," January 4, 1865, Comfort Letters, DUL, and Metz Diary, December 24, 1864, DUL.

54. Diary of Charles W. Wills, January 10, 1865, in Wiley, *Life of Billy Yank*, 106. When Wills's sister edited his diary for publication, she took the liberty of deleting the compliments paid to his Southern sweetheart. For the printed version, see Wills, *Army Life*.

55. Frances Howard Thomas Journal, December 24, 1864, quoted in Jones, *When Sherman Came*, 88–89.

56. King, "Fanny Cohen's Journal," 411, 414; Frances Howard Thomas Journal, December 27, January 21, in Jones, *When Sherman Came*, 90–92. See also Wiley, "Southern Reaction to Federal Invasion," 492.

57. Frances Howard Thomas Journal, December 20, in Jones, *When Sherman Came*, 86; Elizabeth Mackay Stiles to William Stiles, March 2, 1865, Mackay-Stiles Family Papers, SHC.

58. Jones, *When Sherman Came*, 87–89 (quotations, pp. 87–88).

59. Gatell, "A Yankee Views the Agony," 430–31.

60. *Cincinnati Gazette*, January 2, 1865, and *Cincinnati Daily Commercial*, February 16, 1865, both quoted in Lawrence, *A Present for Mr. Lincoln*, 217.

61. WTS to Major General Joseph Wheeler, December 24, 1864, OR 44:800; General Order No. 2, December 24, 1864, OR 44:805. "The people of Savannah are, in a measure, destitute, and will have to be supported, to a certain extent, until such time as the ordinary course of labor and supplies is resumed in the city." John G. Foster to General Halleck, December 26, 1864, OR 44:817.

62. WTS to Ellen Sherman, March 12, June 26, 1864, in Simpson and Berlin, *Sherman's Civil War*, 609, 657. See also Kennett, *Marching through Georgia*, 9.

63. WTS, *Memoirs*, 2:127; Lay Diary, September 28, 1864, NCDAH.

64. Special Field Order No. 143, December 26, 1864, in WTS, *Memoirs*, 2:233; WTS to Caroline Carson, January 20, 1865, WTS Papers, USC.

65. WTS to Wife, December 31, 1864, in Lane, *"War Is Hell,"* 187. See also WTS, *Memoirs*, 2:236.

66. Dyer, "Northern Relief for Savannah," 462–63.

67. Ibid., 464.

68. *New York Times*, January 6, 1865.

69. Dyer, "Northern Relief for Savannah," 466–67.

70. *Savannah and Boston*, 7, 10, Confederate Pamphlets, DUL.

71. Ibid., 40

72. Ibid., 19–20.

73. Ibid., 21–22.

74. Elliott, *Sermon*, 13, Confederate Pamphlets, DUL; Lay Diary, November 25, 1864, NCDAH.

75. *Savannah Daily Herald*, January 30, 1865.

76. *Savannah Republican*, January 17, 1865; *Frank Leslie's Illustrated Newspaper*, February 25, 1865, quoted in Lawrence, *A Present for Mr. Lincoln*, 222.

77. Elizabeth Mackay Stiles to William Stiles, March 2, 1865, Mackay-Stiles

Family Papers, SHC; *Augusta Constitutionalist*, March 1, 1865; Marszalek, *Diary of Miss Emma Holmes*, 394.

78. WTS to Wife, June 27, 1863, December 25, 1864, in Simpson and Berlin, *Sherman's Civil War*, 492, 778; Jones and Mallard, "*Yankees A'Coming*," 81–82; Anna Maria Green Cook Diary, November 24, 1864, in Jones, *When Sherman Came*, 31.

79. Rosa Postell to Son, February 28–April 3, 1865, in Postell, "Sherman's Occupation of Savannah."

80. William S. Basinger to Mother, February 23, 1865, in Lawrence, *A Christmas Present for Mr. Lincoln*, 220.

81. *Frank Leslie's Illustrated Newspaper*, February 1865, quoted in ibid., 228.

82. WTS, *Memoirs*, 2:252; Major James A. Connolly to Wife, January 27, 1865, in Connolly, *Three Years*, 375.

83. George Balloch to Sister, December 25, 1864, Balloch Papers, DUL; Major Henry Hitchcock to Wife, January 7, 1865, in Hitchcock, *Marching with Sherman*, 205.

84. WTS to Wife, January 15, 1865, in Simpson and Berlin, *Sherman's Civil War*, 798.

85. Bradley, December 28, 1864, in Rev. G. S. Bradley, *Star Corps*, 225–26.

86. Lieutenant Samuel Hawkins Marshall Byers, C.S. Military Prison, Columbia, S.C., February 10, 1865, Samuel Byers Papers, USC.

87. Frances Howard Thomas Journal, January 27, 1865, in Jones, *When Sherman Came*, 104; Lieutenant Samuel Hawkins Marshall Byers, C.S. Military Prison, Columbia, S.C., February 10, 1865, Samuel Byers Papers, USC.

Chapter Two

1. Miers, *Diary of Emma LeConte*, 17.

2. Elmore Diary, January 4, USC; Woodward, *Chesnut's Civil War*, 705.

3. Mrs. Kate Burwell Bowyer, "A Woman's Story of the War," in Mrs. Thomas Taylor, *Our Women in the War*, 244.

4. Elmore Diary, January 9, USC. Elmore came from a wealthy and influential South Carolina family that owned a plantation and a home in Columbia. She was twenty-two when she began to chronicle her wartime experiences.

5. Ibid., February 7, 11, 1865.

6. WTS to Admiral David Dixon Porter, January 21, 1865, OR 47:104. See also Marszalek, *Sherman*, 318, and Lewis, *Sherman*, 491.

7. Quaife, *From the Cannon's Mouth*, 385; Lieutenant Samuel Mahon to Lizzie, March 28, 1865, in Mahon, "Civil War Letters," 260; Hitchcock, *Marching with Sherman*, 229. See also Glatthaar, *March to the Sea*, 109–12.

8. Geographer Yi-Fu Tuan ("Place: An Experiential Perspective," 152) argues that at one end of the conceptual spectrum "places are points in a spatial system," whereas at the other "they are strong visceral feelings." See also John A. Jakle ("Time, Space," 1102), who stresses the importance of understanding human awareness of the "spatial alternatives of action."

9. The cultural approach to the study of war has been the subject of recent debate among military historians. John Shy ("Cultural Approach to the History of War," 25) argues that an examination of "motivating belief systems" may be useful. Commenting on Shy's article, Charles Royster suggests that our primary focus should shift from the war itself to how a particular campaign illuminates the story of societies.

10. Hitchcock, *Marching with Sherman*, 220. Hitchcock, a graduate of Yale University, was practicing law in St. Louis when the war broke out. He did not join the army until 1864, making him somewhat unique among the long-time veterans. Sherman had known Hitchcock before the war and was delighted to have him as military secretary. See also Edward W. Benham to "Dear Jennie," February 1, 1865, Benham Papers, DUL, and John Herr to "Dear Sister," January 18, 1865, Herr Papers, DUL.

11. Captain Divine to Captain J. H. Everett, January 29, 1865, Everett Papers, GHS.

12. Morse, *Letters*, 212; George Balloch to Wife, December 22, 1864, January 18, 1865, Balloch Papers, DUL; Eli Ricker to "Sister Mary," January 24, 1865, in Longacre, " 'We Left a Black Track,' " 219. See also Edward Allen to Parents, December 25, 1865, Allen Letters, SHC.

13. Lay Diary, November 12, 1864, NCDAH; WTS to U. S. Grant, December 24, 1864, OR 44:798.

14. Sherman's larger strategy was to continue his march into North Carolina, where he would rendezvous with Union troops on the coast and thereafter squeeze General Robert E. Lee between the vicelike pincers of his own forces and those of General Ulysses S. Grant. He told his superiors that, in his experience, such bold moves were the easiest to execute and that they offered the added advantage of disconcerting the enemy. WTS to Major General H. W. Halleck, December 24, 1864, OR 44:799.

15. WTS to Ellen Sherman, January 15, 1865, in Simpson and Berlin, *Sherman's Civil War*, 797.

16. WTS to Thomas Ewing, December 31, 1864, and to Ellen Sherman, January 5, 1865, in Simpson and Berlin, *Sherman's Civil War*, 782, 792. On the importance of maps, see McElfresh, *Maps and Mapmakers*.

17. Elizabeth Mackay Stiles to William Stiles, March 2, 1865, Mackay-Stiles Family Papers, SHC; Mrs. J. H. B., quoted in Jones, *When Sherman Came*, 144.

18. Corporal John Herr to "Kind Sister," March 14, 1865, Herr Papers, DUL; Hitchcock, *Marching with Sherman*, 216. See also Major James A. Connolly to Wife, January 28, 1865, in Connolly, *Three Years*, 377; Harwell and Racine, *Fiery Trail*, 103, 105; and General Alpheus S. Williams to "My Dear Minnie," January 23, 1865, in Quaife, *From the Cannon's Mouth*, 366.

19. Glatthaar, *March to the Sea*, 27–28, 76–77. Sherman's army constituted four infantry corps; the Fourteenth and Twentieth Corps made up the Army of the Cumberland and the left wing of his march that would feint to Augusta. The right wing consisting of the Fifteenth and Seventeenth Corps comprised the Army of the Tennessee and would feint to Charleston; these two corps would strike Columbia. A unit of cavalry completed this formidable force of approximately sixty thousand men.

20. WTS, *Memoirs*, 2:228, 254.

21. George Balloch to "Jennie," December 22, 1864, January 18, 1865, Balloch Papers, DUL; Sewell Diary, February 4, 1865, DUL. See also Hitchcock, *Marching with Sherman*, 214.

22. William Scofield to Sister, January 25, 1865, and to Father, February 2, 1865, Scofield Family Papers, DUL.

23. Major James A. Connolly to Wife, in Connolly, *Three Years*, 375.

24. Nichols, *Great March*, 131–32. See also Morse, *Letters*, 211.

25. Corporal John Herr to "Dear Sister," February 5, 1865, Herr Papers, DUL.

26. Hitchcock, *Marching with Sherman*, 214; Pepper, *Personal Recollections*, 300.

27. Marszalek, *Diary of Miss Emma Holmes*, 394; Statement of Mrs. Albert Rhett Heyward, March 1865, Heyward Family Papers, USC; Eliza Fludd to Sister, December 11, 1865, Fludd Papers, DUL; Miers, *Diary of Emma LeConte*, 8; Elmore Diary, November 26, 1864, USC. See also H. W. R. Jackson, *Southern Women*. Numerous newspaper accounts of Yankee violations of Southern women had appeared in Georgia and South Carolina following the Union army's attack on Fredericksburg in 1862; see Blair, "Barbarians at Fredericksburg's Gate," 156. As Lee Kennett (*Marching through Georgia*, 306–7) points out, the word "outrage" can be misleading, for it has a wide number of applications. Historians generally agree that the rape of white women was a relatively rare occurrence during the Civil War—see, e.g., Grimsley, *Hard Hand of War*, 199; Fellman, *Citizen Sherman*, 225–26; Faust, *Mothers of Invention*, 200; Rable, *Civil Wars*, 160–61; Brownmiller, *Against Our Will*, 89; and Glatthaar, *March to the Sea*, 73–74. Although most scholars have acknowledged that black women were often the victims of sexual assault, no such modification has been made for poor white women. The dearth of evidence from poor whites makes this a difficult problem to address, but studies of Confederate attitudes toward poor whites suggest

that class was a vital component when it came to acceptable levels of violence against women. See Paludan, *Victims*, and Bynum, *Unruly Women*, 111–50. This issue is discussed further in Chapter 4 below.

28. Mary Akin to Warren Akin, January 19, 1865, in Wiley, *Letters of Warren Akin*, 125; Burr, *Secret Eye*, 250.

29. Marszalek, *Diary of Miss Emma Holmes*, 384–85, 397.

30. Woodward, *Chesnut's Civil War*, 712–13.

31. Marszalek, *Diary of Miss Emma Holmes*, 396.

32. Several geographic texts were published in the Confederacy during the war; see, e.g., Marinda B. Moore, *Primary Geography*, 40, and *Geographical Reader*, and Stewart, *Geography for Beginners*. For textbooks published in the Confederate South, see Stillman, "Education in the Confederate States," 96–254.

33. It is common practice in war for commanders to keep the ordinary soldier ignorant of the larger picture so he will concentrate on the battle at hand and be unable to divulge strategic information to the enemy if captured. Civilians, on the other hand, will frequently have a better grasp of the overall course of the war. Their perceptions might be mistaken, but they will nonetheless fight their vicarious war on the strategic level. I am grateful to Professor Alex Roland for this insight. George Rable (*Confederate Republic*, 121) points out that President Jefferson Davis's increasing concern over the press's effect on troop morale led him to veto an act authorizing newspapers to be mailed to soldiers free of postage, although on this occasion the Confederate Congress overrode him.

34. Burr, *Secret Eye*, 250. See also Smith, Smith, and Childs, *Mason Smith Family Letters*, 162; Holmes, *Burckmeyer Letters*, 462.

35. Elmore Diary, December 31, 1864, USC.

36. Mrs. J. J. Pringle Smith to Mrs. William Mason Smith, March 23, 1865, in Smith, Smith, and Childs, *Mason Smith Family Letters*, 178; Harriett Ravenel, "The Burning of Columbia, 1865," Ravenel Papers, USC; Mrs. H. H. Ravenel to Robert Gourdin, January 21, 1865, Gourdin Papers, DUL; Augustine Smythe to Mother, February 9, 1865, Smythe Letters, SHC. For an extended study of the plight of refugees, see Massey, *Refugee Life*; see also Cashin, "Into the Trackless Wilderness," 29–53.

37. Emily Geiger Goodlett, "The Burning of Columbia by Sherman, February 17, 1865," n.d., Goodlett Papers, USC; Woodward, *Chesnut's Civil War*, 767.

38. Because the state had seen little fighting, blacks in South Carolina did not have the same opportunities as their counterparts in other areas to flee to Union lines.

39. John Bratton to "Dear Bettie," January 27, 1865, Bratton Papers, SHC.

40. Elmore Diary, December 24, 1864, USC.
41. Ibid., February 15, 1865; Statement of Sally Coles Heyward, n.d., Heyward Family Papers, USC.
42. For the special vulnerabilities of female slaves who fled to Union lines, see Glymph, " 'This Species of Property.' "
43. Miers, *Diary of Emma LeConte*, 54.
44. Woodward, *Chesnut's Civil War*, 699.
45. George Balloch to "Jennie," January 26, 1865, Balloch Papers, DUL; Schaum Diary, January 22, 1865, DUL; Samuel Mahon to Lizzie, January 25, 1865, in Mahon, "Civil War Letters," 260; John W. Reid to "Dear Will," March 28, 1865, McCreary Papers, DUL. See also Harwell and Racine, *Fiery Trail*, 83; Hitchcock, *Marching with Sherman*, 247; and Eli Ricker to "Dear Mary," January 23, 1865, in Longacre, "We Left a Black Track," 215.
46. Boltz Diary, January 21, 1865, DUL; Sergeant Rufus Meade to "Dear Folks at Home," January 30, 1865, in Padgett, "With Sherman," 67; Private Charles S. Brown to "All Browns," February 2, 1865, Brown Papers, DUL.
47. Eaton, "Diary of an Officer," 241; Cooper Diary, January 5, 1865, DUL.
48. Hitchcock, *Marching with Sherman*, 229; Conyngham, *Sherman's March*, 301; Meade to "Dear Folks at Home," January 30, 1865, in Padgett, "With Sherman," 68; Fleharty, *Our Regiment*, 138; Rev. G. S. Bradley, *Star Corps*, 250. See also Harwell and Racine, *Fiery Trail*, 105; Burton, *Diary of E. P. Burton*; Barrett, *Sherman's March*, 45; and McPherson, *Battle Cry of Freedom*, 827–28. For the important connections between environmental conditions and war, see Winters, *Battling the Elements*.
49. The focus of this analysis is not the logistics of conquering the landscape, but rather the way these challenges affected soldiers' attitudes toward South Carolina. For the strategic problems that Sherman faced, see Shiman, "Engineering Sherman's March." For the engineering feats involved in crossing mud-drenched roads and swollen rivers, see Glatthaar, *March to the Sea*, 110–12.
50. Force, "Marching across Carolina," *Sketches of the War*, 1861, quoted in Marszalek, *Sherman*, 319; Simms, *Sack and Destruction*, 29. See also Lewis, *Sherman*, 484, and McPherson, *Battle Cry of Freedom*, 828.
51. Morse, *Letters*, 212.
52. Sergeant Rufus Meade, in Padgett, "With Sherman," 68; Corporal Eli Ricker to "Dear Friend Mary," January 6, 1865, in Longacre, "We Left a Black Track,' " 212.
53. Quaife, *From the Cannon's Mouth*, 374; Harwell and Racine, *Fiery Trail*, 92–93; Morse, *Letters*, 211.
54. Mitchell, *Civil War Soldiers*, 96. Half of Sherman's infantry came from Ohio,

Illinois, and Indiana, with an estimated 25 percent from Ohio; see Kennett, *Marching through Georgia*, 42. For the relationship of society and landscape, see Temple, *Posquosin*, 141, where the author suggests that what Northerners often judged as the pathological "laziness" of the rural South may have been the result of a combination of rational choices and geographic features. Joseph Glatthaar (*March to the Sea*, 106) points out just such a misinterpretation regarding the "antiquated hoes" that Union soldiers found so inefficient. They were, in fact, purposely retained by slaveowners, as these older tools were more difficult for slaves to break.

55. Phillips, *American Negro Slavery*, 309.

56. Burke, *Reminiscences of Georgia*, 119–20.

57. Sarah Hicks Williams to Parents, October–November 1853, in Bonner, "Plantation Experiences," 394.

58. Adams, *Education of Henry Adams*, 44, 47. I am grateful to William Blair for bringing this to my attention.

59. Quaife, *From the Cannon's Mouth*, 374. See also Pepper, *Personal Recollections*, 302, and Horton, "Diary of an Officer," 244.

60. Hitchcock, *Marching with Sherman*, 241, 239. See also Pepper, *Personal Recollections*, 302.

61. William Scofield to Sister, January 25, 1865, Scofield Family Papers, DUL; Harwell and Racine, *Fiery Trail*, 110, 118; Pepper, *Personal Recollections*, 336.

62. John Herr to Sister, January 25, 1865, Herr Papers, DUL (emphases added); Lieutenant Samuel Mahon to Lizzie, December 22, 1864, in Mahon, "Civil War Letters," 258 (emphases added).

63. M. Dresbach to Wife, January 19, 1865, quoted in Glatthaar, *March to the Sea*, 79–80 (emphases added).

64. Rose and Ogborn, "Feminism and Historical Geography," 408; Kolodny, *The Land before Her*; Rachel Woodward, " 'It's a Man's Life.' " Geographer James Clifford ("Notes on (Field)notes," 65) argues that "in various Western discourses 'field' is associated with agriculture, property, combat and a 'feminine' place for ploughing, penetration, exploration, and improvements."

65. I use "essentialize" to convey a transhistorical process by which biological aspects of identity are emphasized independent of all other social and cultural forces; see Fox-Genovese, *Within the Plantation Household*. For an example, see Higonnet and Higonnet ("Double Helix," 37–38), who argue that in periods of war, "the masculine struggle for geographic territory is motivated by the symbol of a feminine nation populated by faithful women."

66. hooks, "Feminism and Militarism: A Comment," 92–97.

67. Fleharty, *Our Regiment*, 135; Conyngham, *Sherman's March*, 312.

68. Fleharty, *Our Regiment*, 135.

69. Harwell and Racine, *Fiery Trail*, 107. Joseph T. Glatthaar (*March to the Sea*, 122) explains that the term "bummer" had been used before Sherman's March to refer to a soldier who slacked off whenever possible, yet could be depended on in a crisis. Later, a soldier explained, the word came to identify a "ragged man . . . mounted on a scrawny mule, without a saddle, with a gun, a knapsack, a butcher knife and a plug hat. . . . Keen on the scent of rebels, or bacon, or silverspoons, or corn, or anything valuable." See also Pepper, *Personal Recollections*, 276.

70. Oscar L. Jackson, *Colonel's Diary*, 183.

71. Pepper, *Personal Recollections*, 333, 337; Morse, *Letters*, 211; John W. Reid to "Dear Will," March 28, 1865, McCreary Papers, DUL.

72. Historical anthropologist John Michael Vlach (" 'Not Mansions . . . but Good Enough,' " 109) argues that slaves saw their quarters as the place where "their personal desires and needs mattered most" and where they might find "solace in family and a wider community of black folk." For the political dimension of the "homeplace" in African American history, see hooks, *Yearning*, 42.

73. Pepper, *Personal Recollections*, 276.

74. Major General O. O. Howard to Major General F. P. Blair Jr., Beaufort, S.C., January 10, 1865, OR 47:2:33.

75. AS 2(2):256.

76. Quoted in Schwalm, "*A Hard Fight for We*," 102–3.

77. Ibid., 141.

78. Marszalek, *Diary of Miss Emma Holmes*, 430; Eliza Fludd to "My Dear Sister," December 11, 1865, Fludd Papers, DUL. See also H. J. Cough(?) to General D. H. Hill, November 1865, Hill Papers, NCDAH. Michael Fellman ("Women and Guerrilla Warfare," 153) has described "racism, tied to the license to destroy," as "the deadliest combination."

79. J. Kimball Barnes to George Starbird, December 25, 1862, March 3, 1863, in Mitchell, *Civil War Soldiers*, 122. On the difficulties of obtaining direct testimony from black women on the subject of sexual assault, see Hine, "Rape and the Inner Lives of Black Women in the Middle West," and Ervin L. Jordan, "Sleeping with the Enemy."

80. Glatthaar, *March to the Sea*, 52–65.

81. Edward Benham to "Dear Jennie," February 8, 1865, Benham Papers, DUL; Rev. G. S. Bradley, *Star Corps*, 257.

82. Diary of Lieutenant C. C. Platter, February 18, 1865, Platter Papers, USC; Conyngham, *Sherman's March*, 320–21.

83. Oscar L. Jackson, *Colonel's Diary*, 193–94.

84. AS 2(1):151; Hurmence, *Before Freedom*, 96.

85. AS 3(3):252, 26.

86. Conyngham, *Sherman's March*, 346. See also Harwell and Racine, *Fiery Trail*, 155.

87. Litwack, *Been in the Storm So Long*, 123.

88. AS 2(1):235, 259, 77.

89. Marszalek, *Diary of Miss Emma Holmes*, 403.

90. Bardaglio, "Children of Jubilee," 227. Besides Rawick's *American Slave* (AS), the other main collection of interviews with former slaves was conducted by Fisk University in 1927–30. For a more contemporary collection of documents that emphasizes African Americans' participation in their own emancipation, see Berlin et al., *Free at Last*. Scholars are expressing a growing interest in children's wartime experiences; see Marten, *Children's Civil War*, and Werner, *Reluctant Witnesses*.

91. AS 3(4):186; see also 2(1):98 and 2(2):335.

92. AS 2(2):206; see also 2(1):53 and 3(4):24.

93. AS 2(1):142, 2(2):217.

94. AS 2(2):340, 3(3):54.

95. Thomas, *Confederate Nation*, 107; McFeely, *Sapelo's People*. See also Bindman, "'Outer Bounds of Civilized Creation,'" which discusses slaves' relationship to the land and finds another instance where they returned to the site of their bondage in the immediate postwar period. Leslie Schwalm ("A Hard Fight for We," 140) also finds strong ties to family and place. Although these studies focus on the Sea Islands and Low Country region, where the task system prevailed, evidence exists to suggest that this argument might well be extended to slaves in other areas of the South. See also Stack, *Call to Home*.

96. Mahaffey, "Carl Schurz's Letters from the South," 236; Dennett, *The South as It Is*, 364.

97. Catherine Hammond to M. C. M. Hammond, September 3, 1865, in Faust, *Hammond*, 381–82.

98. AS 2(1):81, 3(4):226; see also 2(1):12, 26.

99. Potter, *The South and the Sectional Conflict*, 15. Potter argues that "the relation between the land and the people remained more direct and more primal in the South than in other parts of the country," a phenomenon he finds to be even truer for blacks than for whites.

100. Mitchell, *Civil War Soldiers*, 116.

101. Mrs. H. J. B., in Jones, *When Sherman Came*, 140–48.

102. Sarah Jane Graham Sams to Robert Randolph Sams, February 8, 1865, Sams Family Papers, USC.

103. Garret S. Byrne Diary, February 21, 1865, in Glatthaar, *March to the Sea*, 72; Grunert, *History of the 129th Regiment*, 181–82.

104. Marszalek, *Diary of Miss Emma Holmes*, 399, 402; McPherson, *For Cause and Comrades*, 39.

105. Heyward Family Papers, March 1865, USC; Mrs. William Moultrie Dwight to Captain Henry A. Gaillard, 22 February 1865, Davis Wyatt Akin Papers, USC.

106. Mrs. E. A. Steele to "My Dear Tody," February 15, 1865, in Jones, *When Sherman Came*, 134; Maria Haynsworth to "Dear Ma," April 28, 1865, Haynsworth Papers, SHC; Eaton, "Diary of an Officer," 245. It is unlikely that these "cruel straggling soldiers" would have physically assaulted this particular woman, even though black and lower-class white women may have been victims of sexual violence.

107. OR ser. 2, 4:885. For a good analysis of this incident, see Faust, *Mothers of Invention*, 207–12.

108. Captain John Bratton to Wife, February 17, 1865, Bratton Papers, SHC. There are numerous examples of Southern women who were accustomed to using firearms. See, e.g., Captain Elliot Welch to Mother, February 24, 1865, Welch Papers, DUL; Elmore Diary, February 17, 1865, USC; and Bryce, *Personal Experiences of Mrs. Campbell Bryce*, 32.

109. Edward W. Benham to "Dear Jennie," February 19, 1865, Benham Papers, DUL.

110. Mitchell, " 'Not the General but the Soldier,' " 91–92.

111. Hitchcock, *Marching with Sherman*, 224.

112. Quaife, *From the Cannon's Mouth*, 373–74.

113. Pepper, *Personal Recollections*, 276.

114. Corporal Eli Ricker to [Sister] Abigail, April 5, 1865, in Longacre, " 'We Left a Black Track,' " 224.

115. Samuel Duncan to Julia Jones, March 15, 1865, in Silber and Sievens, *Yankee Correspondence*, 51.

116. Edward W. Benham to "Dear Jennie and Friends at Home," February 8, 1865, Benham Papers, DUL; Charles S. Brown to "My Dear Etta," April 26, 1865, Brown Papers, DUL.

117. Pepper, *Personal Recollections*, 331.

118. Stormont, *History of the Fifty-eighth*, 287; George Balloch to "My Own Jennie," March 28, 1865, Balloch Papers, DUL; John Herr to "Dear Sister," December 18, 1864, Herr Papers, DUL; Charles S. Brown to "Mother and Etta," December 16, 1864, Brown Papers, DUL; Charles B. Tompkins

to "My Darling Wife," April 12, 1865, Tompkins Papers, DUL. See also Allen Diary, February 18, 1865, SHC.

119. WTS to Ellen Sherman, March 23, 1865, in Howe, *Home Letters*, 335; Trowbridge, *Desolate South*, 303.

120. Morse, *Letters*, 211. See also Pepper, *Personal Recollections*, 331.

121. Mitchell, *Vacant Chair*, 36–37.

122. Charles S. Brown to his "Folks," March–April 1865, Brown Papers, DUL; Rev. G. S. Bradley, *Star Corps*, 275–76; Harwell and Racine, *Fiery Trail*, 107; Sergeant Rufus Meade to "Dear Folks at Home," March 20, 1865, in Padgett, "With Sherman," 72. See also Allen Diary, February 23, 1865, SHC.

123. Grimsley, *Hard Hand of War*, 185, 204, 213. Grimsley builds on Mark Neely's classic article, "Was the Civil War a Total War?," Neely argued that "the essential aspect of any definition of total war asserts that it breaks down the distinction between soldiers and civilians, combatants and noncombatants, and this no one in the Civil War did systematically, including William T. Sherman" (p. 27). Grimsley recasts the image of Sherman as the harbinger of modern total warfare, defining his tactics as "hard war" in which the restraint of soldiers was the remarkable feature. See also Fellman, *Citizen Sherman*, 225–26.

124. Grimsley, *Hard Hand of War*, 190–91, 204. This practice was commonly used by the English during the Hundred Years War of 1337–1453. Grimsley's argument is underscored by the fact that no contemporary commentators remarked on the innovativeness of Sherman's campaign; see Neely, "Was the Civil War a Total War?," 28. Sherman himself cited historical precedent for his strategy using the Duke of Wellington as his model; see Lewis, *Sherman*, 485; see also Marszalek, *Sherman*, 471.

125. Although Sherman's campaign has been described as a psychological rape of the Southern home front, there was never any widespread rape, murder, or removal of populations as occurred in wars against Native American populations in the West or in the civil and global conflicts of the twentieth century. To describe it as such depreciates the horror experienced by those (predominantly African American) women who were actually raped.

126. Fleharty, *Our Regiment*, 140–41; Cooper Diary, February 24, 1865, DUL; Edward W. Benham to "Dear Jennie and Friends at Home," February 19, 1865, Benham Papers, DUL; T. S. Howland to Sister, March 30, 1865, in Glatthaar, *March to the Sea*, 148; Ricker, in Longacre, " 'We Left a Black Track,' " 224. See also Allen Diary, February 18, 1865, SHC.

127. Hacker, "Women and Military Institutions." See also Weelwright, *Amazons and Military Maids*, 18, and Lynn, "Embattled Future," 784–85.

128. Hacker, "Women and Military Institutions," 645, 666. Linda Grant De-Pauw ("Women in Combat") has noted similar changes in the United States. During the American War of Independence women served in George Washington's army in a variety of roles and were subject to military discipline, yet less than a century later these crucial roles had faded from historical memory. The post-Revolutionary period also marked the redefinition of "citizen" as one who bore arms in defense of his country; see Hoffman and Albert, *Women in the Age of the American Revolution*, 30. Military historians are reluctant to recognize women's support roles as essential to military efforts. I think it is indicative of my argument that, once professionalized and masculinized, the Quartermaster Corps was considered vital.

129. Stormont, *History of the Fifty-eighth*, 481.

130. Hitchcock, *Marching with Sherman*, 264.

131. Ricker, in Longacre, " 'We Left a Black Track,' " 223; Major S. S. Farwell to his home paper, March 27, 1865, in Farwell, "Palmetto Flag," 61; "Madame Sosnowski's Account of the Burning of Columbia," Sosnowski-Schaller Family Papers, USC.

Chapter Three

The chapter title is a quotation from Miers, *Diary of Emma LeConte*, 67.

1. Massey, *Refugee Life*, 37, 82. See also Kaufman, "Treasury Girls."

2. Simms, *Sack and Destruction*, 29.

3. Trowbridge, *Desolate South*, 298. See also Jesse S. Bean Diary, February 17, 1865, SHC. The repeated requests from Confederate generals to President Davis for reinforcements from Virginia and North Carolina fell on deaf ears; see OR 47:1083–84.

4. De Treville, "Extracts from the Letters of a Confederate Girl," 183–84; LeConte, " 'Ware Sherman,' " 86, 89; Woodward, *Chesnut's Civil War*, 728. See also Augustus Robert Taft Diary, February 25, 1865, USC.

5. As of this writing, the best account of this episode is Lucas, *Sherman and the Burning of Columbia*. For a representative Union soldier's account, see Harwell and Racine, *Fiery Trail*, 127–32.

6. For a recent argument that women on the home front increasingly saw their sacrifice as useless and withdrew their support, see Faust, *Mothers of Invention*. My assertion engages with intriguing new scholarship suggesting that common suffering could lead to greater resolve on the home front as well as the battlefront. See Blair, *Virginia's Private War*, and Gallagher, *Confederate War*.

7. Miers, *Diary of Emma LeConte*, 39; Simms, *Sack and Destruction*, 34; WTS, *Memoirs*, 2:278.

8. Mrs. J. J. Pringle Smith to Mrs. William Mason Smith, March 23, 1865, in Smith, Smith, and Childs, *Mason Smith Family Letters*, 173; Miers, *Diary of Emma LeConte*, 41.

9. Elmore Diary, February 17, 1865, USC; Goodlett Papers, USC; Sewell Diary, March 8, 1865, DUL; Simms, *Sack and Destruction*, 43.

10. Sergeant Henry H. Wright to "Dear Folks at Home," March 28, 1865, in Monnett, " 'The Awfulest Time I Ever Seen,' " 286. See also Glatthaar, *March to the Sea*, 76.

11. Sergeant Robert Hoadley to "Cousin Em," April 8, 1865, Hoadley Papers, DUL.

12. Elmore Diary, February 18, 1865, USC.

13. Anonymous Mother to "My Dear Gracia," March 3, 1865, in Jones, *When Sherman Came*, 176.

14. WTS to Major General H. W. Halleck, December 24, 1865, in WTS, *Memoirs*, 2:227; Cooper Diary, January 23, 1865, DUL. Although three of Sherman's four corps were made up of Western troops, the Fifteenth Corps had acquired a reputation for being particularly destructive. For a geographic breakdown of the native origins of Sherman's men, see Kennett, *Marching through Georgia*, 42–43.

15. Mrs. W. K. Bachman to Kate Bachman, March 27, 1865, Bachman Family Papers, USC; Lily Logan to "My Precious Brother," March 2, 1865, in Jones, *When Sherman Came*, 194; Simms, *Sack and Destruction*, 42.

16. Elmore Diary, February 18, 1865, US; Harriett Ravenel "The Burning of Columbia, 1865," Ravenel Papers, USC.

17. Conyngham, *Sherman's March*, 346; Mary Leverette to "My Dear Caroline," March 18, 1865, Leverette Papers, USC.

18. Harriett Ravenel, "The Burning of Columbia, 1865," Ravenel Papers, USC.

19. Simms, *Sack and Destruction*, 49.

20. Harriott Middleton to Susan, March 10, 1865, in Leland, "Middleton Family Correspondence," 105; Elmore Diary, March 7, 1865; Mrs. H. H. Simons, "The Burning of Columbia, February, 1865," Simons Papers, USC.

21. Sosnowski, "Burning of Columbia," 205; Harriett Ravenel, "The Burning of Columbia, 1865," Ravenel Papers, USC; Harriott Middleton to Susan, March 2, 1865, in Leland, "Middleton Family Correspondence," 103. The Middletons were an extensive family with several plantations and a town home in Charleston; for more background, see Hunt, "High with Courage."

22. Conyngham, *Sherman's March*, 322; Bryce, *Experiences of Mrs. Campbell Bryce*, 23; Elmore Diary, February 17, 1865, USC.

23. Anonymous Mother to "My Dear Gracia," March 3, 1865, in Jones, *When Sherman Came*, 177; Lily Logan to "My precious Brother," ibid., 165; Mrs. J. J. Pringle Smith to Mrs. William Mason Smith, March 23, 1865, in Smith, Smith, and Childs, *Mason Smith Family Letters*, 175; Harriott to Susan, February 28, March 2, 1865, in Leland, "Middleton Family Correspondence," 102, 104.

24. Mrs. W. K. Bachman to Kate Bachman, March 27, 1865, and Wade Hampton Manning to Mrs. W. K. Bachman, n.d., Bachman Family Papers, USC. See also Dr. Toomer Porter to Lieutenant General Wade Hampton, February 18, 1865, Brooks Papers, DUL. Reverend Porter commended the behavior of an Illinois officer to Confederate forces to ensure that, if this Yankee fell into enemy hands, he would be treated with leniency. The officer in question was also a member of the Fifteenth Corps.

25. Simms, *Sack and Destruction*, 39.

26. Ibid., 81; Spencer, *Last Ninety Days*, 187. See also Jones and Mallard, "Yankees A'Coming," 77.

27. Mrs. W. K. Bachman to Kate Bachman, March 27, 1865, Bachman Family Papers, USC; Sosnowski, "Burning of Columbia," 206. See also Barrett, *Sherman's March*, 86. On the need for an analysis of racial attitudes along regional lines, see Gallagher, "Blueprint for Victory," 32. Even after the war Emma LeConte commented on the treatment of blacks by the garrison of Western soldiers who "far from fraternizing with the negroes, seem to hold them in profound disgust"; Miers, *Diary of Emma LeConte*, 105.

28. Miers, *Diary of Emma LeConte*, 51.

29. Simms, *Sack and Destruction*, 55.

30. Sosnowski, "Burning of Columbia," 203.

31. John Bennett Walters, "Sherman and Total War" (Ph.D. diss., Vanderbilt University, 1947), quoted in Barrett, *Sherman's March*, 89; Affidavits, n.d., in Trezevant Papers, USC.

32. Elmore Diary, February 19, March 6, 1865, USC; Harwell and Racine, *Fiery Trail*, 155.

33. Robert Finley to "Friend Mary," March 30, 1865, Finley Papers, SHC; Connolly, *Three Years*, 387; Burton, *Diary*, 63; Pepper, *Personal Recollections*, 308; Conyngham, *Sherman's March*, 333–34.

34. Appendix to Bean Diary, SHC; Rev. G. S. Bradley, *Star Corps*, 263.

35. Platter Diary, February 18, 1865, Platter Papers, USC; Samuel Snow to Parents, March 28, 1865, Snow Family Papers, DUL. See also Conyngham, *Sherman's March*, 331, and Ward Diary, February 17, 1865, USC.

36. Harwell and Racine, *Fiery Trail*, 131; Connolly, *Three Years*, 388; George Balloch to "My Own Jennie," March 12, 1865, Balloch Papers, DUL.

37. Simms, *Sack and Destruction*, 86; Harriott Middleton to Susan, February 28, 1865, in Leland, "Middleton Family Correspondence," 103. See also Trowbridge, *Desolate South*, 296.

38. Elmore Diary, February 19, 1865, USC; Reverend Shand to Mrs. Howard Kennedy, March 9, 1868, Shand Papers, USC; Harriett Ravenel, "The Burning of Columbia," Ravenel Papers, USC. See also Mrs. W. K. Bachman to Kate Bachman, March 26, 1875, Bachman Family Papers, USC; Harriott to Susan, February 28, 1865, in Leland, "Middleton Family Correspondence," 100–101; and Trowbridge, *Desolate South*, 296.

39. Arbuckle, *Civil War Experiences*, 135.

40. Simons, "The Burning of Columbia," Simons Papers, USC; Miers, *Diary of Emma LeConte*, 58. See also Bryce, *Experiences of Mrs. Campbell Bryce*, 32.

41. McPherson, *For Cause and Comrades*, 88–89. McPherson argues that "cohesion is a renewable resource" and that "ideological attachments" can provide "sustaining motivation" in the face of destruction.

42. Faust, *Mothers of Invention*. See also Rable, *Civil Wars*. These informative studies consider the Confederacy as a whole and offer general conclusions based on detailed research. I do not suggest that their conclusions are erroneous, but rather that they might be modified by attention to the tenacity of female nationalism in specific areas of the South, particularly where women met the enemy face-to-face.

43. Blair, *Virginia's Private War*, 79; Gallagher, *Confederate War*, 56, 78.

44. Logue, "Coping with Defeat Rhetorically." Drawing on studies of bereavement and disaster, Logue argues that "during the last months of the fighting, mythic appeals were smelted from suffering and defiance, tempered in a hostile environment, and molded for use after the war politically and economically" (p. 62). Although not an exact fit in South Carolina, the model is useful in illuminating the dynamics of the recovery process. The increasing hostility of Southerners in the postwar years is discussed in the Epilogue to this book.

45. Reverent Robert Boykin to Peter Shand, February ?, 1865, Boykin Papers, SHC.

46. Governor Andrew Magrath to Mayor T. J. Goodwyn, February 27, 1865, Magrath Papers, SCDAH. I am grateful to Lisa Frank for bringing this letter to my attention; see her " 'To Cure Her of Her Pride and Boasting.' "

47. Mrs. W. K. Bachman to Kate Bachman, March 27, 1865, Bachman Family Papers, USC; Mary Leverette to "My Dear Caroline," March 18, 1865, Leverette Papers, USC; Harriott Middleton to Susan, March 21, 1865, in

Leland, "Middleton Family Correspondence," 105; Lily Logan to Brother, March 2, 1865, in Jones, *When Sherman Came*, 193; R. S. C. to Husband, February 27, 1865, Cheves Papers, DUL.

48. Andrew McBride to Wife, March 16, 1865, McBride Papers, DUL; Greenville Ladies Association Minutes, typescript, DUL.

49. Julia Gott to Sister, February 27, 1865, Gott Letters, USC; Mary Elinor Poppenheim Diary, March 1, 1865, in Jones, *When Sherman Came*, 246; Mrs. Emily Caroline Ellis Diary, Ellis Family Papers, USC; Caroline R. Ravenel to Isabella Middleton Smith, March 31, 1865, in Smith, Smith, and Childs, *Mason Smith Family Letters*, 187; Ravenel Papers, USC; Conyngham, *Sherman's March*, 335–36; Pepper, *Personal Recollections*, 330.

50. McPherson, *What They Fought For*, 18; Elmore Diary, March 4, 1865, USC; Mary Elinor Poppenheim Diary, February, 27, 1865, in Jones, *When Sherman Came*, 245; Miers, *Diary of Emma LeConte*, 60, 66.

51. Potter, "Historian's Use of Nationalism," warns us that the argument that Southern nationalism was inherently weak because it was unsuccessful leads us to overemphasize inner conflicts. He contends that nationalism could embrace a multiplicity of loyalties. See also Gallagher, *Confederate War*, 63–111. According to Gallagher, Potter's essay remains "the best exploration of the dangers inherent in exploring the topic of Confederate nationalism" (p. 189).

52. Elmore Diary, March 4, 1865, USC; Harriott Middleton to Susan, March 2, 1865, in Leland, "Middleton Family Correspondence," 103; Miers, *Diary of Emma LeConte*, 66, 49.

53. Mrs. W. K. Bachman to Kate Bachman, Bachman Family Papers, March 27, 1865, USC; Miers, *Diary of Emma LeConte*, 68; Harriott Middleton to Susan, March 2, 1865, in Leland, "Middleton Family Correspondence," 103.

54. Faust, "Confederate Women and Narratives of War," in Clinton and Silber, *Divided Houses*, 198.

55. Unsigned to My Dear Willie, March 31, 1865, DeSaussure Papers, DUL; R. S. C. to Husband, February 27, 1865, Cheves Papers, DUL; Marszalek, *Diary of Miss Emma Holmes*, 407.

56. Lily Logan to "My Precious Brother," March 2, 1865, in Jones, *When Sherman Came*, 194; Elliot Welch to Mother, February 24, 1865, Welch Papers, DUL.

57. Miers, *Diary of Emma LeConte*, 68; Sallie I. Lowndes to Mrs. William Mason Smith, March 18, 1865, in Smith, Smith, and Childs, *Mason Smith Family Letters*, 171; Elliot Welch to My Darling Mother, March 20, 1865, Welch

Papers, DUL. See also Andrew Baxter Spring to F. B. Sexton, December 15, 1864, Springs Letters, UNCC.

58. Miers, *Diary of Emma LeConte*, 77; Elmore Diary, March 4, 1865, USC; Elizabeth Stiles to William Stiles, March 2, 1865, Mackay-Stiles Family Papers, SHC. See also Rosa Postell to Son, February 28, 1865, in Postell, "Sherman's Occupation of Savannah," 112. William Blair (*Virginia's Private War*, 251) has found similar sentiments in Virginia, where people refused to give up hope as long as Lee's army stood. See also Gallagher's *Confederate War*, 58–59, which argues that Lee's mystique lasted to the very end of the conflict.

59. Message to the Senate and House of Representatives of the Confederate States of America, Richmond, November 7, 1864, in Richardson, *Messages and Papers*, 1:485.

60. Sarah Sams, for example, who lived in the much smaller town of Barnwell, was left with few provisions. She wrote to her husband about the loneliness she felt and prayed for a speedy end to the war. Sarah Jane Sams to Husband, March 9, 1865, Sams Family Papers, USC.

61. McPherson, *For Cause and Comrades*, 147.

Chapter Four

The chapter title is a quotation from Bartholomew F. Moore to D. L. Swain, April 8, 1865, Swain Papers, SHC.

1. Harwell and Racine, *Fiery Trail*, 171.

2. General Order No. 8, OR 47:719; Special Order No. 63, OR 47:760–61.

3. WTS, *Memoirs*, 2:292, 299. Johnston had been removed from his command by Jefferson Davis, who was frustrated by the general's retreat before Atlanta. The Confederate president had now only reluctantly reinstated him at the request of General Robert E. Lee. See Special Order No. 3, OR 47:1248.

4. Harwell and Racine, *Fiery Trail*, 199–200. Johnston's army contained many Western soldiers who had survived Confederate defeats in Nashville and Franklin, Tennessee, and traveled across country to join Johnston's forces in North Carolina. But due to problems of transportation and lack of supervision, only 9,000 had arrived in April 1865, by which time Sherman had received 25,000 reinforcements. See Grimsley, "Learning to Say 'Enough.' "

5. Civil War scholars have neglected Sherman's North Carolina campaign and have instead focused on the inner tensions, particularly those across class lines, that fueled disloyalty on the home front and encouraged Con-

federate soldiers to desert their ranks. The clearest articulation of this argument is Escott's *Many Excellent People*. Escott contends that the state's low population density and the inhabitants' personal independence minimized the importance of social class in the antebellum period, but that the war brought people face-to-face in a new way and consequently highlighted class divisions. See also Durrill, *War of Another Kind*, and Bynum, *Unruly Women*. Beringer et al. (*Why the South Lost*) maintain that class discontent in North Carolina was a "drain on the limited supply of Confederate nationalism" (p. 434).

6. WTS to Ellen Sherman, April 9, 1865, in Howe, *Home Letters*, 343; Fleharty, *Our Regiment*, 151; Diary of George Williamson Balloch, March 7, 1865, and Balloch to Wife, March 28, 1865, Balloch Papers, DUL. See also Barrett, *Sherman's March*, 121, and Glatthaar, *March to the Sea*, 107.

7. Farwell, "Palmetto Flag," 66; Lieutenant Robert Stuart Finley to "Friend Mary," March 30, 1865, Finley Papers, SHC; WTS, *Memoirs*, 2:296. See also Rev. G. S. Bradley, *Star Corps*, 274; Connolly, *Three Years*, 384; Wills, *Army Life*, 362; Hitchcock, *Marching with Sherman*, 270; OR 47:679; and Barrett, *Sherman's March*, 192.

8. Wills, *Army Life*, 358; Nichols, *Great March*, 222.

9. Pepper, *Personal Recollections*, 343; Samuel Snow to Parents, March 28, 1865, Snow Family Papers, DUL; Charles S. Brown to "My Dear Etta," April 26, 1865, Brown Papers, DUL; Oscar L. Jackson, *Colonel's Diary*, 197–98.

10. John Herr to "Kind Sister," March 12, 1865, Herr Papers, DUL; Robert Hoadley to "Cousin Em," April 8, 1865, Hoadley Papers, DUL. See also Y. J. Powell to Ellen Aumack, March 27, 1865, Aumack Papers, DUL, and Morse, *Letters*, 212.

11. Wills, *Army Life*, 364; Edward W. Benham to "Dear Jennie," March 9, 1865, Benham Papers, DUL; Fleharty, *Our Regiment*, 154; WTS to Wife, April 9, 1865, in Howe, *Home Letters*, 342; Winther, *With Sherman to the Sea*, 158.

12. Andrew Barnard to Z. B. Vance, December, 30, 1864, and John Roberts to Vance, December 16, 1864, Vance Papers, NCDAH; OR ser. 4, 2:1061–62.

13. Nicholas Gibson Diary, Appendix, Gibson Papers, UNCC; OR 47:1203, 1234. See also Blair, *Virginia's Private War*, 121.

14. J. M. Worth to Jonathan Worth, March 9, 1865 (1:364), J. J. Jackson to Jonathan Worth, March 12, 1865 (1:365), and Anon to Jonathan Worth, March 2, 1865 (1:261–62), in Hamilton, *Correspondence of . . . Worth*.

15. Easter [Robins] to Marmaduke Robins, March 13, 1865, and "A Quaker" to M. S. Robins, January 20, 1865, Robins Papers, SHC; W. J. Foust to Jonathan Worth, February 3, 1865 (1:343), J. M. Worth to Jonathan Worth, March 9, 1865 (1:356), and Jonathan Worth to ?, January 8, 1865 (1:338), in

Hamilton, *Correspondence of . . . Worth*. See also Tilgham Diary, February 11, 1865, SHC; Captain J. E. Rheims to Z. B. Vance, January 9, 1865, and The Mayor and Commissioners of High Point to Vance, December 1864, Vance Papers, NCDAH; Bynum, *Unruly Women*, 120; Escott, *Many Excellent People*, 68–69.

16. Robert E. Lee to Z. B. Vance, February 24, 1865, OR 47:1270; Beringer et al., *Why the South Lost*, 334.

17. Reid, "Test Case of the 'Crying Evil.' " Confederate soldiers often took 'french leave'—a brief absence from the ranks to assist family members with the full intention of returning to their units; as several scholars have argued, it was the motive, rather than the act, that constituted desertion. See Reid and White, " 'Mob of Stragglers and Cowards,' " 64; Blair, *Virginia's Private War*, 129–30; Lonn, *Desertion*; and Bearman, "Desertion as Localism."

18. Petition from North Carolina Soldiers of Lee's Army to Z. B. Vance, January 24, 1865, Vance Papers, NCDAH.

19. Susan C Wooker to Z. B. Vance, April 3, 1864, quoted in Yearns and Barrett, *North Carolina Civil War Documentary*, 262–63; Mrs. Sue O. Conly to Vance, January 5, 1865, Vance Papers, NCDAH; Harriett McMasters to Marmaduke Robins, February 16, 1865, Robins Papers, SHC.

20. Dodge, "Cave-Dwellers of the Confederacy," 519. See also Bynum, *Unruly Women*, 132.

21. Brigadier General Theophilus Holmes to General S. Cooper, January 31, 1865, Holmes Papers, DUL; Harriett McMasters to Marmaduke Robins, February 16, 1865, Robins Papers, SHC.

22. Petition from North Carolina Soldiers of Lee's Army to Z. B. Vance, January 24, 1865, and Mrs. Sue O. Conly to Vance, January 5, 1865, Vance Papers, NCDAH; Harriett McMasters to Marmaduke Robins, February 16, 1865, Robins Papers SHC; Bynum, *Unruly Women*, 146.

23. OR 51:1054–65.

24. Dodge, "Cave-Dwellers of the Confederacy," 519. This article might be considered as postwar apologia; nevertheless, it provides contemporary evidence of the added burdens that desertion placed on women.

25. Escott, *Many Excellent People*, 20; Bynum, *Unruly Women*, 143–44; McKinney, "Women's Role," 43.

26. Thomas Settle to Z. B. Vance, October 4, 1864, Settle Letters, NCDAH.

27. Paludan, *Victims*, 896.

28. Escott, *Many Excellent People*, xviii–xix; Edwards, "Law, Domestic Violence," 742–43. Escott contends that a tradition of violence in defense of their rights was common among yeomen, and elites always saw them as

a potential threat. He does not, however, consider the role of women. Kirsten Fischer (*Bodies of Evidence*) also finds North Carolina a particularly disorderly state. Victoria Bynum (*Unruly Women*, 131) argues that North Carolina women were both victims and perpetrators of aggressive behavior, although the disorderly behavior of women during the Civil War was a break with tradition.

29. Escott, *Many Excellent People*, 65–66; Bynum, *Unruly Women*, 125–26, 134, 145.

30. In considering whether or not such actions were disloyal, an interesting comparison could be made between the food riots, in which women sought a solution to economic injustices, and the New York draft riots that erupted in July 1863, in which women played a prominent role in resisting the war effort. Diaries describe "the fury of the low Irish women . . . all cursing the 'bloody draft' and egging on their men to mischief" and women crowding around the lynched body of an African American, cutting off "parts of his body as souvenirs." *Diary of George Templeton Strong* and *Diary of a Union Lady*, respectively, quoted in Linden and Pressly, *Voices from the House Divided*, 116, 118, 119–20. James McPherson (*Drawn with the Sword*, 123) finds the Northern draft riots "much more violent and threatening" than the bread riots of the South.

31. I have borrowed the term "moral economy" from E. P. Thompson ("Moral Economy of the English Crowd," 126), who argues that the food riots of eighteenth-century England were a result of people defending traditional rights. He describes these riots as a "pattern of social protest which derives from a consensus as to the moral economy of the commonweal in times of dearth." Drew Gilpin Faust (*Creation of Confederate Nationalism*, 52) argues that these riots are a clear example of such "moral economy."

32. Blair, *Virginia's Private War*, 132.

33. During the Revolutionary War American women also used petitions as political devices. See Hoffman and Albert, *Women in the . . . American Revolution*, 19.

34. "A Southern Woman" to Z. B. Vance (December 12, 1864), "Nina" to Vance (December 30, 1864), and H. Nutt to Vance (December 12, 1864), Vance Papers, NCDAH. See also S. E. Grandy to Vance, December 15, 1865, ibid.

35. Sue O. Conly to Z. B. Vance, January 5, 1865, and Harriet S. Briley to Vance, December 30, 1865, Vance Papers, NCDAH. See also Mrs. Richard Drake to Vance (December 27, 1864), M. L. Wiggens to Vance (January 1, 1865), and Mary Newton to Vance (January 10, 1975), ibid.

36. George Rable (*Civil Wars*, 74) asserted that these women "seemed patheti-

cally parochial" in assuming that authorities would devote attention to their plight. I prefer to give them more credit; after all, ordinary citizens sent similar personal appeals to the president and first lady in the 1930s. Similarly, Paul Escott (*Many Excellent People*, 67) interprets female protest as an "unconscious" continuation of ancient European rituals rather than informed political acts. For a recent revisionist argument, see Murrell ("Of Necessity and Public Benefit"), who interprets appeals by Southern families as "narratives of negotiation, rather than of protest" (p. 79).

37. WTS to Major General Q. A. Gilmore, March 14, 1865, and Robert E. Lee to Z. B. Vance, February 24, 186, OR ser. 1, 47:857, 1270; North Carolina Officers to W. A. Graham, February 27, 1865, Graham Papers, SHC; Spencer, *Last Ninety Days*, 147. Even scholars who identify weak Confederate nationalism as the prime determinant of Southern defeat still recognize that Vance's personal influence "headed off and to some extent pacified more serious discontent"; Beringer et al., *Why the South Lost*, 210.

38. Vance's Proclamation to the people of North Carolina, February 14, 1865, OR 47:1187–92.

39. Crabtree and Patton, "*Journal of a Secesh Lady*," 666; Letter to the editor of the *Conservative*, February 7, 1865, and Easter to Marmaduke Robins, March 12, 1865, Robins Papers, SHC. See also Robert Strange to Robert Strange Jr., February 1865, Strange Jr. Papers, SHC.

40. Blair, *Virginia's Private War*, 76, 79.

41. AS 15(2):123.

42. Mayor of Greensboro to Z. B. Vance, January 19, 1865, Vance Papers, NCDAH; David Schenck Diary, February 1865, SHC. See also Mayor and Commissioners of High Point to Vance, December 25, 1864, Vance Papers, NCDAH, and Durrill, *War of Another Kind*, 164–65.

43. Justices of Peace, Richmond County, to Z. B. Vance (December 9, 1864), H. Nutt to Vance (December 10, 1864), and Anon to Vance (December 13, 1864), Vance Papers, NCDAH; Webb Diary, December 22, 1864, DUL; Conyngham, *Sherman's March*, 355. See also Mary Mosby to Vance (December 10, 1864), R. D. McDonald to Vance (December 12, 1864), and Ralph P. Buxton to Vance (December 14, 1864), Vance Papers, NCDAH.

44. WTS to U. S. Grant, March 12, 1865, OR 47:794–95; WTS to Major General Terry, March 12, 1865, ibid., 803; Nichols, *Great March*, 252; Harwell and Racine, *Fiery Trail*, 184, 186.

45. AS 14(1):136, 178, 15(2):190.

46. AS 14(1):387, 97, 271, 15(2):111, 288. See also Spencer, *Last Ninety Days*, 51.

47. Janie Smith to ?, April 12, 1865, Webb Papers, NCDAH.

48. AS 15(2):149–50, 75; see also 14(1):361.

49. AS 14(1):425, 459; see also 14(1):293, 430, 455, and 15(2):190, 224. See also Janie Smith to ?, April 12, 1865, Webb Papers, NCDAH.

50. Simms, *Sack and Destruction*, 53–54, 82; Esther Alden Diary, March 14, 15, 1865, in Jones, *When Sherman Came*, 362–63; AS 15(2):190; Testimony of Violet Guntharpe, in Hurmence, *Before Freedom*, 96; Sally Hawthorne Memoirs, in Jones, *When Sherman Came*, 284; Excerpt from *Winnsboro Courier*, n.d., typed transcript, Mordecai Family Papers, SHC. See also Goodlett Papers and Elmore Diary, March 6, 1865, both in USC; AS 15(2):224; and Elizabeth Hinsdale to "My Darling Child," March 23, 1865, Hinsdale Family Papers, DUL.

51. AS 14(1):149–50, 11; 15(2):149–50.

52. Nellie Worth to "My Dear Cousin," March 21, 1865, in Jones, *When Sherman Came*, 261; Annie I. Jones to ?, March 6, 1865, Jones Papers, SHC; Elizabeth Hinsdale to John Hinsdale, n.d., and to "My Darling Child," March 23, 1865, Hinsdale Family Papers, DUL. For a Union soldier's account of such an incident, see Charles S. Brown to "My Dear Etta," April 26, 1865, Brown Papers, DUL.

53. Bruce Cauthen, "Opposing Forces," 15. Cauthen argues that this was a policy of "ethnocide" aimed not at depriving people of their lives, but of their "cultural and communal identity."

54. Edmund J. Cleveland Diary, April 16, 1865, Cleveland SHC; John Metzgar to Wife, April 14, 1865, Metzgar Papers, SHC. See also John MacRae to "Dear Don," April 3, 1865, MacRae Letters, DUL, and Stormont, *History of the Fifty-eighth*, 514.

55. These actions may have been intended to destroy Southern cultural identity, but in fact they often served to actively form a renewed Confederate identity, especially in the postwar world. This reshaping of identities is discussed more fully in the Epilogue.

56. Charles S. Brown to "My Dear Etta," April 26, 1865, Brown Papers, DUL; Burton, *Diary*, 70; Pepper, *Personal Recollections*, 331. See also Glatthaar, *March to the Sea*, 148–49.

57. Jones, *When Sherman Came*, 268, 284; AS 15(2):217. See also Collier Diary, April 20, 1865, SHC; Washington Sandford Chaffin Diary, March 9, 10, 1865, Chaffin Papers, DUL; and Spencer, *Last Ninety Days*, 66–67.

58. George Rable (*Civil Wars*, 173) described this as tearing into the "sinews of memory that bound families together and to past generations."

59. Crabtree and Patton, "Journal of a Secesh Lady," 696.

60. Mrs. J. J. B. in Jones, *When Sherman Came*, 143; Loula to Poss, May 22, 1865, in Ash, *When the Yankees Came*, 40. See also Esther Alden Diary, in Jones,

When Sherman Came, 251, and Eliza Fludd to "My Dear Friend," September 25, 1865, Fludd Papers, DUL.

61. On March 16 Confederate and Union forces met at the Battle of Averasboro, which proved to be little more than a delaying action. On March 19–21 a much bloodier battle was fought at Bentonville. For a detailed analysis of this much overlooked encounter, see Mark L. Bradley, *Last Stand in the Carolinas*, and Hughes, *Bentonville*.

62. Janie Smith to Janie Robeson, April 12, 1865, typed transcript, Webb Papers, NCDAH; Baxter Smith Reminiscences, in Mark L. Bradley, *Last Stand in the Carolinas*, 135. See also WTS, *Memoirs*, 2:301; Fleharty, *Our Regiment*, 157–59; and Barrett, *Sherman's March*, 156.

63. Jones, *When Sherman Came*, 284, 274–75, 290, 301; Elizabeth Hinsdale to "My Darling Child," March 23, 1865, Hinsdale Family Papers, SHC.

64. Crabtree and Patton, "*Journal of a Secesh Lady*," 677; Pepper, *Personal Recollections*, 333; Private Charles S. Brown to "My Dear Etta," April 26, 1865, Brown Papers, DUL; Spencer, *Last Ninety Days*, 61.

65. James C. Scott, *Domination*, 23. Scott argues that, although usually seen as secondary to material exploitation, assaults to dignity and autonomy are powerful stimulators of resistance.

66. Janie Smith to Janie Robeson, April 12, 1865, typed transcript, Webb Papers, NCDAH; Elizabeth Hinsdale to "My Darling Child," March 23, 1865, Hinsdale Family Papers, DUL. Such sentiments were fueled by confusing rumors about the outcome of the North Carolina battles. Many civilians heard that Sherman had suffered serious losses.

67. Robert Shalhope ("Republicanism and Early American Historiography," 355) refers to this as the "sociopsychological dimensions of ideology."

68. Unidentified Woman from Fayetteville, N.C., March 22, 1865, typed transcript, Mordecai Family Papers, SHC. David Potter ("Nature of Southernism," 53) argues that if a people have sufficient reason to believe they have cause to be a unified group (in this case, the presence of an army of invasion was ample cause), "the conviction itself may unify them, and thus may produce the nationalism which it appears to reflect."

Chapter Five
The chapter title is a lyric from a Southern postwar song quoted in Edward L. Ayers, ed. "*A House Divided*": *A Century of Great Civil War Quotations* (New York: Wiley, 1997), 215.

1. Mark L. Bradley, *Last Stand in the Carolinas*, 302, 405–8; Barrett, *Sherman's March*, 182–83.

2. Jonathan Worth to J. J. Jackson, in Hamilton, *Correspondence of . . . Worth*,

1:371. See also Edward L. Wells to Sabina Elliott Wells, March 20, 1865, in Smith, Smith, and Childs, *Mason Smith Family Letters*, 172; Crabtree and Patton, "Journal of a Secesh Lady," 682; Webb Diary, March 22, 1865, DUL; and Washington Sandford Chaffin Diary, March 26, 1865, Chaffin Papers, DUL.

3. Hitchcock, *Marching with Sherman*, 273. See also Harwell and Racine, *Fiery Trail*, 199, and Sewell Diary, April 10, 1865, DUL.

4. Charles B. Tompkins to "My Darling Wife," April 12, 1865, Tompkins Papers, DUL; John J. Metzgar to "Dear Carrie," April 14, 1865, Metzgar Papers, SHC.

5. Gary Gallagher (*Confederate War*, 95) argues that Lee and his army were of such importance to the Confederacy that, despite the fact that he surrendered only a fraction of the Southern armies, "few Confederates contemplated serious resistance after Appomattox."

6. Nichols, *Great March*, 310.

7. Johnston's reluctance to continue the war by guerrilla tactics has been interpreted as a weak sense of nationalism. My argument is that although military and geographic conditions were ideal for guerrilla warfare, the culture was not. The chaos and conflict that would ensue was antithetical to the type of Confederate nation Southerners envisaged, one based on social stability. A partisan war could not have sustained morale, nor would it have produced a viable Confederate nation that could earn the recognition of other world powers. It was not that the South lacked the will to fight, but rather it chose not to fight the only type of war that could have prolonged the struggle. William Blair (*Virginia's Private War*, 150) asserts that "guerrilla war demanded unpalatable choices."

8. Sherman had promised members of the Savannah Chamber of Commerce that "when war is done we can soon bring order out of chaos, and prosperity out of ruin & destruction." Sherman's Response to Resolutions of the Savannah Chamber of Commerce, January 15, 1865, in Royster, *Destructive War*, 354. See also Simpson, "*Let Us Have Peace.*"

9. Others argued that the truculence of the South was the fruit of leniency— see, e.g., Tourgée, *Fool's Errand*. This, of course, highlights the irony that many Southerners were in political agreement with Sherman, yet constructed a postbellum image of him as the devil incarnate.

10. Marszalek, *Diary of Miss Emma Holmes*, 432; Elmore Diary, April 27, 1865, USC; Woodward, *Chesnut's Civil War*, 794; Crabtree and Patton, "Journal of a Secesh Lady," 695–96; Collier Diary, April 20, 1865, SHC; Miers, *Diary of Emma LeConte*, 89–90. See also Bonner, *Journal of a Milledgeville Girl*, 73; Eliza Frances Andrews, *War Time Journal*, 171; Mrs. Carolina S. Jones to

Mrs. Mary Jones, April 30, 1865, in Myers, *Children of Pride*, 1268; and Dennett, *The South as It Is*, 192. Similar sentiments were expressed by elite women across the Confederacy—see, e.g., Diary of Cornelia Peake Mc-Donald, April 1865, in Sullivan, *The War the Women Lived*, 283; McGuire, *Diary of a Southern Refugee*, 353; and Sarah Wadley Diary, April 20, 1865, SHC.

11. Oscar L. Jackson, *Colonel's Diary*, 209; Pepper, *Personal Recollections*, 403; Conyngham, *Sherman's March*, 384.

12. Nellie Worth to "My Dear Cousin," March 21, 1865, in Jones, *When Sherman Came*, 261; Marszalek, *Diary of Miss Emma Holmes*, 436; Eliza Frances Andrews, *War Time Journal*, 172; OTC to Father, April 21, 1865, in Glatthaar, *March to the Sea*, 72; Burr, *Secret Eye*, 260–61.

13. Wyatt-Brown, *Southern Honor*, 155. Wyatt-Brown argues that shame can be avoided only by a "congruence of social and personal perception."

14. Barrett, *Sherman's March*, 239–41; Marszalek, *Sherman*, 349. On the question of "property" Sherman was intentionally vague. He believed that the institution of slavery was dead and that the position of the freed people could be negotiated in detail with the individual states. Ensuring the political rights of blacks was never a priority for Sherman, who believed that they should remain in the South as a cheap form of labor. WTS to Ellen Sherman, May 10, 1865, in Howe, *Home Letters*, 353.

15. WTS to Ellen Sherman, April 18, 1865, in Simpson and Berlin, *Sherman's Civil War*, 867; WTS to Lieutenant General U. S. Grant, or Major General Halleck, April 18, 1865, ibid., 864.

16. Jonathan Worth to J. J. Jackson, April 21, 1865, in Hamilton, *Correspondence of . . . Worth*, 381; D. L. Swain to WTS, April 19, 1865, and WTS to D. L. Swain, April 22, 1865, in Clark Papers, NCDAH; Crabtree and Patton, "*Journal of a Secesh Lady*," 705–6.

17. WTS, *Memoirs*, 2:350, 358. In a meeting on April 24, Grant informed Sherman that Lincoln had instructed his generals not to enter into any political negotiations with the enemy. Sherman had thus overstepped his authority; he was ordered to demand the surrender of Johnston's army on the same terms given to General Lee.

18. Marszalek, *Sherman*, 346–48; Barrett, *Sherman's March*, 273–76.

19. Mahon, "Civil War Letters," 262; Winther, *With Sherman to the Sea*, 167; Wills, *Army Life*, 377–78.

20. Stormont, *History of the Fifty-eighth*, 524, 526–27; Conyngham, *Sherman's March*, 366; Charles B. Tompkins to Wife, May 7, 1865, Tompkins Papers, DUL; Ellen Sherman to WTS, April 26, in Howe, *Home Letters*, 344, 348. See also Webb Diary, May 9, 1865, DUL.

21. As early as June 1863, Sherman had identified Southern women as an unparalleled example of "deep & bitter enmity." Simpson and Berlin, *Sherman's Civil War*, 492.

22. Burr, *Secret Eye*, 265; Bonner, *Journal of a Milledgeville Girl*, 188–89; George Anderson Mercer, "Diary and Notebook," in Lawrence, *A Present for Mr. Lincoln*, 245; Collier Diary, April 25, May 9, 1865, SHC; Crabtree and Patton, "Journal of a Secesh Lady," 710–11; Eliza Fludd to Sister, December 11, 1865, Fludd Papers, DUL.

23. Woodward, *Chesnut's Civil War*, 800; Marszalek, *Diary of Miss Emma Holmes*, 436–37; Elmore Diary, May 2, 1865, USC; Miers, *Diary of Emma LeConte*, 97.

24. Miers, *Diary of Emma LeConte*, 99.

25. Trowbridge, *Desolate South*, 306; Dennett, *The South as It Is*, 362.

26. Marszalek, *Diary of Miss Emma Holmes*, 439.

27. North Carolina had been one of the last states to secede; see Escott, *Many Excellent People*, 50, and Dennett, *The South as It Is*, 162. William Blair (*Virginia's Private War*, 135) argues that Confederate Virginians also believed that they could restore their antebellum world.

28. Crabtree and Patton, "Journal of a Secesh Lady," 709.

29. Dennett, *The South as It Is*, 111, 146, 116, 118, 183; Trowbridge, *Desolate South*, 312, 315. See also Sidney Andrews, *The South since the War*, 157, and Reid, *After the War*, 34.

30. Eliza Frances Andrews, *War Time Journal*, 315–16; Stock, *Shinplasters and Homespun*, 35; Crabtree and Patton, "Journal of a Secesh Lady," 719; Burr, *Secret Eye*, 275.

31. AS 15(2):268, 14(1):186, 15(2):429, 14(1):361; Dennett, *The South as It Is*, 176–77. See also Escott, *Many Excellent People*, 113–35.

32. Reid, *After the War*, 33; Dennett, *The South as It Is*, 362, 368–69; Trowbridge, *Desolate South*, 316–17.

33. Simpson and Berlin, *Sherman's Civil War*, 878, 886, 889. See also Simpson, "Facilitating Defeat."

34. Burr, *Secret Eye*, 264; Eliza Frances Andrews, *War Time Journal*, 198, 217.

35. Spencer, *Last Ninety Days*, 153, 61. Spencer's history elicited harsh criticism from both North and South; see Massey, *Women in the Civil War*, 194.

36. For the soldiers' alienation thesis, see Linderman, *Embattled Courage*. Those who argue that Union soldiers' retained their peacetime values include Mitchell, *Vacant Chair*, and Grimsley, *Hard Hand of War*. McPherson (*For Cause and Comrades*) extends this analysis to soldiers on both sides of the conflict.

37. Faust, *Mothers of Invention*, 252; Whites, *The Civil War as a Crisis in Gender*, 149–50.

38. Woodward, *Chesnut's Civil War*, 716; Miers, *Diary of Emma LeConte*, 90.

39. Collier Diary, July 9. 1865, SHC; Crabtree and Patton, "Journal of a Secesh Lady," 708.

40. Weiner, *Heritage of Woe*, 176.

41. Marszalek, *Sherman*, 333.

42. Merton E. Coulter ("Sherman and the South") argues that the lack of balanced analysis between Sherman's actions as warrior and as peacemaker has produced a distorted picture.

43. Rable, *Civil Wars*, 238. Cynthia Enloe (*Bananas Beaches, & Bases*, 44) contends that "nationalism typically has sprung from masculinized memory, masculinized humiliation, and masculinized hope."

Epilogue

1. Paludan, *Victims*, 121.

2. General Wade Hampton to President Johnson, 1866, Brooks Papers, DUL; Address by Jubal Early on the anniversary of Robert E. Lee's death, 1872, in Gallagher, *Confederate War*, 170–71; *Augusta Chronicle & Constitutionalist*, November 1, 1878, clipping in Jones Papers, box 4, DUL; Address at Davidson College by Robert Dabney, in Foster, *Ghosts of the Confederacy*, 29.

3. The reinterpretation of Confederate women's power from courage and defiance to domestic devotion and sacrifice also occurred in Northern rhetoric as conciliation transformed the "secesh" woman from "political viper" to "flirtatious belle." See Silber, "Northern Myth," 130.

4. Studies of reunion and the development of Lost Cause ideology are voluminous. See, e.g., Silber, *Romance of Reunion*; William R. Taylor, *Cavalier and Yankee*; Foster, *Ghosts of the Confederacy*; and Wilson, *Baptized in Blood*.

5. Blight, *Race and Reunion*; Hodes, "Sexualization of Reconstruction Politics"; Hall, *Revolt against Chivalry*, xx. Hall argues that "the racism that caused white men to lynch black men cannot be understood apart from the sexism that informed their policing of white women and their exploitation of black women."

6. Faust, *Southern Stories*, 9; Dowler, " 'And They Think I'm Just a Nice Old Lady,' " 160. Both scholars note this simultaneous reinforcement and disruption of women's roles during war; I argue, however, that it also affected men.

7. Michelle Rosaldo ("Woman, Culture, and Society," 28) contends that "a woman becomes a woman by following in her mother's footsteps," whereas "masculinity is never fully possessed, but must be perpetually achieved, asserted and renegotiated," a theory that meshes perfectly with

the gendered discourse of war that offers men the opportunity to display and prove their manhood. See also Roper and Tosh, *Manful Assertions*, 18.

8. Wyatt-Brown, *Southern Honor*, 35. John Lynn ("Embattled Future," 786) has found a similar appeal among aristocratic men in seventeenth-century France, where an honor code dictated that "it was not enough to be brave; one must be seen as being brave by one's peers."

9. James L. Huston, "Property Rights in Slavery," 266. Huston argues that the significant increase of wage earners by the 1830s modified the republican vision of producing an independent virtuous population into a "free labor ideology"; thus men were forced to endure a period of "dependency on their road to economic independence." See also Rotunda, *American Manhood*, and Bederman, *Manliness & Civilization*, although both authors date this job market crisis at the end of the nineteenth century.

10. Mitchell, *Civil War Soldiers*, 161. See also Escott, *After Secession*, 117–18.

11. Silber, *Romance of Reunion*, 23–24. On the changing values from "manly" characteristics of self-control and strength of character to a celebration of "masculine" strength and virility, see Rotunda, *American Manhood*, and Bederman, *Manliness & Civilization*. See also Bourke, *Dismembering the Male*, 250. Bourke argues that during World War I "the male body was subjected to callous treatment during war and then to the renewed sanitizing of disciplines of peace."

12. Tourgée, *Fool's Errand*, 171 (emphasis added).

13. Pollard, *Southern History of the War*, 608–9. Interestingly, Pollard's deconstruction of the nature of military leaders does not appear in the later facsimile editions. Gallagher, *Confederate War*, 59. Thomas L. Connelly (*Marble Man*) places the creation of a "Lee Cult" at the end of the nineteenth century while ignoring the presence of a wartime "Lee Cult" in the Confederacy.

14. Davis, *Rise and Fall of the Confederate Government*; Marszalek, "Celebrity in Dixie."

15. Address by Mrs. August Kohn, reprinted in *The State* (Columbia), April 30, 1911.

16. Brockett and Vaughan, *Women's Work in the Civil War*, quoted in Schultz, "Women at the Front," 19. See also Attie, *Patriotic Toil*.

17. Meriwether, Recollections, SHC.

BIBLIOGRAPHY

MANUSCRIPTS
Georgia
    Savannah: Georgia Historical Society
        Delannoy, J. D., Papers
        Everett, J. H., Papers
        Paine, W. W., Papers
North Carolina
    Chapel Hill: Southern Historical Collection, University of North Carolina
        Allen, Edward W., Letters and Diary
        Barnes, David Alexander, Papers
        Bean, Jesse S., Diary
        Boykin, Reverend Robert Wilson, Papers
        Bratton, John S., Papers
        Cleveland, Edmund J., Papers
        Collier, Elizabeth, Diary
        Confederate Miscellany
        Duryea, D. H., Letters
        Finley, Robert Stuart, Papers
        Graham, William Alexander, Papers
        Grimball, Margaret Ann Meta Morris, Diary
        Haynsworth, Maria L., Papers
        Hutson, Charles Woodward, Papers
        Hyde, Anne Bachman, Papers
        Jones, Cadwallader, Papers
        Mackay-Stiles Family Papers
        Meriwether, Elizabeth Avery, Recollections
        Metzgar, John J., Papers
        Mitchell, Elisha, Papers
        Mordecai Family Papers
        Noble Family Letters
        Pettigrew Family Papers
        Philips-Myers Family Papers

Polk, Leonidas Lafayette, Papers
Ramsey, James Gettys McGready, Papers
Robins, Marmaduke S., Papers
Schenck, David, Diary
Smythe, Augustine Thomas, Letters
Spencer, Cornelia Phillips, Papers
Strange, Robert, Jr., Papers
Swain, David L., Papers
Terry Family Papers
Tilgham, Tench, Diary
Wadley, Sarah, Diary
Wilson, Norvell Winsboro, Diary
Worth, Jonathan, Papers
Charlotte: Special Collections, Atkins Library, University of North Carolina
Clark, Richard Lee, Papers
Gibson, Nicholas Biddle, Papers
Goodwin, Virginia Caroline, Papers
Siewers, Nathaniel Shober, Papers
Springs, Andrew Baxter, Letters
Wilkes Family Papers
Durham: Special Collections, Perkins Library, Duke University
Aumack, Ellen, Papers
Balloch, George, Papers
Beardsley, Alonzo G., Correspondence
Benham, Edward W., Papers
Boltz, Ferdinand F., Diary
Brooks, Ulysses R., Papers
Brown, Charles S., Papers
Calder, William, Papers
Chaffin, Washington Sanford, Papers
Cheves, Rachel Susan, Papers
Comfort, Joshua and Merrit, Letters
Confederate Miscellany
Confederate Pamphlets
Elliott, Reverend Stephen. *A Sermon Preached in Christ's Church,
    Savannah, September 1864.* Macon, Ga.: Burke, Boydin and Co.,
    1864.
*Savannah and Boston: Account of the Supplies Sent to Savannah with the
    Last Appeal of Edward Everett in Fanuiel Hall.* Boston: Press of John
    Wilson and Son, 1865.

Confederate Survivors Association Addresses
Cooper, Lieutenant John Snider, Diary
Craven-Pegram Family Papers
DeSaussure, Henry William, Papers
Fisher, John W., Diary
Fludd, Eliza Burden, Papers
Gourdin, Robert Newman, Papers
Gray, Mrs. Hiram, Papers
Greenville Ladies Association Minutes
Herr, John, Papers
Hinsdale Family Papers
Hoadley, Robert Bruce, Papers
Holmes, Theophilus Hunter, Papers
Jarratt-Puryear Family Papers
Johnson, John, Diary
Jones, Charles Colcock, Jr., Papers
Ledbetter, William J., Papers
Long, Augustus White, Papers
MacRae, Hugh, Letters
McBride, Andrew Jay, Papers
McCreary, William G., Papers
Metz, George P., Diary
Nixon, Thomas, Papers
Schaum, William, Diary
Scofield Family Papers
Sewell, Captain Thomas, Diary
Sherman, William T., Papers
Simpson, William Dunlap, Papers
Snow Family Papers
Stetson, Joseph M., Papers
Tompkins, Charles B., Papers
Van Duzer, John, Diary
Walkup, Samuel Hoey, Diary
Webb, Lewis H., Diary
Welch, Elliot Stephen, Papers
Wheeler, Joseph, Papers
Raleigh: North Carolina Division of Archives and History
Clark, Walter Manus, Papers
Hawthorne, Sally, Papers
Hill, General Daniel H., Papers

      Lay, Henry Champlin, Diary
      Martin, Mrs. Margaret Craig, Papers
      Meyers, Thomas J., Papers
      Mordecai, Pattie, Papers
      Patterson Family Papers
      Settle, Thomas, Jr., Letters
      Thayer, Will F., Diary
      Vance, Zebulon Baird, Letter Book and Papers
      Webb, Mrs. Thomas H., Papers
South Carolina
    Columbia: Caroliniana Library, University of South Carolina
      Akin, David Wyatt, Papers
      Bachman Family Papers
      Byers, Samuel, Papers
      Ellis Family Papers
      Elmore, Grace Brown, Diary
      Goodlett, Emily Geiger, Papers
      Goodwyn, Thomas Jefferson, Letters
      Gott, Julia Frances, Letters
      Heyward Family Papers
      Huggins, George, Papers
      Leverette, Mary, Papers
      Palmer Family Papers
      Platter, C. C., Papers
      Ravenel, Mrs. Harriett Horry, Papers
      Sams Family Papers
      Shand, Reverend Peter Johnson, Papers
      Sherman, William T., Papers
      Simons, Mrs. H. H., Papers
      Sosnowski-Schaller Family Papers
      Taft, Augustus Robert, Diary
      Trezevant, Daniel Heyward, Papers
      Ward, Charles G., Diary
    Columbia: Division of Archives and History
      Magrath, Andrew, Papers

NEWSPAPERS
  Augusta Constitutionalist
  Chicago Tribune
  Cincinnati Daily Commercial

Cincinnati Gazette
Frank Leslie's Illustrated Newspaper
Georgia Countryman
New York Times
Savannah Daily Herald
Savannah Republican

PUBLISHED PRIMARY SOURCES

Adams, Henry. *The Education of Henry Adams: An Autobiography*. Boston: Houghton Mifflin, 1918.

Andrews, Eliza Frances. *The War Time Journal of a Georgia Girl, 1864–1865*. Edited by Spencer Bidwell King Jr. Macon, Ga.: Ardivan Press, 1960.

Andrews, Sidney. *The South since the War as Shown by Fourteen Weeks of Travel and Observation in Georgia and the Carolinas*. 1866. Reprint, Boston: Houghton Mifflin, 1971.

Arbuckle, John C. *Civil War Experiences of a Foot-Soldier Who Marched with Sherman*. Columbus, Ohio: N.p., 1930.

Berlin, Ira, Barbara J. Fields, Steven F. Miller, Joseph P. Reidy, and Leslie S. Rowland, eds. *Free at Last: A Documentary History of Slavery, Freedom, and the Civil War*. New York: New Press, 1992.

Boggs, Marion, ed. *The Alexander Letters*. Athens: University of Georgia Press, 1980.

Bonner, James C. "Plantation Experiences of a New York Woman." *North Carolina Historical Review* 33 (July 1956): 384–412; (October 1956): 529–46.

———, ed. *The Journal of a Milledgeville Girl, 1861–1867*. Athens: University of Georgia Press, 1964.

Bradley, Reverend G. S. *The Star Corps, or Notes of an Army Chaplain during Sherman's Famous "March to the Sea."* Milwaukee: Jermain and Brightman, 1865.

Bryce, Campbell. *The Personal Experiences of Mrs. Campbell Bryce during the Burning of Columbia, South Carolina by W. T. Sherman's Army, February 17, 1865*. Philadelphia: Lippincott Press, 1899.

Burke, Emily. *Reminiscences of Georgia*. Oberlin, Ohio: N.p., 1850.

Burr, Virginia Ingraham, ed. *The Secret Eye: The Journal of Ella Gertrude Clanton Thomas, 1848–1889*. Chapel Hill: University of North Carolina Press, 1990.

Burton, E. P. *Diary of E. P. Burton, Surgeon*. Des Moines, Iowa: Historical Records Survey, 1939.

Connolly, Major James A. *Three Years in the Army of the Cumberland*. Edited by Paul M. Angle. Bloomington: Indiana University Press, 1959.

Conyngham, Captain David P. *Sherman's March through the South*. New York: Sheldon and Co., 1865.

Crabtree, Beth Gilbert, and James W. Patton, eds. *"Journal of a Secesh Lady": The Diary of Catherine Ann Devereaux Edmondston, 1860–1865*. Raleigh: Division of Archives and History, 1979.

Davis, Jefferson. *The Rise and Fall of the Confederate Government*. 1881. Reprint, New York: Thomas Yoseloff, 1958.

Dennett, John Richard. *The South as It Is, 1865–1866*. Edited by Henry M. Christman. New York: Viking, 1965.

De Treville, Mary Darby. "Extracts from the Letters of a Confederate Girl." In *South Carolina Women in the Confederacy*, edited by Mrs. Thomas Taylor, 183–84. Columbia: The State Co., 1903.

Eaton, Clement, ed. "Diary of an Officer in Sherman's Army Marching through the Carolinas." *Journal of Southern History* 9 (May 1943): 238–54.

Farwell, Sewell S. "The Palmetto Flag: Letter of Major S. S. Farwell to His Home Paper from the Field." *Annals of Iowa* 15 (July 1925): 61–66.

Fleharty, D. F. *Our Regiment: A History of the 102nd Illinois Infantry Volunteers*. Chicago: Brewster and Hanscom Printers, 1865.

Franklin, John Hope, ed. *Civil War Diary of James T. Ayers*. Springfield: Illinois State Historical Society, 1947.

Friedel, Frank, ed. *Union Pamphlets of the Civil War*. Cambridge: Harvard University Press, 1967.

Gragg, Rod, ed. *The Illustrated Confederate Reader*. New York: Harper and Row, 1989.

Green, Anna. *Journal of a Milledgeville Girl*. Edited by James C. Bonner. Athens: University of Georgia Press, 1964.

Grunert, William. *History of the 129th Regiment Illinois Volunteer Infantry*. Winchester, Ill.: R. B. Dedman, 1866.

Hamilton, J. G. de Roulhac, ed. *The Correspondence of Jonathan Worth*. 4 vols. Raleigh: Edwards and Broughton Printing Co., 1909.

——. *The Papers of Thomas Ruffin*. 3 vols. Raleigh: Edwards and Broughton Printing Co., 1920.

Harwell, Richard, and Philip N. Racine, eds. *The Fiery Trail: A Union Officer's Account of Sherman's Last Campaigns*. Knoxville: University of Tennessee Press, 1986.

Hitchcock, Henry. *Marching with Sherman*. Edited by M. A. DeWolfe Howe. Lincoln: University of Nebraska Press, 1995.

Holmes, Charlotte R., ed. *The Burckmeyer Letters, March 1863–June 1865*. Columbia, S.C.: State Co., 1926.

Howe, M. A. DeWolfe, ed. *Home Letters of General Sherman.* New York: Scribner's, 1909.

Hundley, Daniel R. *Social Relations of Our Southern States.* New York: Henry B. Price, 1860.

Hurmence, Belinda, ed. *Before Freedom.* New York: Penguin Books, 1990.

Jackson, H. W. R. *The Southern Women and the Second American Revolution: Their Trials, &c., Yankee Barbarities Illustrated.* Atlanta: Intelligencer Steam-Power Press, 1959.

Jackson, Oscar Lawrence. *The Colonel's Diary: Journals Kept before and during the Civil War by the Late Colonel Oscar L. Jackson . . . Sometime Commander of the 63rd Regiment, O.V.I..* Sharon? Pa.: N.p., 1922.

Johnston, Joseph Eggleston. *Narrative of Military Operations Directed during the Late War between the States.* New York: D. Appleton and Co., 1874.

Jones, Katherine M., ed. *Heroines of Dixie.* New York: Bobbs-Merrill, 1955.

———. *When Sherman Came: Southern Women and the "Great March."* Indianapolis: Bobbs-Merrill, 1964.

Jones, Mary Sharpe, and Mary Jones Mallard. *"Yankees A'Coming": One Month's Experience during the Invasion of Liberty County, Georgia, 1864–1865.* Edited by Haskell Monroe. Tuscaloosa, Ala.: Confederate Publishing Co., 1959.

King, Spencer B., Jr. "Fanny Cohen's Journal of Sherman's Occupation of Savannah." *Georgia Historical Quarterly* 41 (December 1957): 407–16.

Lane, Mills, ed. *"War Is Hell": William T. Sherman's Personal Narrative of His March through Georgia.* Savannah: Beehive Press, 1974.

LeConte, Joseph. *'Ware Sherman: A Journal of Three Months' Personal Experience in the Last Days of the Confederacy.* Berkeley: University of California Press, 1937.

Leland, Isabella Middleton, ed. "Middleton Family Correspondence, 1861–1865." *South Carolina Historical Magazine* 64 (April 1964): 98–109.

Linden, Glenn M., and Thomas J. Pressly, eds. *Voices from the House Divided: The United States Civil War as Personal Experience.* New York: McGraw-Hill, 1995.

Longacre, Edward G. " 'We Left a Black Track in South Carolina': Letters of Corporal Eli S. Ricker, 1865." *South Carolina Historical Magazine* 82 (July 1981): 210–24.

Mahaffey, Joseph H., ed. "Carl Schurz's Letters from the South." *Georgia Historical Quarterly* 35 (September 1951): 222–57.

Mahon, John K., ed. "The Civil War Letters of Samuel Mahon, Seventh Iowa Infantry." *Iowa Journal of History* 51 (July 1953): 233–66.

Marszalek, John F., ed. *The Diary of Miss Emma Holmes.* Baton Rouge: Louisiana State University Press, 1979.

McGuire, Judith W. *Diary of a Southern Refugee during the War by a Lady of Virginia.* Lincoln: University of Nebraska Press, 1995.

Miers, Earl Schenck, ed. *When the World Ended: The Diary of Emma LeConte.* New York: Oxford University Press, 1957.

Monnett, Howard Norman, ed. " 'The Awfulest Time I Ever Seen': A Letter from Sherman's Army." *Civil War History* 8 (September 1962): 283–89.

Moore, Marinda B. *Geographical Reader for the Dixie Children.* Raleigh: Branson and Farrar, 1863.

———. *Primary Geography Arranged as a Reading Book for Common Schools with Questions and Answers Attached.* 2d ed. Raleigh: Branson and Farrar, 1864.

Morse, Charles Fessenden. *Letters Written during the Civil War.* Privately printed, 1898.

Myers, Robert Manson, ed. *The Children of Pride: A True Story of Georgia and the Civil War.* Book II, "The Edge of the Sword, 1860–1865." New York: Popular Library, 1972.

Nichols, George Ward. *The Story of the Great March.* New York: Harper, 1865.

Padgett, James A., ed. "With Sherman through Georgia and the Carolinas: Letters of a Federal Soldier." *Georgia Historical Quarterly* 33 (March 1949): 48–81.

Pepper, Captain George W. *Personal Recollections of Sherman's Campaigns in Georgia and the Carolinas.* Zanesville, Ohio: Hugh Dunne, 1866.

Pollard, E. A. *Southern History of the War.* New York: Charles B. Richardson, Publisher, 1866.

Postell, Rosa. "Sherman's Occupation of Savannah: Two Letters." *Georgia Historical Quarterly* 50 (March 1966): 109–15.

Quaife, Milo M., ed. *From the Cannon's Mouth: The Civil War Letters of General Alpheus S. Williams.* Detroit: Wayne State University Press, 1959.

Racine, Philip N., ed. *Piedmont Farmer: The Journals of David Golightly Harris, 1855–1870.* Knoxville: University of Tennessee Press, 1990.

Rawick, George P., gen. ed. *The American Slave: A Composite Autobiography.* 19 vols., 12 vols. in supplement. Westport, Conn.: Greenwood Publishing Co., 1972.

Reid, Whitelaw. *After the War: A Tour of the Southern States, 1865–1866.* Edited by C. Vann Woodward. New York: Harper and Row, 1965.

Richardson, James D., ed. *Messages and Papers of the Confederacy.* 2 vols. Nashville, Tenn.: U.S. Publishing Co., 1906.

Sherman, William T. *Memoirs of General William T. Sherman.* New York. 2 vols. 1875. Reprint, New York: Da Capo Press, 1984.

Silber, Nina, and Mary Beth Sievens, eds. *Yankee Correspondence: Civil War Letters* between *New England Soldiers and the Home Front*. Charlottesville: University Press of Virginia, 1996.

Simms, William Gilmore. *Sack and Destruction of the City of Columbia, South Carolina*. 1865. Reprint, Alexander Samuel Salley, ed., Atlanta: Oglethorpe University Press, 1937.

Simpson, Brooks D., and Jean V. Berlin, eds. *Sherman's Civil War: Selected Correspondence of William T. Sherman, 1860–1865*. Chapel Hill: University of North Carolina Press, 1999.

Smith, Daniel E. Huger, Alice R. Huger Smith, and Arney R. Childs, eds. *Mason Smith Family Letters, 1860–1865*. Columbia: University of South Carolina Press, 1950.

Sosnowski, Madame S. "Burning of Columbia." *Georgia Historical Quarterly* 13 (September 1924): 195–214.

Spencer, Cornelia Phillips. *The Last Ninety Days of the War in North Carolina*. New York: Watchman Publishing Co., 1865.

Stewart, K. J. *A Geography for Beginners*. Richmond, Va.: J. W. Randolph, 1864.

Stock, Mary Wright, ed. *Shinplasters and Homespun: The Diary of Laura Nisbet Boykin*. Rockville, Md.: Printex, 1975.

Stormont Gilbert R., ed. *History of the Fifty-eighth Regiment of Indiana Volunteer Infantry: Its Organization, Campaigns, and Battles from 1861–1865: From the Manuscript Prepared by the Late Chaplain John I. Hight during His Service with the Regiment in the Field*. Princeton, N.J.: Press of the Clarion, 1895.

Sullivan, Walter J., ed. *The War the Women Lived: Female Voices from the Confederate South*. Nashville, Tenn.: J. S. Sanders and Co., 1995.

Taylor, Mrs. Thomas, ed. *Our Women in the War—The Lives They Lived; The Deaths They Died*. Charleston, S.C.: N.p., 1885.

Throne, Mildred, ed. "A Commissary in the Union Army: Letters of C. C. Carpenter." *Iowa Journal of History* 53 (January 1955): 59–88.

Tourgée, Albion W. *A Fool's Errand*. New York: Fords, Howard, and Hulbert, 1879.

Trezevant, Daniel Heyward. *The Burning of Columbia, South Carolina: A Review of Northern Assertions and Southern Facts*. Columbia: South Carolinian Power Press, 1866.

Trowbridge, John T. *The Desolate South, 1865–1866: A Picture of the Battlefields and of the Devastated Confederacy*. Edited by Gordon Carroll. Boston: Little, Brown, 1956.

U.S. Government. *The War of the Rebellion: A Compilation of the Official Records of the Union and Confederate Armies*. 128 vols. Washington, D.C.: GPO, 1880–1901.

Volwiler, Albert Tangeman, ed. "Letters from a Civil War Officer." *Mississippi Valley Historical Review* 14 (March 1928): 508–29.

Weiner, Marli F. *A Heritage of Woe: The Civil War Diary of Grace Brown Elmore, 1861–1868*. Athens: University of Georgia Press, 1997.

Wiley, Bell Irvin, ed. *Letters of Warren Akin, Confederate Congressman*. Athens: University of Georgia Press, 1959.

Willey, R., ed. *"I Soldiered for the Union": The Civil War Diary of William Bluffton Miller*. Privately published, n.d.

Wills, Charles W. *Army Life of an Illinois Soldier*. Washington, D.C.: Globe Printing Co., 1906.

Winther, Oscar Osburn, ed. *With Sherman to the Sea: The Civil War Letters, Diaries, & Reminiscences of Theodore F. Upson*. Bloomington: Indiana University Press, 1985.

Woodward, C. Vann, ed. *Mary Chesnut's Civil War*. New Haven, Conn.: Yale University Press, 1981.

Yearns, W. Buck, and John G. Barrett, eds. *North Carolina Civil War Documentary*. Chapel Hill: University of North Carolina Press, 1980.

SECONDARY SOURCES

Books

Anderson, Benedict. *Imagined Communities: Reflections on the Origins and Spread of Nationalism*. London: Verso Press, 1983.

Ash, Stephen V. *When the Yankees Came: Conflict and Chaos in the Occupied South, 1861–1865*. Chapel Hill: University of North Carolina Press, 1995.

Attie, Jeanie. *Patriotic Toil: Northern Women and the American Civil War*. Ithaca, N.Y.: Cornell University Press, 1998.

Ayers, Edward L. *Vengeance and Justice: Crime and Punishment in the Nineteenth-Century American South*. New York: Oxford University Press, 1984.

Bailey, Anne J. *War and Ruin: William T. Sherman and the Savannah Campaign*. Wilmington, Del.: Scholarly Resources, Inc., 2003.

Barnes, Trevor J., and James S. Duncan, eds. *Writing Worlds: Discourse, Text, and Metaphor in the Representation of Landscape*. London: Routledge, 1992.

Barrett, John G. *Sherman's March through the Carolinas*. Chapel Hill: University of North Carolina Press, 1956.

Bederman, Gail. *Manliness & Civilization: A Cultural History of Gender and Race in the United States, 1880–1917*. Chicago: University of Chicago Press, 1995.

Beringer, Richard E., Herman Hattaway, Archer Jones, and William N. Still Jr. *Why the South Lost the Civil War*. Athens: University of Georgia Press, 1986.

Blair, William. *Virginia's Private War: Feeding Body and Soul in the Confederacy, 1861–1865*. New York: Oxford University Press, 1998.

Bleser, Carol, ed. *In Joy and in Sorrow: Women, Family, and Marriage in the Victorian South*. New York: Oxford University Press, 1991.

Blight, David W. *Race and Reunion: The Civil War in American Memory*. Cambridge: Harvard University Press, 2001.

Bourke, Joanna. *Dismembering the Male: Men's Bodies, Britain, and the Great War*. Chicago: University of Chicago Press, 1996.

Boydston, Jeanne. *Home & Work: Housework, Wages, and the Ideology of Labor in the Early Republic*. New York: Oxford University Press, 1990.

Bradley, Mark L. *Last Stand in the Carolinas: The Battle of Bentonville*. Campbell, Calif.: Savas Woodbury Publishers, 1996.

Brownmiller, Susan. *Against Our Will: Men, Women, and Rape*. New York: Bantam Books, 1976.

Bynum, Victoria. *Unruly Women: The Politics of Social and Sexual Control in the Old South*. Chapel Hill: University of North Carolina Press, 1992.

Campbell, Edward D., Jr., and Kym S. Rice, eds. *A Woman's War: Southern Women, Civil War, and the Confederate Legacy*. Charlottesville: University Press of Virginia, 1996.

Cashin, Joan E. *A Family Venture: Men and Women on the Southern Frontier*. Oxford: Oxford University Press, 1991.

Cauthen, Charles Edward. *South Carolina Goes to War, 1860–1865*. James Sprunt Hill Studies. Chapel Hill: University of North Carolina Press, 1950.

Clinton, Catherine. *The Plantation Mistress: Woman's World in the Old South*. New York: Pantheon Books, 1982.

———, ed. *Southern Families at War: Loyalty and Conflict in the Civil War South*. New York: Oxford University Press, 2000.

Clinton, Catherine, and Nina Silber, eds. *Divided Houses: Gender and the Civil War*. New York: Oxford University Press, 1992.

Clinton, Catherine, and Michele Gillespie, eds. *The Devil's Lane: Sex and Race in the Early South*. New York: Oxford University Press, 1997.

Connell, R. W. *Gender and Power: Society, the Person, and Sexual Politics*. Stanford: Stanford University Press, 1987.

Connelly, Thomas Lawrence. *The Marble Man: Robert E. Lee and His Image in American Society*. New York: Knopf, 1977.

Cott, Nancy F. *The Bonds of Womanhood: "Woman's Sphere" in New England, 1780–1835*. New Haven, Conn.: Yale University Press, 1977.

Cott, Nancy F., and Elizabeth H. Pleck, eds. *A Heritage of Her Own: Toward a New Social History of American Women*. New York: Simon and Schuster, 1979.

De Pauw, Linda Grant. *Battle Cries and Lullabies: Women in War from Prehistory to the Present.* Norman: Oklahoma University Press, 1998.

Durrill, Wayne K. *War of Another Kind: A Southern Community in the Great Rebellion.* New York: Oxford University Press, 1990.

Elshtain, Jean Bethke. *Women and War.* New York: Basic Books, 1987.

Enloe, Cynthia. *Does Khaki Become You?: The Militarization of Women's Lives.* Boston: South End Press, 1983

———. *Bananas, Beaches, & Bases: Making Feminist Sense of International Politics.* Berkeley: University of California Press, 1990.

Escott, Paul D. *After Secession: Jefferson Davis and the Failure of Confederate Nationalism.* Baton Rouge: Louisiana State University Press, 1978.

———. *Many Excellent People: Power and Privilege in North Carolina, 1850–1900.* Chapel Hill: University of North Carolina Press, 1985.

Fahs, Alice. *The Imagined Civil War: Popular Literature of the North and South, 1861–1865.* Chapel Hill: University of North Carolina Press, 2001.

Farnham, Christie Anne, ed. *Women of the American South: A Multi-Cultural Reader.* New York: New York University Press, 1997.

Faust, Drew Gilpin. *James Henry Hammond and the Old South: A Design for Mastery.* Baton Rouge: Louisiana State University Press, 1982.

———. *The Creation of Confederate Nationalism: Ideology and Identity in the Civil War South.* Baton Rouge: Louisiana State University Press, 1988.

———. *Southern Stories: Slaveholders in Peace and War.* Columbia: University of Missouri Press, 1992.

———. *Mothers of Invention: Women of the Slaveholding South in the American Civil War.* Chapel Hill: University of North Carolina Press, 1996.

Fellman, Michael. *Citizen Sherman: A Life of William Tecumseh Sherman.* Cambridge: Cambridge University Press, 1995.

Fischer, Kirsten. *Bodies of Evidence: The Racial Politics of Illicit Sex in Colonial North Carolina.* Ithaca, N.Y.: Cornell University Press, 2002.

Foster, Gaines M. *Ghosts of the Confederacy: Defeat, the Lost Cause, and the Emergence of the New South.* New York: Oxford University Press, 1987.

Foucault, Michel. *Power/Knowledge: Selected Interviews and Other Writings.* Edited by Colin Gordon. New York: Pantheon, 1980.

Fox-Genovese, Elizabeth. *Within the Plantation Household: Black and White Women of the Old South.* Chapel Hill: University of North Carolina Press, 1988.

Freehling, William W. *The South vs. the South: How Anti-Confederate Southerners Shaped the Course of the Civil War.* New York: Oxford University Press, 2001.

Friedman, Jean E. *The Enclosed Garden: Women and Community in the Evangelical South, 1830–1900.* Chapel Hill: University of North Carolina Press, 1985.

Gallagher, Gary W. *The Confederate War: Popular Will, Nationalism, and Strategy.* Cambridge: Harvard University Press, 1997.

———, ed. *Decision on the Rappahannock: Causes and Consequences of the Fredericksburg Campaign.* Chapel Hill: University of North Carolina Press, 1995.

Glatthaar, Joseph T. *The March to the Sea and Beyond: Sherman's Troops in the Savannah and Carolinas Campaigns.* Baton Rouge: Louisiana State University Press, 1985.

Grimsley, Mark. *The Hard Hand of War: Union Military Policy toward Southern Civilians, 1861–1865.* Cambridge: Cambridge University Press, 1995.

Grimsley, Mark, and Brooks D. Simpson, eds. *The Collapse of the Confederacy.* Lincoln: University of Nebraska Press, 2002.

Hall, Jacquelyn Dowd. *Revolt against Chivalry: Jessie Daniel Ames and the Women's Campaign against Lynching.* Rev. ed. New York: Columbia University Press, 1993.

Helly, Dorothy O., and Susan M. Reverby, eds. *Gendered Domains: Rethinking Public and Private in Women's History.* Ithaca, N.Y.: Cornell University Press, 1992.

Higonnet, Margaret Randolph, Jane Jenson, Sonya Michel, and Margaret Collins Weitz, eds. *Behind the Lines: Gender and the Two World Wars.* New Haven, Conn.: Yale University Press, 1978.

Hodes, Martha. *White Women, Black Men: Illicit Sex in the Nineteenth-Century South.* New Haven, Conn.: Yale University Press, 1997.

Hoffman, Ronald, and Peter J. Albert, eds. *Women in the Age of the American Revolution.* Charlottesville: University Press of Virginia, 1990.

hooks, bell. *Talking Back: Thinking Feminist, Thinking Black.* Boston: South End Press, 1989.

———. *Yearning: Race, Gender, and Sexual Politics.* London: Turnaround Press, 1991.

Hughes, Nathaniel C. *Bentonville: The Final Battle of Sherman and Johnston.* Chapel Hill: University of North Carolina Press, 1996.

Johnson, Guion Griffis. *Ante-Bellum North Carolina: A Social History.* Chapel Hill: University of North Carolina Press, 1937.

Kammen, Michael. *The Mystics Chords of Memory: The Transformation of Tradition in American Culture.* New York: Knopf, 1991.

Keegan, John. *The Face of Battle.* New York: Penguin Books, 1976.

Kennett, Lee. *Marching through Georgia: The Story of Soldiers & Civilians during Sherman's Campaign.* New York: HarperCollins, 1995.

———. *Sherman: A Soldier's Life.* New York: HarperCollins, 2001.

Kolodny, Annette. *The Land before Her: Fantasy and Experience of the American Frontiers, 1630–1860.* Chapel Hill: University of North Carolina Press, 1984.

Lawrence, Alexander A. *A Present for Mr. Lincoln: The Story of Savannah from Secession to Sherman*. Macon, Ga.: Ardivan Press, 1961.

Lewis, Lloyd. *Sherman: Fighting Prophet*. New York: Harcourt, Brace, 1931.

Linderman, Gerald F. *Embattled Courage: The Experience of Combat in the Civil War*. New York: Free Press, 1987.

Litwack, Leon F. *Been in the Storm So Long: The Aftermath of Slavery*. New York: Ramdom House, 1979.

Lonn, Ella. *Desertion during the Civil War*. New York: Century, 1928.

Lucas, Marion Brunson. *Sherman and the Burning of Columbia*. College Station: Texas A&M University Press, 1976. Reprint, Columbia: University of South Carolina Press, 2000.

Marszalek, John F. *Sherman: A Soldier's Passion for Order*. New York: Free Press, 1993.

Marten, James. *The Children's Civil War*. Chapel Hill: University of North Carolina Press, 1998.

Massey, Mary Elizabeth. *Refugee Life in the Confederacy*. Baton Rouge: Louisiana State University Press, 1964.

———. *Women in the Civil War*. Lincoln: University of Nebraska Press, 1994 (originally published as *Bonnett Brigades* [New York: Knopf, 1966]).

McCurry, Stephanie. *Masters of Small Worlds: Yeoman Households, Gender Relations, and the Political Culture of the Antebellum South Carolina Low Country*. New York: Oxford University Press, 1995.

McElfresh, Earl B. *Maps and Mapmakers of the Civil War*. New York: Harry N. Abrams, Inc., Publishers, 1999.

McFeely, William S. *Sapelo's People: A Long Walk into Freedom*. New York: Norton, 1994.

McPherson, James M. *Battle Cry of Freedom*. New York: Ballantine Books, 1988.

———. *What They Fought For, 1861–1865*. Baton Rouge: Louisiana State University Press, 1994.

———. *Drawn with the Sword: Reflections on the American Civil War*. New York: Oxford University Press, 1996.

———. *For Cause and Comrades: Why Men Fought in the Civil War*. New York: Oxford University Press, 1997.

McPherson, James M., and William J. Cooper Jr., eds. *Writing the Civil War: The Quest to Understand*. Columbia: University of South Carolina Press, 1998.

Mitchell, Reid. *Civil War Soldiers*. New York: Viking, 1988.

———. *The Vacant Chair: The Northern Soldier Leaves Home*. New York: Oxford University Press, 1993.

Mohr, Clarence L. *On the Threshold of Freedom*. Athens: University of Georgia Press, 1986.

Moore, John Hammond. *Columbia and Richland County: A South Carolina Community, 1740–1990*. Columbia: University of South Carolina Press, 1993.

Morton, Patricia, ed. *Discovering the Women in Slavery: Emancipating Perspectives on the American Past*. Athens: University of Georgia Press, 1996.

Ownby, Ted, ed. *Black & White: Cultural Interaction in the Antebellum South*. Jackson: University Press of Mississippi, 1993.

Paludan, Phillip Shaw. *Victims: A True Story of the Civil War*. Knoxville: University of Tennessee Press, 1981.

———. *A People's Contest: The Union and Civil War, 1861–1865*. 1988. 2d ed. Lawrence: University of Kansas Press, 1996.

Pencak, William, and William Blair, eds. *Making and Remaking Pennsylvania's Civil War*. University Park: Pennsylvania State University Press, 2001.

Phillips, Ulrich B. *American Negro Slavery*. 1918. Reprint, Baton Rouge: Louisiana State University Press, 1966.

Potter, David M. *The South and the Sectional Conflict*. Baton Rouge: Louisiana State University Press, 1968.

Rable, George C. *Civil Wars: Women and the Crisis of Southern Nationalism*. Urbana: University of Illinois Press, 1989.

———. *The Confederate Republic: A Revolution against Politics*. Chapel Hill: University of North Carolina Press, 1994.

Roper, Michael, and John Tosh, eds. *Manful Assertions: Masculinities in Britain since 1800*. London: Routledge Press, 1991.

Rosaldo, Michelle Zimbalist, and Louise Lamphere, eds. *Woman, Culture, and Society*. Stanford, Calif.: Stanford University Press, 1974.

Rose, Gillian. *Feminism and Geography: The Limits of Geographical Knowledge*. Minneapolis: University of Minnesota Press, 1993.

Royster, Charles. *The Destructive War: William T. Sherman, Stonewall Jackson, and the Americans*. New York: Random House, 1993.

Schwalm, Leslie A. *"A Hard Fight for We": Women's Transition from Slavery to Freedom in South Carolina*. Urbana: University of Illinois Press, 1997.

Scott, Anne F. *The Southern Lady: From Pedestal to Politics, 1830–1930*. Chicago: University of Chicago Press, 1970.

Scott, James C. *Domination and the Arts of Resistance: Hidden Transcripts*. New Haven, Conn.: Yale University Press, 1990.

Silber, Nina. *The Romance of Reunion: Northerners and the South, 1865–1900*. Chapel Hill: University of North Carolina Press, 1993.

Simpson, Brooks D. *Let Us Have Peace: Ulysses S. Grant and the Politics of War and Reconstruction, 1861–1868*. Chapel Hill: University of North Carolina Press, 1997.

Snitow, Ann, Christine Stansell, and Sharon Thompson, eds. *Powers of Desire: The Politics of Sexuality*. New York: Monthly Review Press, 1983.

Spain, Daphne. *Gendered Spaces*. Chapel Hill: University of North Carolina Press, 1992.

Stack, Carol B. *Call to Home: African Americans Reclaim the Rural South*. New York: Basic Books, 1996.

Taylor, Rosser H. *Ante-Bellum South Carolina: A Social and Cultural History*. Chapel Hill: University of North Carolina Press, 1942.

Taylor, William Robert. *Cavalier and Yankee: The Old South and American National Character*. New York: Braziller, 1961. Reprint, New York: Oxford University Press, 1993.

Temple, Jack Kirby. *Posquosin: A Study of Rural Landscape and Society*. Chapel Hill: University of North Carolina Press, 1995.

Thomas, Emory M. *The Confederate Nation, 1861–1865*. New York: Harper and Row, 1979.

Ulrich, Laurel Thatcher. *Good Wives: Images and Reality in the Lives of Women in Northern New England, 1650–1750*. New York: Random House, 1980.

Vinovskis, Maris A. *Towards a Social History of the American Civil War*. Cambridge: Cambridge University Press, 1990.

Vlach, John Michael. *Back of the Big House: The Architecture of Plantation Slavery*. Chapel Hill: University of North Carolina Press, 1993.

Weelwright, Julie. *Amazons and Military Maids: Women Who Dressed as Men in Pursuit of Life, Liberty, and Happiness*. London: Pandora Press, 1989.

Werner, Emmy E. *Reluctant Witnesses: Children's Voices from the Civil War*. Boulder, Colo.: Westview Press, 1998.

Whites, Lee Ann. *The Civil War as a Crisis in Gender: Augusta, Georgia, 1860–1890*. Athens: University of Georgia Press, 1995.

Wiley, Bell I. *The Life of Johnny Reb: The Common Soldier of the Confederacy*. 1943. Reprint, Baton Rouge: Louisiana State University Press, 1993.

———. *The Life of Billy Yank*. 1952. New ed., Baton Rouge: Louisiana State University Press, 1993.

———. *Confederate Women*. 1975. New ed., New York: Greenwood Press, 1994.

Wilson, Charles Reagan. *Baptized in Blood: The Religion of the Lost Cause, 1865–1920*. Athens: University of Georgia Press, 1980.

Winters, Harold A. *Battling the Elements: Weather and Terrain in the Conduct of War*. Baltimore: Johns Hopkins University Press, 1998.

Woodward, C. Vann. *The Burden of Southern History*. 3d ed. Baton Rouge: Louisiana State University Press, 1993.

Wyatt-Brown, Bertram. *Southern Honor: Ethics and Behavior in the Old South*. New York: Oxford University Press, 1982.

——. *The Shaping of Southern Culture: Honor, Grace, and War, 1760s–1880s.* Chapel Hill: University of North Carolina Press, 2001.

Articles

Baker, Paula. "The Domestication of Politics: Women and American Political Society, 1780–1920." In *Unequal Sisters: A Multi-Cultural Reader in U.S. Women's History,* edited by Vicki L. Ruiz and Ellen Carol DuBois, 85–110. 2d ed. New York: Routledge Press, 1994.

Bardaglio, Peter. "The Children of Jubilee: African American Childhood in Wartime." In *Divided Houses: Gender and the Civil War,* edited by Catherine Clinton and Nina Silber, 213–29. New York: Oxford University Press, 1992.

Bearman, Peter S. "Desertion as Localism: Army Unit Solidarity and Group Norms in the U.S. Civil War." *Social Forces* 70 (December 1991): 321–42.

Blair, William. "Barbarians at Fredericksburg's Gate." In *The Fredericksburg Campaign: Decision on the Rappahannock,* edited by Gary W. Gallagher, 142–70. Chapel Hill: University of North Carolina Press, 1995.

Bonner, James C. "Sherman at Milledgeville in 1864." *Journal of Southern History* 22 (August 1965): 273–91.

Cashin, Joan E. " 'Into the Trackless Wilderness': The Refugee Experience in the Civil War." In *A Woman's War: Southern Women, Civil War, and the Confederate Legacy,* edited by Edward D. Campbell Jr. and Kym S. Rice, 29–53. Charlottesville: University Press of Virginia, 1996.

Cohen, Patricia Cline. "Safety and Danger: Women on American Public Transport, 1750–1850." In *Gendered Domains: Rethinking Public and Private in Women's History,* edited by Dorothy O. Helly and Susan M. Reverby, 109–22. Ithaca, N.Y.: Cornell University Press, 1992.

Cott, Nancy F. "Passionlessness: An Interpretation of Victorian Sexual Ideology, 1790–1850." In *A Heritage of Her Own,* edited by Cott and Elizabeth H. Pleck, 162–81. New York: Simon and Schuster, 1979.

Coulter, Ellis Merton. "Sherman and the South." *North Carolina Historical Review* 8 (January 1931): 41–54.

DeLaubenfels, D. J. "Where Sherman Passed." *Geographical Review* 47 (1954): 381–95.

DePauw, Linda Grant. "Women in Combat: The Revolutionary War Experience." *Armed Forces and Society* 7 (Winter 1981): 209–26.

Dodge, David. "The Cave-Dwellers of the Confederacy." *Atlantic Monthly* 68 (1891): 514–21.

Dowler, Lorraine. " 'And They Think I'm Just a Nice Old Lady': Women and War in Belfast, Northern Ireland." *Gender, Place, and Culture* 5 (July 1988): 159–76.

Drago, Edmund L. "How Sherman's March through Georgia Affected the Slaves." *Georgia Historical Quarterly* 57, no. 3 (1973): 361–75.

Dyer, John P. "Northern Relief for Savannah during Sherman's Occupation." *Journal of Southern History* 19 (November 1953): 457–72.

Edwards, Laura F. "Law, Domestic Violence, and the Limits of Patriarchal Authority in the Antebellum South." *Journal of Southern History* 65 (November 1999): 733–70.

Ericson, Christina. " 'The World Will Little Note nor Long Remember': Gender Analysis of Civilian Responses to the Battle of Gettysburg." In *Making and Remaking Pennsylvania's Civil War*, edited by William Pencak and William Blair, 81–102. University Park: Pennsylvania State University Press, 2001.

Escott, Paul D. "Poverty and Government Aid for the Poor in Confederate North Carolina." *North Carolina Historical Review* 61 (October 1984): 462–80.

———. " 'The Cry of the Sufferers': The Problem of Welfare in the Confederacy." *Civil War History* 23 (September 1977): 228–40.

———. "The Moral Economy of the Crowd in Confederate North Carolina." *Maryland Historian* 13 (Spring–Summer 1982): 1–17.

Fahs, Alice. "The Feminized Civil War: Gender, Northern Popular Literature, and the Memory of the War, 1861–1900." *Journal of American History* 85 (March 1999): 1461–94.

Faust, Drew Gilpin. "Altars of Sacrifice: Confederate Women and Narratives of War." *Journal of American History* 76 (March 1990): 1200–28.

———. "Altars of Sacrifice: Confederate Women and Narratives of War." In *Divided Houses: Gender and the Civil War*, edited by Catherine Clinton and Nina Silber, 171–99. New York: Oxford University Press, 1992.

———. " 'Trying to Do a Man's Business': Gender, Violence, and Slave Management in Civil War Texas." In *Southern Stories: Slaveholders in Peace and War*, edited by Faust, 174–92. Columbia: University of Missouri Press, 1992.

Fellman, Michael. "Women and Guerrilla Warfare." In *Divided Houses: Gender and the Civil War*, edited by Catherine Clinton and Nina Silber, 147–65. New York: Oxford University Press, 1992.

Gallagher, Gary W. "Blueprint for Victory: Northern Strategy and Military Policy." In *Writing the Civil War: The Quest to Understand*, edited by James M. McPherson and William J. Cooper Jr., 8–35. Columbia: University of South Carolina Press, 1988.

Gatell, Frank Otto. "A Yankee Views the Agony of Savannah." *Georgia Historical Quarterly* 43 (December 1959): 428–31.

Glymph, Thavolia. " 'This Species of Property': Female Slave Contrabands in the Civil War." In *A Woman's War: Southern Women, Civil War, and the Confederate Legacy*, edited by Edward D. Campbell Jr. and Kym S. Rice, 55–71. Charlottesville: University Press of Virginia, 1996.

Green, Mary Fulton. "A Profile of Columbia in 1850." *South Carolina Historical Magazine* 70 (January 1969): 104–21.

Grimsley, Mark. "Learning to Say 'Enough': Southern Generals and the Final Week of the Confederacy." In *The Collapse of the Confederacy*, edited by Grimsley and Brooks D. Simpson, 40–79. Lincoln: University of Nebraska Press, 2001.

Hacker, Barton C. "Women and Military Institutions in Early Modern Europe: A Reconnaissance." *Signs* 6 (Summer 1981): 647–66.

Hallock, Judith Lee. "The Role of the Community in Civil War Desertion." *Civil War History* 29 (July 1983): 123–34.

Hewitt, Nancy A. "Beyond the Search for Sisterhood: American Women's History in the 1980's." *Social History* 10 (October 1985): 299–321.

Higonnet, Margaret R., and Patrice L. R. Higonnet. "The Double Helix." In *Behind the Lines: Gender and the Two World Wars*, edited by Margaret Randolph Higonnet, Jane Jenson, Sonya Michel, and Margaret Collins Weitz, 31–47. New Haven, Conn.: Yale University Press, 1987.

Hine, Darlene Clark. "Rape and the Inner Lives of Black Women in the Middle West: Preliminary Thoughts on the Culture of Dissemblance." *Signs* 14 (Summer 1989): 12–20.

Hodes, Martha. "The Sexualization of Reconstruction Politics: White Women and Black Men in the South after the Civil War." *Journal of the History of Sexuality* 3, no. 3 (1993): 402–17.

hooks, bell. "Feminism & Militarism: A Comment." *Yearning: Race, Gender, and Sexual Politics*, 92–97. London: Turnaround Press, 1991.

Huff, Lawrence. " 'A Bitter Draught We Had to Quaff': Sherman's March through the Eyes of Joseph Addison Turner." *Georgia Historical Quarterly* 62 (Summer 1988): 306–26.

Hunt, Judith Lee. " 'High with Courage and Hope': The Middleton Family's Civil War." In *Southern Families at War: Loyalty and Conflict in the Civil War South*, edited by Catherine Clinton, 101–17. New York: Oxford University Press, 2000.

Huston, James L. "Property Rights in Slavery and the Coming of the Civil War." *Journal of Southern History* 65 (May 1999): 249–86.

Huston, Nancy. "Tales of War and Tears of Women." *Women's Studies International Forum* 5, no. 3/4 (1982): 271–82.

Inscoe, John C. "The Civil War Empowerment of an Appalachian Woman: The

1864 Slave Purchases of Mary Bell." In *Discovering the Women in Slavery*, edited by Patricia Morton, 61–81. Athens: University of Georgia Press, 1996.

Jakle, John A. "Time, Space, and the Geographic Past: A Prospectus for Historical Geography." *American Historical Review* 74 (October 1971): 1074–1103.

James, Clifford. "Notes on (Field)notes." In *Fieldnotes: The Makings of Anthropology*, edited by Roger Sanjek, 47–70. Ithaca, N.Y.: Cornell University Press, 1990.

Jordan, Ervin L. "Sleeping with the Enemy: Sex, Black Women, and the Civil War." *Western Journal of Black Studies* 18, no. 21 (1994): 55–63.

Kaufman, Janet E. "Treasury Girls." *Civil War Times Illustrated* (May 1986): 32–38.

Kay, Jeanne. "Landscapes of Women and Men: Rethinking the Regional Historical Geography of the United States and Canada." *Journal of Historical Geography* 17, no. 3 (1991): 435–52.

Kerber, Linda K. "Separate Spheres, Female Worlds, Woman's Place: The Rhetoric of Women's History."*Journal of American History* 75 (June 1988): 9–39.

Logue, Cal M. "Coping with Defeat Rhetorically: Sherman's March through Georgia." *Southern Communication Journal* 58 (Fall 1992): 55–66.

Lynn, John A. "The Embattled Future of Academic Military History." *Journal of Military History* 61 (October 1977): 777–89.

Marszalek, John F. "Celebrity in Dixie: Sherman Tours the South, 1879." *Georgia Historical Quarterly* 66 (Fall 1982): 368–83.

McKinney, Gordon B. "Women's Role in Civil War Western North Carolina." *North Carolina Historical Review* 69 (January 1992): 37–56.

McNeill, William J. "A Survey of Confederate Soldier Morale during Sherman's Campaign through Georgia and the Carolinas." *Georgia Historical Quarterly* 55 (Spring 1971): 1–25.

Mitchell, Reid. " 'Not the General but the Soldier': The Study of Civil War Soldiers." In *Writing the Civil War: The Quest to Understand*, edited by James M. McPherson and William J. Cooper Jr., 81–95. Columbia: University of South Carolina Press, 1998.

Morgan, Philip D. "The Ownership of Property by Slaves in the Mid-Nineteenth-Century Low Country." *Journal of Southern History* 49 (August 1983): 399–420.

Murrell, Amy E. " 'Of Necessity and Public Benefit': Southern Families and Their Appeals for Protection." In *Southern Families at War: Loyalty and Conflict in the Civil War South*, edited by Catherine Clinton, 77–99. New York: Oxford University Press, 2000.

Neely, Mark. "Was the Civil War a Total War?" *Civil War History* 37, no. 1 (1992): 5–28.

Potter, David M. "The Historian's Use of Nationalism and Vice Versa." *The South and the Sectional Conflict*, 34–83. Baton Rouge: Louisiana State University Press, 1968.

Reid, Brian Holden, and John White. " 'A Mob of Stragglers and Cowards': Desertion from the Union and Confederate Armies, 1861–65." *Journal of Strategic Studies* 8 (March 1985): 64–77.

Reid, Richard. "A Test Case of the 'Crying Evil': Desertion among North Carolina Troops during the Civil War." *North Carolina Historical Review* 58, no. 3 (1981): 234–62.

Rosaldo, Michelle Zimbalist. "Woman, Culture, and Society: A Theoretical Overview." In *Woman, Culture, and Society*, edited by Rosaldo and Louise Lamphere, 17–42. Stanford, Calif.: Stanford University Press, 1974.

Rose, Gillian, and Miles Ogburn. "Feminism and Historical Geography." *Journal of Historical Geography* 14 (October 1988): 404–9.

Royster, Charles. "Comments on John Shy: 'The Cultural Approach to the History of War.' "*Journal of Military History*, Special Issue 57 (October 1993): 59–62.

Shalhope, Robert W. "Republicanism and Early American Historiography." *William and Mary Quarterly* 39 (April 1982): 334–56.

Shy, John. "The Cultural Approach to the History of War." *Journal of Military History*, Special Issue 57 (October 1993): 13–26.

Silber, Nina. "The Northern Myth of the Rebel Girl." In *Women of the American South: A Multi-Cultural Reader*, edited by Christie Anne Farnham, 120–32. New York: New York University Press, 1997.

Simpson, Brooks D. "Facilitating Defeat: The Union High Command and the Collapse of the Confederacy." In *The Collapse of the Confederacy*, edited by Mark Grimsley and Simpson, 80–103. Lincoln: University of Nebraska Press, 2001.

Stiehm, Judith Hicks. "The Protected, the Protector, the Defender." *Women's Studies International Forum* 5, no. 3/4 (1982): 367–76.

Swift, Jacquie. "Common Place, Common Sense." *Women's Studies International Forum* 20, no. 3 (1997): 351–60.

Thompson, E. P. "The Moral Economy of the English Crowd in the Eighteenth Century." *Past and Present* 50 (February 1971): 76–136.

Tuan, Yi-Fu. "Place: An Experiential Perspective." *Geographical Review* 65 (April 1975): 151–65.

Vlach, John Michael. " 'Not Mansions . . . but Good Enough': Slave Quarters as Bi-Cultural Expressions." In *Black and White: Cultural Interaction in the*

Antebellum South, edited by Ted Ownby, 89–114. Jackson: University Press of Mississippi, 1993.

Wiley, Bell I. "Southern Reaction to Federal Invasion." *Journal of Southern History* 16 (November 1950): 491–510.

Woodward, Rachel. " 'It's a Man's Life': Soldiers, Masculinity, and the Countryside." *Gender, Place, and Culture* 5, no. 3 (1988): 277–300.

Dissertations, Theses, and Unpublished Papers

Bindman, Jacqueline A. " 'The Outer Bounds of Civilized Creation': Power, Space, and Meaning on an Ante-bellum Sea Island." M.A. thesis, Duke University, 1995.

Cauthen, Bruce. "Opposing Forces: Confederate Nationalism and Familial Disintegration in the Civil War South." Paper given at Family at War Conference, University of Richmond, April 24–25, 1998.

Frank, Lisa Tendrich. " 'To Cure Her of Her Pride and Boasting': The Gendered Implications of Sherman's March." Ph.D. diss., University of Florida, 2001.

Krug, Donna Rebecca Dondes. "The Folks Back Home: The Confederate Home Front during the Civil War." Ph.D. diss., University of California, Irvine, 1990.

McNeill, William James. "The Stress of War: The Confederacy and William Tecumseh Sherman during the Last Year of the Civil War." Ph.D. diss., Rice University, 1973.

Rubin, Anne S. "Redefining the South: Confederates, Southerners, and Americans, 1863–1868." Ph.D. diss., University of Virginia, 1998.

Seidman, Rachel Filene. "Beyond Sacrifice: Women and Politics on the Pennsylvania Home Front during the Civil War." Ph.D. diss., Yale University, 1995.

Shiman, Philip L. "Engineering Sherman's March: Army Engineers and the Management of Modern War, 1862–1865." Ph.D. diss., Duke University, 1991.

Shultz, Jane E. "Women at the Front: Gender and Genre in the Literature of the American Civil War." Ph.D. diss., University of Michigan, 1988.

Stillman, Rachel Bryan. "Education in the Confederate States of America, 1861–1865." Ph.D. diss., University of Illinois at Urbana-Champaign, 1976.

INDEX

Adams, Henry, 43
African Americans (Southern): on
Yankees, 3, 4, 47–50, 85–87,
100–101; Union army's treatment
of, 4, 16, 18, 39, 45–49, 65, 66,
100, 127 (n. 125); decisions of, to
leave or stay on plantations, 16–
18, 33, 38–39, 45–50, 66; Southern whites on, 17–18, 38–39, 49,
66, 99–100; Union troops' attitudes toward, 17–18, 45, 47, 65–
66, 86–87, 100–101, 116 (n. 41),
141 (n. 14); as Union army fol-
lowers, 17–18, 47, 86, 115 (n. 38),
121 (n. 38); after Civil War, 49,
101, 106, 143 (n. 5); plundering
by, 59–60; emancipation of, 99–
101, 106, 115 (n. 36); suffrage for,
101. See also Slavery; Slaves;
Women (Southern black)
Akin, Mrs. Warren, 36
Alden, Esther, 87
Alexander County (North Carolina),
84
Allen, Julian, 24–25
Allen, Lawrence, 105
American Revolution, 128 (n. 128),
136 (n. 33)
Andrews, Eliza, 95, 98, 100, 101
Army. See Confederate army and
government; Union army

Army of Northern Virginia, 37, 69,
72, 73, 79, 93
Army of the Cumberland, 120
(n. 19)
Army of the Potomac, 8
Army of the Tennessee, 111 (n. 2),
120 (n. 19)
Arnold, Richard, 8, 22
Ash, Stephen V., 113 (n. 17)
Atlanta, Ga.: Sherman's campaign
to take, 4–5, 9, 111 (n. 2); Sher-
man in, 23, 26; evacuation of,
37–38; and Johnston, 133 (n. 3)
Augusta, Ga., 33, 34, 36, 120 (n. 19)
Averasboro, N.C., 139 (n. 61)

B., Mrs. H. J., 50
Bachman, Mrs. W. K., 61, 64, 70, 72
Balloch, George, 9, 29, 33–34, 54,
68
Barnwell, S.C., 50, 51, 133 (n. 60)
Battlefront: as home front. See
Home front
Battle of Averasboro (North Car-
olina), 139 (n. 61)
Battle of Bentonville (North Car-
olina), 93, 139 (n. 61)
Beaufort, S.C., 46
Bentonville, N.C., 93, 139 (n. 61)
Beringer, Richard E., 133 (n. 5)
Bindman, Jacqueline A., 125 (n. 95)

Blair, William, 112 (n. 5), 123 (n. 58); on Virginia, 69, 85, 133 (n. 58), 142 (n. 27); on guerrilla warfare, 140 (n. 7)
Boston, Mass., 25–26
Bourke, Joanna, 144 (n. 11)
Boykin, Laura, 100
Bradley, G. S., 15, 29
Branchville, S.C., 33, 36
Bread riots, 82–83, 136 (n. 30)
Briggs, George, 49–50
Briley, Harriet S., 84
Brown, Charles, 40, 54, 55, 78
Brown, Sara, 49
"Bummers," 45, 54–56, 61, 124 (n. 69)
Butler, Benjamin, 26, 52
Byers, Samuel, 29
Bynum, Victoria, 136 (n. 28)

Camden, S.C., 36, 46
Campbell, Alice, 91
Campbell, John A., 81
Carolinas: Sherman's campaign across, 4, 5, 30–92. See also North Carolina; South Carolina
Cauthen, Bruce, 138 (n. 53)
Chapel Hill, N.C., 96
Charleston, S.C., 33, 34, 36, 37, 58, 120 (n. 19)
Charlotte, N.C., 85
Chestnut, Mary, 39, 58–59, 94, 98, 102
Chevauchée, 55, 56
Cheves, Susan, 72
Children, 48–49
Chivalry. See Honor
Civilians. See African Americans; Children; Women
Class: and violence, 81–83, 120

(n. 27), 135 (n. 28); and deserters, 133 (n. 5)
Clifford, James, 123 (n. 64)
Cohen, Fanny, 20
Collier, Elizabeth, 94, 98
Columbia, S.C.: Union army's burning of, 3, 6, 58–74; Confederate fundraising in, 31, 32; as Sherman's objective in South Carolina, 34, 57, 120 (n. 19); refugees in, 38, 58, 73; postwar sentiments in, 98
Confederate army and government: white women as fierce supporters of, 3, 4, 6, 7, 13–16, 20, 21, 26–28, 33, 44, 50–53, 62–63, 68–74, 91–92, 106, 142 (n. 21); fighting by, 4, 76, 93, 113 (n. 17); question of disloyalty toward, 6, 76–77, 79–85, 91–92, 133 (n. 5); plundering by, 10, 59–60, 78–82; feeding of, 21; leadership of, 41, 77–78, 82–84, 108; and Columbia's burning, 59; desertion in, 76, 79–82, 85, 133 (n. 5); postwar camaraderie of, with Union veterans, 94–95, 102–3, 107–8, 110. See also Deserters; Honor; Lost Cause ideology; Military; Morale; Nationalism; Plundering; Women (Southern white); specific soldiers, officers, and officials
Connelly, Thomas L., 144 (n. 13)
Connolly, James A., 19, 28–29, 35, 67–68
Conyngham, David, 48, 67, 95, 97, 116 (n. 38)
Cooper, John, 40, 56
Coulter, Merton E., 143 (n. 42)

Davis (Fifteenth Army Corps private), 64, 65

Davis, Heddie, 48
Davis, Jefferson (Confederate president), 10, 28, 73, 108, 121 (n. 33), 133 (n. 3)
Davis, Jefferson (Union general), 114 (n. 38)
Demonization: of Sherman, 6, 23, 26, 72–73, 94, 103, 108, 110, 140 (n. 9); of Southern women by Union army, 14; of Union troops by Southern women, 61–63, 69, 72–73
DePauw, Linda Grant, 128 (n. 128)
Deserters, Confederate, 76, 79–82, 85, 133 (n. 5)
Devil imagery. See Demonization
Divine (Union captain), 8–9
Duncan, Samuel, 53
Dunn, Fannie, 86

Eastern states, 64
Edmonston, Catherine, 91, 94, 96, 98, 100, 103
Elberton, Ga., 36
Elliot, Stephen, 17, 26
Ellis, Emily, 70
Elmore, Grace: on Sherman's approach, 33; slaves of, 38–39; on Columbia, S.C., 60, 62, 63, 66–68, 71, 73; on Fifteenth Army Corps, 61; on Confederacy's surrender, 94; background of, 118 (n. 4)
Enloe, Cynthia, 143 (n. 42)
Escott, Paul D., 133 (n. 5), 135 (n. 28), 137 (n. 36)
"Ethnocide," 138 (n. 53)

Farwell, S. S., 57, 77
Faust, Drew, 69, 113 (n. 19), 131 (n. 42), 136 (n. 31)

Fayetteville, N.C., 91, 92, 100
Fellman, Michael, 124 (n. 78)
Fessenden, Charles, 41–42
Fifteenth Army Corps, 61, 64, 65, 120 (n. 19), 129 (n. 14), 130 (n. 24)
Finley, Robert, 77
Fischer, Kirsten, 136 (n. 28)
Fleharty, George, 56
Fludd, Eliza, 36, 98
Food riots, 82–83, 136 (n. 30)
Foraging. See Plundering
Fort Fisher (North Carolina), 36
Fourteenth Army Corps, 120 (n. 19)
14th New Hampshire Volunteers, 53
Frank, Lisa, 131 (n. 46)
Franklin, Tenn., 36

Gallagher, Gary, 115 (n. 36), 132 (n. 51); on resistance, 69; on Lee, 108, 133 (n. 58), 140 (n. 5)
Geary, John White, 18
Gender: ideology of, for women, 4, 11–14, 26, 44, 51–53, 56–57, 62, 82–83, 115 (n. 24); and Southern honor, 6, 28, 71–72, 95, 104–9; attributed to landscapes and regions, 43–44, 108; ideology of, for men, 54–56, 71, 72, 107; and war, 56–57, 73–74, 102–3, 106–7, 128 (n. 128), 143 (n. 7); and military roles, 56–57, 128 (n. 128); and postwar healing, 102–3; and nationalism, 103–10, 143 (n. 43). See also Men; Women
Geography: civilians' vs. soldiers' knowledge of, 36–38, 121 (n. 33). See also Land; Maps; specific places
Georgia: Sherman's advance across,

4–5, 8–30, 32, 85; destruction in, 10. See also specific towns and cities
Georgia Countryman, 10, 14
Glatthaar, Joseph, 123 (n. 54), 124 (n. 69)
Goldsboro, N.C., 75
Goodlett, Emily, 38
Gott, Julia, 70
Grant, Ulysses S., 26, 119 (n. 14); Sherman's communications with, 4, 18–19, 141 (n. 17)
Greensboro, N.C., 82–83
Greenville Ladies Relief Association, 70
Griffin, Ga., 10
Grimsley, Mark, 55, 113 (n. 9), 116 (n. 41), 127 (n. 123)
Guntharpe, Violet, 47

Hall, Jacquelyn Dowd, 143 (n. 5)
Halleck, H. W., 29, 61
Hammond, Catherine, 49
Hammond, James Henry, 49
Hampton, Wade, 105
Hardee, William J., 8, 21, 40
Hard Hand of War (Grimsley), 55, 113 (n. 9), 116 (n. 41), 127 (n. 123)
Hawthorne, Sally, 91
Haynesworth, Maria, 51
Herr, John, 35, 54, 78
Heyward family, 39
Hill, Kitty, 87
Hinsdale, Elizabeth, 91, 92
Hitchcock, Henry, 33, 34, 36, 43, 52–53, 119 (n. 10)
Hoadley, Robert, 60–61
Holmes, Emma: on South Carolina campaign, 36–37, 99; and Union troops, 51, 72; on Confederacy's surrender, 94, 95, 98

Holmes, Theophilus, 81
Home front: as Southern battle-front, 3, 5, 11–16, 28, 33, 44, 50–57, 69–74, 76, 88–90. See also Households
Honor: Southern concepts of female, 6, 28, 71–72; Georgians' sense of, 10; Southern concepts of male, 95, 104–9; definition of, 114 (n. 21)
Hood, John Bell, 19
Horton, Dexter, 40, 52
Hospitals, 76, 90–91
Households: Union invasions of Southern, 4, 5, 9–11, 15–16, 28, 33, 44–45, 48–50, 53, 55–56, 61–62, 65, 69–74, 76, 78, 86–92, 103; as political center of South, 4, 12–14, 44, 71; as hospitals, 76, 90–91; Confederate deserters' raids on, 78–82. See also Home front; Housing; Plundering; Women
Housing: regional differences in, 41–43, 77. See also Households; Plundering
Howard, Frances, 20–21, 30
Howard, O. O., 46
Hundred Years War, 127 (n. 124)
Hunter, Hester, 49
Huston, James L., 144 (n. 9)

Illinois, 42
Indiana, 42

Jackson, Oscar L., 11–12, 19, 45, 47, 78, 95
Jakle, John A., 119 (n. 8)
Jasper County (Georgia), 13
Johnson, Andrew, 49

Johnson, Jimmie, 49
Johnston, Joseph E., 111 (n. 2); on
  South Carolina campaign, 40–41;
  on North Carolina campaign, 75,
  79, 133 (nn. 3, 4); peace treaty
  negotiated by, 93–97, 101, 140
  (n. 9), 141 (n. 17)
Jones, Annie, 88
Jones, Mary, 15–17, 27–28

Kennett, Lee, 120 (n. 27)

Lamar, Charles, 64
Land: attachment to, 49–50, 125
  (n. 99). See also Maps
Lay, Henry, 23, 26
LeConte, Emma, 39, 95, 98, 102,
  130 (n. 27); on Columbia, S.C.,
  59, 60, 66, 69, 71–73
LeConte, Joseph, 11
Lee, Robert E., 84, 119 (n. 14), 133
  (n. 3); in Petersburg, Va., 4; Sherman on, 29; Confederate glorification of, 72, 73, 94, 103, 108,
  133 (n. 58); and plundering of
  North Carolina, 79–80; surrender
  by, 93–94, 110, 140 (n. 5), 141
  (n. 17); Northern invasion by, 113
  (n. 19)
Leverette, Mary, 70
Liberty County (Georgia), 11, 15–17,
  27–28, 113 (n. 17). See also Savannah, Ga.
Lincoln, Abraham, 4–5, 46, 96, 100,
  141 (n. 17); Savannah as Christmas present for, 5, 8, 19
Lincolnton, N.C., 58
Livestock, 87–88, 91. See also
  Plundering
Logan, Lily, 61, 63–64, 70, 72

Logue, Cal M., 131 (n. 44)
Lost Cause ideology, 98, 105
Louisiana, 22–23
Lynn, John, 144 (n. 8)

Magrath, Andrew, 70
Mahon, Samuel, 43, 97
Many Excellent People (Escott), 133
  (n. 5), 135 (n. 28), 136 (n. 36)
Maps: Union, 34, 41; Confederate,
  37. See also Geography
"March from the Sea," 111 (n. 2);
  goals of, 5, 10, 22–23, 69; over-
  looking of women's resistance
  to, 102. See also Georgia; North
  Carolina; Sherman, William
  Tecumseh; South Carolina;
  Union army
"March to the Sea," 8, 111 (n. 2); as
  obscuring march from the sea, 4;
  as neither grueling nor devastating, 5, 8–9, 32, 113 (nn. 9, 11). See
  also Atlanta, Ga.
Marszalek, John, 108
McMasters, Harriet, 81
McPherson, James, 69, 71, 73–74
Meade, Rufus, 40, 55
Memory: cultural politics of, 108–
  10, 143 (n. 43)
Men (Southern white): as hiding
  from Union army, 11–14, 81; prewar authority of, 13; essentializing of, 44, 102, 123 (n. 65);
  Southern women's common
  goals with, 73–74; violence
  against Southern white women
  by, 81–82, 105; postwar camaraderie of, with Union veterans,
  94–95, 102–3, 107–8, 110; postwar rehabilitation of authority of,

at Southern women's expense, 104, 105–9; link between sexism and racism among, 108–9, 143 (n. 5). *See also* Confederate army and government; Gender; Honor

Meriwether, Elizabeth, 109–10

Metzgar, John, 88

Middleton, Harriott, 63, 70–72

Midway, S.C., 38

Military: as cultural entity, 3; Confederate women's identification with, 101–4, 106. *See also* Confederate army and government; Home front; Union army; War

Milledgeville, Ga., 10, 28

Mississippi, 113 (n. 9)

Mitchell, Reid, 107

Morale, Southern: among Confederate troops, 3, 36, 121 (n. 33); Sherman's attempts to destroy, 5, 9–10, 37–38, 55–56, 69, 76, 88–92; Southern women's resistance to attacks on, 6, 25–26, 28, 59, 69–74, 91–92, 112 (n. 5). *See also* Deserters, Confederate; Resistance

Moral economy (of war), 6, 82–84, 91–92, 136 (n. 31)

Murrell, Amy E., 136 (n. 36)

Nationalism, Confederate: women's role in, during war, 7, 12–13, 15, 71–74, 112 (n. 5); and masculinity, 13, 103–10, 143 (n. 43); women's postwar role in, 91–92, 94–95, 97–98, 101–4, 108; invasion's link to, 139 (n. 68). *See also* Confederate army and government; Women (Southern white):

as fierce supporters of Confederacy

Native Americans, 66, 127 (n. 125)

Neely, Mark, 127 (n. 123)

New York, N.Y.: Savannah trade with, 24, 25; on Sherman-Johnston peace treaty, 96–97; draft riots in, 136 (n. 30)

New York Herald, 11, 48

New York Times, 27

New York Tribune, 75

Nichols, George, 77, 93

Nichols, Lila, 87, 88

North: and Atlanta stalemate, 4; on Sherman and Johnston's peace treaty, 6, 94, 96–97; on Confederate women, 14, 21, 28; on Savannah relief program, 24–25; South perceived as culturally inferior to, 32–33, 41–44, 50; as feminine, 108; Lee's invasion of, 113 (n. 19); women's resistance to war in, 136 (n. 30). *See also* Union army

North Carolina: resistance to Sherman's campaign across, 6, 85–92; and Unionist sympathies, 75–78, 105; Sherman's campaign in, 75–92, 111 (n. 2), 119 (n. 14); question of disloyalty in, 76, 79–85, 91–92, 133 (n. 5). *See also* specific towns and cities

Ohio, 42, 47

Ohio Infantry Volunteers, 47

Osborn, Thomas, 41, 55, 67, 75, 76

Palmetto State. *See* South Carolina

Peace treaty, Sherman and Johnston's, 6–7, 93–97, 101, 140 (n. 9), 141 (n. 17)

Pennsylvania, 113 (n. 19)

Pepper, George: on Savannah, 18; on South Carolina, 36, 43, 67; on bummers, 45, 54; on North Carolina, 77–78

Perry, Amy, 47

Petersburg, Va., 4

Pillaging. See Plundering

Platter, C. C., 47, 67

Plundering: by Union troops, in Georgia, 9–11, 15–16, 23; by Confederates, 10, 59–60, 78–82; by Union troops, in South Carolina, 44–45, 47–51, 53–56, 59–60, 62, 64, 65, 87; by African Americans, 59–60; Fifteenth Army Corps' reputation for, 61, 64, 65; by Union troops, in North Carolina, 76, 78, 86–92

Pollard, E. A., 108, 144 (n. 13)

Pool, Parker, 86

Poppenheim, Mrs., 70, 71

Porter, Toomer, 130 (n. 24)

Potter, David M., 125 (n. 99), 132 (n. 51), 139 (n. 68)

Prostitutes, 17, 52, 106. See also Rape

Rable, George, 112 (n. 5), 121 (n. 33), 131 (n. 42), 136 (n. 36), 138 (n. 58)

Racial attitudes, 3; and rape, 11, 39, 44, 120 (n. 27), 127 (n. 125); and power in the South, 12–13; of white Union troops, 17–18, 45, 47, 65–66, 86–87, 100–101, 116 (n. 41), 141 (n. 14); in the West, 65–66, 130 (n. 27)

Raleigh, N.C., 88

Rape: of black women by Union troops, 4, 38, 39, 45–48, 66, 127

(n. 125); racial differences in, 11, 39, 44, 120 (n. 27), 127 (n. 125); lack of, among Southern white women during Civil War, 11, 120 (n. 27); exaggeration of reports of, 23; fears of, 36; allegations of black-on-white, 106, 108–9, 143 (n. 5); and women's class, 120 (n. 27). See also Prostitutes; Violence

Rations: of Union army, 9; in Columbia, S.C., 69–71. See also Food riots; Plundering; Relief programs

Ravenel, Harriett, 38, 62, 68, 70

Reconstruction, 106, 107–8

Regionalism: of gender ideology for women, 12–14, 51–53, 57, 114 (n. 20), 115 (n. 24); and housing, 41–43, 77; East-West, as issue in Union army, 61, 64–66, 129 (n. 14), 130 (n. 27). See also North; South

Relief programs: in South, 22–27, 70, 94

Resistance: by Southern white women during Civil War, 3, 4, 6, 7, 13–16, 20–22, 26–28, 33, 44, 50–53, 62–63, 68–74, 91–92, 106, 142 (n. 21); connection between despondency and, 6, 59, 69–74, 92, 106, 112 (n. 5), 138 (n. 55), 139 (n. 65); by Northern women to war, 136 (n. 30). See also Military; Nationalism, Confederate; Revenge

Revenge: Union troops' desire for, in South Carolina, 32–33, 35–36, 43–44, 53–54, 67; Southern white women's postwar feelings of, 91–92, 97–98, 102–3, 109–10. See also Resistance

Revolutionary War, 128 (n. 128), 136 (n. 33)
Rhiza, John, 113 (n. 11)
Richmond, Va., 36
Ricker, Eli, 41, 53, 56, 57
Rise and Fall of the Confederate Nation (Davis), 108
Roland, Alex, 120 (n. 33)
Rosaldo, Michelle, 143 (n. 7)
Royster, Charles, 119 (n. 9)

Sams, Sarah Jane, 50, 133 (n. 60)
Savannah, Ga., 37; as starting point of Sherman's March from the Sea, 4, 5; as Christmas present for Lincoln, 5, 8, 19; surrender of, 5, 8, 94; Union occupation of, 5–6, 11, 17–30, 32, 36, 38, 73, 113 (n. 17); Union relief program in, 22–27, 94
Savannah Daily Herald, 27
Savannah Republican, 27
Schaum, William, 40
Schurz, Carl, 49
Schwalm, Leslie, 125 (n. 95)
Scofield, William, 35, 43
Scott, James C., 139 (n. 65)
Second Division, Twentieth Corps (Union Army), 18
Separate sphere ideology (in North), 12, 56–57
Seventeenth Army Corps, 120 (n. 19)
Seward, William Henry, 21
Shand, Peter, 68
Sherman, Ellen (Mrs. William Tecumseh), 22, 23, 34, 96, 97
Sherman, William Tecumseh: Union soldiers on destruction under, 3, 33, 53–56, 64, 67–68, 76, 91; demonization of, 6, 23, 26, 72–

73, 94, 103, 108, 110, 140 (n. 9); peace treaty negotiated by, 6, 93–97, 101, 140 (n. 9), 141 (n. 17); and slaves following Union army, 17–18, 47, 86; on occupation of Savannah, 18–19, 22–27; knowledge of South of, 22–23, 34, 95, 101; reputation concerns of, 22–23, 26, 94; on Northern profiteers, 28; Union soldiers on, 29, 33–36, 40, 68, 97; and South Carolina campaign, 31–74; discipline over troops of, 68, 75; and North Carolina campaign, 75–92; Spencer on, 101–2. See also "March from the Sea"; "March to the Sea"; Union army
"Sherman puddings," 31
"Sherman's bummers," 45
Shy, John, 119 (n. 9)
Simms, William, 41, 58, 59–62, 66, 68, 87
Slavery: defenders of, 17, 65, 66–67; and Sherman's peace treaty, 96, 141 (n. 14). See also Slaves
Slaves: decisions of, to leave or stay on plantations, 16–18, 33, 38–39, 45–50, 66; fugitive, 17, 85, 86; as intermediaries between Union soldiers and Southern white women, 20–21, 60; and Sherman's approach, 38–39, 45–50, 65–66; white fears of insurrection by, 76, 85–86; emancipation of, 99–101, 106, 115 (n. 36). See also African Americans (Southern)
Smith, Janie, 90, 92
Smith, Mrs. Pringle, 64
Snow, Samuel, 78

Sorghum pudding, 31
South: household as political center of, 4, 12–14, 44, 71; status of, in Sherman and Johnston's peace treaty, 6, 95–96; link of race to power in, 12–13; Unionist sympathies in, 18, 21, 26, 75–78, 105; Sherman's personal knowledge of, 22–23, 34, 95, 101; relief programs in, 22–27, 70, 94; Northern profiteers in, 24–25, 28; North perceived as culturally superior to, 32–33, 41–44, 50; Union destruction of items associated with heritage of, 88–90. See also African Americans (Southern); Confederate army and government; Home front; Households; Men (Southern white); Women (Southern white); names of specific places
South Carolina: Sherman's army in, 5, 30–75; as "cradle of secession," 30, 32, 35, 57, 67; Union troops' desire for revenge in, 32–33, 35–36, 43–44, 53–54, 67; postwar sentiments toward Northerners in, 99. See also specific towns and cities
South Carolina Railroad depot (Columbia), 59–60
Spencer, Cornelia, 91, 101–2
Stanton, Edwin M., 96
Stealing. See Plundering
Steele, Mrs. A. E., 51
Stiles, Elizabeth, 20–21

Temple, Jack Kirby, 123 (n. 54)
Tennessee, 19, 36
Thomas, Ella, 36, 95, 97–98, 100, 101

Thompson, E. P., 136 (n. 31)
Tompkins, Charles, 54
Tourgée, Albion, 108, 140 (n. 9)
Tuan, Yi-Fu, 119 (n. 8)
Twentieth Army Corps, 18, 120 (n. 19)

Union army: Southern white women's resistance to, 3, 4, 6, 7, 13–16, 20–22, 26–28, 33, 44, 50–53, 62–63, 68–74, 91–92, 106, 142 (n. 21); on their destruction of the South, 3, 33, 53–56, 64, 67–68, 76, 91; invasion of Southern households by, 4, 5, 9–11, 15–16, 28, 33, 44–45, 48–50, 53, 55–56, 61–62, 65, 69–74, 76, 78, 86–92, 103; African Americans' treatment by, 4, 16, 18, 38, 39, 45–49, 66, 100, 127 (n. 123); Savannah's occupation by, 5–6, 11, 17–30, 32, 36, 38, 73, 113 (n. 17); rations of, 9; Southern white women as facing, alone, 11–16, 44–45, 50–51, 62–64, 69, 70, 72, 74, 88, 102–3, 106; on Southern white women, 14, 21, 28; attitudes of, toward African Americans, 17–18, 45, 47, 65–66, 86–87, 100–101, 116 (n. 41), 141 (n. 14); African Americans following, 17–18, 47, 86, 115 (n. 38), 121 (n. 38); Southern white women's reactions to, 19–21, 26, 60–61, 63–64, 70–74, 95; on Sherman, 29, 33–36, 40, 68, 97; in South Carolina, 32–74; maps used by, 34, 41; regional differences among men in, 61, 64, 65, 129 (n. 14); in North Carolina, 75–92; in Virginia, 85; Southern heritage destroyed by, 88–90; postwar camaraderie of, with Confederate veterans, 94–95, 102–3, 107–8, 110; substitutes for draftees in, 107. See also Army of the Potomac; Households; North; Plundering; Unionist sympathies; specific soldiers and officers

Union County (South Carolina), 49–50

Unionist sympathies (in South), 18, 21, 26, 75–78, 105

United Daughters of the Confederacy, 109

United States. See American Revolution; Regionalism

Vance, Zebulon, 80, 82–85

Violence: and gender, 81–82, 105; and class, 81–83, 120 (n. 27), 135 (n. 28). See also Plundering; Rape; War

Virginia: morale in, 69, 133 (n. 58); supplies for Confederate troops in, 79; Union troops in, 85, 113 (n. 9). See also specific towns and cities

Vlach, John Michael, 124 (n. 72)

War: as culturally sanctioned violence, 3, 5, 57; moral economy of, 6, 82–84, 91–92, 136 (n. 31); women's knowledge of geographic elements of, 36–38, 121 (n. 33); and gender, 56–57, 73–74, 102–3, 106–7, 143 (n. 7); guerrilla, 91, 93, 96, 140 (n. 7); cultural approach to study of, 119 (n. 9); total, 127 (n. 123). See also American Revolution; Confeder-

ate army and government; Gender; Home front; Military; Morale, Southern; Nationalism, Confederate; Plundering; Rape; Union army; Violence

Washington, George, 128 (n. 128)

Washington, Nancy, 48–49

Wellington, Duke of, 127 (n. 124)

Western states: Fifteenth Corps from, 61, 64, 65, 129 (n. 14); racial attitudes in, 65–66, 130 (n. 27)

Wheeler, Joseph, 10, 22, 60, 115 (n. 38)

Williams, Alpheus S., 18, 32, 43, 53

Wills, Charles W., 116 (n. 54)

Wilmington, N.C., 36

Winthrop College (South Carolina), 109

Women (Northern white): resistance to war by, 136 (n. 30)

Women (Southern black): rape of, by Union troops, 4, 38, 39, 45–48, 66, 127 (n. 125); as following Union army, 17–18, 47, 86

Women (Southern white): as fierce supporters of Confederacy, 3, 4, 6, 7, 13–16, 20–22, 26–28, 33, 44, 50–53, 62–63, 68–74, 91–92, 106, 142 (n. 21); ideology regarding, 4, 11–14, 26, 44, 51–53, 56–57, 62, 82–83, 115 (n. 24); resistance of, to Union army, 4, 6, 12–16, 20–22, 26–28, 33, 44, 50–57, 62–63, 68, 69–74, 88, 92, 103, 106, 109–10, 112 (n. 5), 131 (n. 44), 139 (n. 65); honor among, 6, 28, 71–72; resistance of, to attacks on morale of, 6, 25–26, 28, 59, 69–74, 91–92, 112

(n. 5); obscuring of role of, in shaping Confederate nationalism, 7, 102–10; city vs. country, 11, 38, 113 (nn. 17, 19); not raped by Union army officers, 11, 120 (n. 27), 127 (n. 125); as facing Union army alone, 11–16, 44–45, 50–51, 62–64, 69, 70, 72, 74, 88, 102–3, 106; reactions of, to Union soldiers, 19–21, 26, 60–61, 63–64, 70–74, 95; economic survival tactics of, 20–21, 28, 82–84; geographic knowledge of, 36–38, 121 (n. 33); essentializing of, 44, 102, 123 (n. 65); Lee's glorification by, 72, 73, 94; Southern men's common goals with, 73–74; scarcity afflicting, and soldiers' desertion, 80; as targets of Southern male violence, 81–82, 105; postwar enmity of, toward North, 91–92, 94–95, 97–98, 102–3, 109–10, 131 (n. 44); on Confederacy's surrender, 94, 95. *See also* Gender; Honor; Military; Resistance

Woodberry, Genia, 50

World War I, 144 (n. 11)

Worth, Jonathan, 93, 96

Worth, Josephine, 89

Worth, Nellie, 88, 95

Wright, Henry, 60

Wyatt-Brown, Bertram, 114 (n. 21), 141 (n. 13)

Yankees. *See* Union army